Youth and Community Work in Ireland

Critical Perspectives

Edited by
Catherine Forde
Elizabeth Kiely
and Rosie Meade

BLACKHALL
Publishing

PUBLISHED BY BLACKHALL PUBLISHING
Lonsdale House
Avoca Avenue
Blackrock
Co. Dublin
Ireland

e-mail: info@blackhallpublishing.com
www.blackhallpublishing.com

ISBN: 978-1-84218-173-7

A catalogue record for this book is available from the British Library.

Printed in the UK by Athenaeum Press Ltd.

Acknowledgements

We wish to thank the contributors without whose time, commitment and goodwill the book would not have been possible. Thanks are also extended to Elizabeth Brennan of Blackhall Publishing for her advice and assistance over the last two years. We would like to acknowledge the support of the Faculty of Arts, Celtic Studies and Social Sciences in University College Cork in providing funding towards the publication of this book.

Contents

Section III: Futures

About the Contributors

Seamus Bane has had a long involvement in voluntary youth work at club, county and national level. After a number of years working in industry he returned to full-time education in 1994 and completed a B.Soc.Sc. and an M.Soc.Sc. (Youth and Community Work) in University College Cork. Following graduation he worked for a number of years on the Local Development Social Inclusion Programme with the Obair Newmarket-on-Fergus Community Partnership. Following this he worked with the Clare Lifelong Learning Network, an initiative funded under the EU EQUAL 2 programme. In 2007 he became youth development officer with Co. Clare Vocational Education Committee (VEC). A native of Co. Clare, he lives in Shannon with his wife Gemma and their son Oisín. The views expressed are not necessarily those of Co. Clare VEC.

Maurice Devlin, Ph.D. is senior lecturer in Applied Social Studies at NUI Maynooth. He is a member of the National Youth Work Advisory Committee, joint chair of the North-South Education and Standards Committee for Youth Work and Irish correspondent for the European Knowledge Centre on Youth Policy. He chairs the editorial board of the journal *Youth Studies Ireland* and is co-author (with Kevin Lalor and Áine de Róiste) of *Young People in Contemporary Ireland* (Gill & Macmillan, 2007).

Eilish Dillon is programme co-ordinator for the postgraduate/MA programme in Development Studies at the Kimmage Development Studies Centre, Dublin, where she teaches the sociology of development and qualitative research methods. Her research interests include development organisations and development work, and development co-operation policy in Ireland. She has been involved in development education in Ireland for many years.

Catherine Forde is a lecturer in the Department of Applied Social Studies in University College Cork. She has a background in community work and is course coordinator of the B.Soc.Sc. (Youth and

Community Work). Her research interests include community development, state–civil society relations, educational disadvantage and local government reform. She has conducted research and published in each of these areas.

Elizabeth Kiely is a senior lecturer in Social Policy in the Department of Applied Social Studies, University College Cork. Her teaching and research areas include youth policy and practice, penal policy, research methodology and women's studies. In the field of youth work, she has published research in the areas of youth policy and practice, sexuality education, drug policy and second chance education for young people.

Chris McInerney currently works as a programme specialist in Rural and Community Development at Tipperary Institute in Thurles, having completed his Ph.D. on the theme of local governance and social inclusion at the University of Limerick. His principal research interests include the relationship between the domains of democracy, governance and social exclusion; the role of civil society in democracy and development; and the functioning of institutions in promoting social inclusion, in both Irish and international contexts. Previously, Chris worked in a variety of different settings: with the United Nations Development Programme in East Timor; as co-ordinator of the Community Workers Co-operative; and as executive secretary of the rural development initiative, Developing the West Together.

Sinéad McMahon is currently programme leader for the BA (Hons) in Social and Community Studies at Tipperary Institute and has previously taught on a number of other youth and community work courses. She has been interested in youth work issues for many years and has worked as a voluntary board member of Regional Youth Services. She has undertaken research work on youth and youth services which included evaluating programmes and services, and conducting strategic planning exercises.

Rosie Meade is a lecturer in the Department of Applied Social Studies in University College Cork. Her teaching and research interests include community development, social movements, cultural democracy, critical media analysis and 'alter' globalisation. She is currently a member of the editorial board of the *Community Development Journal*, where she is joint reviews editor with her colleague Orla O'Donovan. She has been involved in a range of activist and community groups over the years, and is currently chairperson of Cork Community Artlink. She can be contacted at r.meade@ucc.ie.

Hilary Tovey is a senior lecturer in the Department of Sociology at Trinity College Dublin, Ireland, and a Fellow of TCD. She has been president of the European Society for Rural Sociology and a council member of the International Rural Sociological Association. Her research interests cover food, environment, rural development, social movements and the sociology of knowledge; recent publications include *Environmentalism in Ireland: Movement and Activists* (Institute of Public Administration, 2007) and (with Perry Share and Mary Corcoran) *A Sociology of Ireland* (3rd edition, Gill & Macmillan, 2007).

David Treacy is education officer with the City of Dublin Vocational Education Committee (CDVEC) with special responsibility for all adult education programmes and services, including workplace education, literacy and community education, and adult guidance services. Prior to this, he worked at all levels in youth work over a thirty-year period and held senior posts in Catholic Youth Care and Youth Work Ireland. He was Assessor of Youth Work in the Department of Education for two years in the 1990s before becoming director of the City of Dublin Youth Service Board, the youth service of the CDVEC. He is currently a nominee of the Irish Vocational Education Association (IVEA) on the North–South Education and Training and Standards Committee and the National Youth Work Advisory Committee, and has been heavily involved in the preparation of the National Youth Work Development Plan and the preparations for the implementation of the Youth Work Act 2001.

Introduction

Voluntary youth work and community development have been long-standing and important, if not always high-profile or well-resourced features of Irish society. This book traces the changing youth and community work landscape over the last thirty years, recognising in particular how the State has become a significant player in directing the focus and outcomes of youth and community work initiatives.

Coinciding with State involvement, there has been a notable improvement in the status and visibility of these so-called 'sectors' through, for example, their inclusion in the 'Social Pillar' of national social partnership. As the contributors to this volume highlight and analyse key trends in youth and community work, they acknowledge the emergence of new definitions and sociological understandings of the terms 'youth' and 'community'. They also explore the political and ethical implications of the professionalisation of youth and community work, moves towards partnership with the State and the apparent globalisation of all aspects of political, economic and cultural life. Furthermore, because the sectorisation of youth and community work obscures the diversity of these fields, contributors attempt to re-assert the differentiated, pluralised and ambiguous nature of both youth and community work organisations and their constituencies.

Youth and community work draw on a common value base, invoking terms such as 'empowerment', 'participation', 'voluntarism', 'collective action' and 'social change'. As this book critically deconstructs this language, it creates a much needed intellectual space in which alternative perspectives, ideas and approaches may be explored. Moreover, because it recognises the need for a constant interchange between theory and practice, this collection brings together for the first time an interesting mix of contributors from academic and practice settings, all of whom are grappling with the contradictions and tensions that beset these fields.

For academics and activists who are engaged in youth work and community development practice, the very limited amount of Irish published material in these areas poses significant problems. We have been excessively dependent on British theoretical and research literature, which does not analyse the nuances of the Irish historical, policy and cultural context. We welcome the recent emergence of two journals that focus specifically on youth and community work in Ireland – *Youth Studies Ireland* and *Working for Change: The Irish Journal of Community Work*. This book explicitly seeks to address the deficiency in Irish material by theorising the policy and practice of youth and community work in this country. In doing so, individual authors introduce and revisit important ideas from other contexts, but attempt to assess and explicate their relevance to Ireland in the twenty-first century.

The book is envisaged as a textbook for degree, diploma and postgraduate students in youth and community work, and for students on related courses such as social studies, social work, adult and community education, and social care. It is also intended as a resource for youth and community work practitioners. The breadth and diversity of the projected readership reflects the growing recognition, application and adaptation of youth work and community development approaches in contemporary Ireland. An increasing number of Government departments and State bodies, local authorities, private sector organisations and of course locality- and interest-based communities have declared their willingness to promote these approaches. As a consequence there has been a significant rise in the number of paid personnel who claim to be engaging in youth and community work. The State now funds a major proportion of youth and community work activity, although the continuity of funding is never guaranteed and is particularly susceptible to cutbacks and austerity during recessionary times.

Given the recent and unprecedented upswing in their popularity, we believe the time is right for a critical analysis of community development and youth work, by which we mean a considered reappraisal of the values, intentions and outcomes associated with each field. In engaging in this reappraisal we assert that action or intervention in the lives of communities and their young people is never straightforward. It is overlaid with conflicting assumptions about the nature and composition of those communities, what they need and deserve, who is responsible and who is best placed to speak on their behalf. This might seem like a statement of the obvious, but in our view it requires constant reassertion, not least because – as a number of chapters demonstrate – youth and community work have become synonymous with certain progressive values, an unreflexive invocation of which may serve to deflect public appraisal and debate. As the chapters in this volume illustrate, youth work and community development are dialectical in their potential. Sometimes they encourage and resource people to transcend the limitations of the here and now, to imagine better futures and to activate latent skills and understandings. They can also do the opposite, however, encouraging people to 'put up and shut up', to accept received wisdoms about what is politically possible and socially desirable. This book attempts to analyse how this dialectic is played out in Irish society where the illusion of social consensus and harmony often masks real conflicts and inequalities. We ask if and how the 'progressive' values of community development and youth work can be invested with meaning and we seek to identify the forces and interests that work against the realisation of their transformative potential.

Key Themes: Commonalities and Controversies

As Terry Eagleton (2008: 354) observes, we should not 'expect theory and practice to dance a harmonious minuet hand-in-hand throughout history' and it is true that even if this book succeeds in offering useful insights into what is happening on the ground, there is no guarantee that this critical wisdom can or will change anything. We are living in difficult times, where media and discursive spaces are being narrowed and where marketisation threatens 'the very existence of critique and creativity itself' (Lynch, 2006: 8). If the self-styled and comparatively privileged intellectuals of the university sphere seem unwilling and unable to withstand the forces of neoliberalism (see Lynch, 2006), why should we expect the volunteers and less securely positioned workers of the voluntary sector to do so? None of the contributors to this volume pretends that critique or resistance is easy and, indeed, they may even differ as to the degree to which protest strategies are likely to bring about significant change. However, they all agree that, at a minimum, youth and community workers desperately need time, space and opportunities within which to interrogate their practice. As the State extends and tightens its control over the funding, management and content of work on the ground, many youth and community organisations are being drawn into agendas and outcomes not of their own design. In a market-driven context where action, delivery and results constitute the dominant logic, taking time to theorise and critically analyse is a political act. It is certainly not an end in itself but, as most of our authors agree, it is a vital first step towards political re-engagement.

Students of the social sciences will be all too familiar with 'contested and constructed' concepts which evade easy definition but which must be interrogated as a starting point on the road to critical understanding. Across all the contributions to this volume there is a shared appreciation of the nebulousness of the fields of youth work and community development, where even our base concepts of 'community' and 'youth' are up for discussion and negotiation. In Chapters 2 and 4, Maurice Devlin and Hilary Tovey guide us through some of the most long-standing and influential theorisations of 'youth' and 'community', reminding us as they go that sociological theory can be 'really useful'. Theory is useful not because it can be applied crudely or grafted on to practice relations but because it helps us to identify and own up to the dynamics behind what we do. For example, how do we respond to the following questions? Are young people incomplete adults in a state of 'becoming' or are they a diverse and complex grouping with multiple insights and interests? Do we invest too much hope in locality- and area-based communities? Can associational life withstand modernisation and individualisation? Should we target resources at the most disadvantaged or alienated young people or should we prioritise universal provision instead? Is the State a monolithic entity or is it more complex and multifaceted? These might seem like big concerns, far removed from the daily reality of youth and community work, but the various chapters in this book demonstrate that they are fundamental questions which have significant practice implications. The elevated status that youth and community work now enjoy is premised upon and reflects particular understandings – whether overt or covert – of how those questions might be answered. Contributors to this volume identify and critically analyse these interpretations but they also try to move beyond them in order to begin the difficult process of imagining alternatives.

In the broad international and Irish youth work and community development literature, the State features as a key concept and writers are acutely concerned with the shape and quality of relationships between the statutory sector and organisations on the ground. In this volume, the centrality of those relationships is foregrounded in chapters by Sinéad McMahon (Chapter 5), Catherine Forde (Chapter 6) and Seamus Bane (Chapter 7), but also emerges as a significant theme in other contributions – in particular those from Elizabeth Kiely (Chapter 1), David Treacy (Chapter 8) and Chris McInerney (Chapter 9).

Furthermore, as Eilish Dillon (Chapter 10) recognises, the phenomenon of globalisation transcends the power of nation-states and offers both definite possibilities and threats for youth and community work in Ireland. Authors avoid a simplistic and unidirectional discussion of State power with its familiar caricature of youth and community workers as 'good guys' and State officials as 'demons'. Instead they incline towards a poststructuralist analysis which views the State as a complex and highly differentiated entity comprising 'a diverse range of agencies, apparatuses and practices producing varied mechanisms of control and varied forms of knowledge' (Finlayson and Martin, 2006: 167).

Youth and community work interests are amongst the agents that make up the differentiated State. Within this remit they play a part in shaping the State while in their turn they are shaped by it. Thus, while contributors are critical of both the tone and content of State policy, they highlight how the extension of State involvement in youth and community work was actively courted by some of the most vocal and high-profile sector organisations, and how the youth work and community development sectors constitute significant power blocks and interest groups in their own right. This power may be manifested through social closure and professional exclusivity (Chapter 7), through the pursuit of sectoral recognition or through hollow promises to speak on behalf of constituencies that are not adequately consulted (see Chapters 1, 3, 5 and 6). The discursive and persuasive force associated with claims of participation, empowerment or 'starting where people are at' can obscure unimaginative or even destructive practice on the part of youth and community work bodies (see Chapters 1, 3 and 8). Alternatively, the power of youth and community work organisations can be used in more oppositional ways, to actively disrupt dominant economic and political arrangements and to create new discursive spaces in co-operation with young people and disadvantaged communities (see Chapters 6, 7, 8, 9 and 10).

Contributors recognise the realities that currently inform and shape youth and community work, including the considerable threat that the current recession and retrenchment in public spending poses to these sectors. At the same time they seek to identify and pursue transformative possibilities that are sometimes latent within these approaches. Ideas range from interesting possibilities for day-to-day practice (see Chapters 3, 8 and 10) to consideration of the future direction of youth work and community development (Chapters 1, 5, 6, 8, 9 and 10). While these ideas differ, there is agreement that youth work and community development are unique activities which can and do enrich the lives of young people, local communities and the wider society. The challenge for workers and scholars alike is to seek ways to maintain this distinctiveness whilst guarding against its diminishment from within or without the youth and community work fields. We hope that this book will inspire students, activists, academics and policy makers to engage in a process of reflection that will precipitate the attainment of this goal.

Structure of the Book

Although we recognise that there are strong parallels between the issues impacting on and the values expressed by youth work and community development organisations, this book also explores the distinctive history and operational context of both fields of practice. The book is divided into three sections: the first is concerned with conceptual themes in youth work and community development; the second deals with the opportunities and challenges that projects or organisations face in the current policy context; and the third looks at future possibilities, both positive and negative. Section I (Concepts) directly addresses the question 'What do we mean by youth work or community development?' in Chapters 1 and 3. As Elizabeth Kiely and Rosie Meade critically deconstruct the values associated with these fields, they recognise how rhetoric and aspiration can obscure the messy and contradictory realities of practice, particularly when those values are being claimed by such a wide diversity of interest groups. This section also includes chapters that review the current sociological status of 'youth' (Chapter 2) and 'community' (Chapter 4). In doing so, these authors expose and transcend some of the taken-for-granted assumptions that lie behind both the policy and everyday usage of those concepts.

Section II (Contexts) begins with a detailed evaluation of the quality of relationships between the youth work and community sectors and the State. Chapters 5 and 6 explore the historical, policy and political factors that have shaped those relationships and question the extent to which the enhanced status of the sectors has translated into meaningful benefits for young people and disadvantaged communities. The thorny issue of 'professionalisation' is considered in Chapter 7, which integrates a discussion of sociological theories of the professions with an analysis of the factors contributing to the professionalisation of youth and community work in contemporary Ireland. The implications and potential tensions associated with these trends are also explored.

Section III (Futures) recognises the constraints currently affecting community development and youth projects, but also attempts to identify possible new directions for practice. As noted earlier, youth work and community development are dialectical in their potential, capable of generating both progressive and regressive outcomes. In Chapter 8 David Treacy argues that youth projects, in the main, work to slot young people into society and its institutions, rarely asking fundamental questions about inequality and its causes. He asks if it is possible to develop a more consciously political and reflexive youth work that celebrates the importance of relationships with and accountability to young people. Community development is often seen as a political activity, in a way that youth work is not. In Chapter 9 Chris McInerney assesses the extent to which community organisations can breach narrow definitions and structures of democracy in favour of more participatory and discursive approaches. As he introduces theories of deliberative and participatory democracy, he suggests that there is an absence of political will, particularly within the State sector, to facilitate the emergence of more egalitarian structures and processes. Chapter 10, the concluding chapter, focuses on the multidimensional and contested concept of globalisation. Eilish Dillon presents core issues and themes from the sociological literature and makes them relevant to a youth and community work audience. Her original research with local organisations highlights some of the challenges associated with communicating, explaining, resisting and taking advantage of globalisation at the grassroots level.

I

Concepts

1

Irish Youth Work Values: A Critical Appraisal

Elizabeth Kiely

Introduction

In Ireland, the voluntary youth work sector emerged out of a number of diverse traditions, each with their own very distinctive value stances, as evident in different styles of working and different priorities governing their work (see Hurley, 1992*a* and 1999). Youth work is thus best understood as an ambivalent set of practices in the Irish context, yet there are high-minded or progressive values at the core of youth work, which supposedly give it a certain style and mark it out as a distinct practice.[i] The youth work sector is largely comprised of voluntary youth organisations (though not exclusively). It consists of large providers of youth work services (e.g. National Youth Council of Ireland, Youth Work Ireland, Foróige, Ógra Chorcaí, YMCA) to smaller interest-based organisations (Young Greens, ECO-UNESCO, Experiment in International Living, Labour Youth). The sector also includes the scouting and guiding organisations. The City of Dublin Youth Service Board is a statutory body responsible for youth services in its particular catchment area. The National Youth Council of Ireland (NYCI) is the recognised representative body for voluntary youth work organisations in Ireland.

In the contemporary Irish context, the youth work sector has sought to represent itself as making a remarkable and unique contribution to the lives of young people to ensure its survival and its relevance into the future as a distinct form of practice. The progressive core values and ideals underpinning youth work have thus been reasserted in literature and policy documents (Department of Education and Science, 2003*a*; Jenkinson, 2000; National Youth Council of Ireland, 2008). In these sources youth work is defined as being universal and informal in orientation. The values of empowerment, equality and inclusiveness, respect, involvement of young people in decision making, partnership and voluntary participation purportedly give youth work character and meaning. Adherence to these values is readily assumed to distinguish youth work from other more 'controlling' modes of intervention (e.g. schooling, social work or policing) with young people. However, while youth work has indeed the potential to engage in a radical and transformative practice, its history reveals few incidences where this potential has been actually realised (Davies and Gibson, 1967; Hurley, 1992*a*; Jenkinson, 1996). The long-standing contribution youth work practice has made and continues to make to inducing social conformity, promoting the status quo and imposing the habits of one class over another tend to be obscured when the 'progressive' value base of youth work is being projected.[ii] Furthermore, tracing youth work policy over time reveals that, in policy discourses, the value base of youth work is something of a moveable feast. For example, in the Republic of Ireland, youth work's role in the pursuit of social change, which was invoked in the Costello Report (Department of Labour, 1984), has featured much less in youth policy discourses since the Costello Report (Kiely and Kennedy, 2005). Similarly, in the Northern Irish context, a strategy setting out the delivery of youth work participation identified personal and social development and peace building as key values underpinning the work. However, as McCready (2006) observed, no reference was made to other values typically associated with youth work, such as empowerment, working collectively, social justice or social change.

As this chapter will show, a lack of clarity underpins many of the terms frequently used to communicate the value base of youth work. They tend to give youth work its spin because they are trotted out as general synonyms for practising youth work without adequate theoretical reflection or attention as to how they are actually embodied in the life of projects. As terms, they are invested with progressive and radical meaning, and if they are allowed tell the whole story they draw attention away from the controlling anti-democratic strains that also pervade youth work practice. Critical 'post' theories[iii] enable a thoughtful, if indeed a troublesome, inquiry into the claims made in the name of youth work practice. They compel us to unpick youth work discourses riddled with concepts that evade clear meaning. Poststructuralist insights[iv] encourage us to disrupt many of the commonsense assumptions or the articles of faith upon which the practices of youth work are based. They encourage us to be more questioning and a lot more humble about what youth work can achieve. It seems that this kind of critical project is necessary if youth work is to continue to have meaning in contemporary society.

In terms of understanding youth work purposes and practices, frameworks of theories and conceptual models derived from the discipline of sociology have been typically employed in the literature (e.g. character building, personal development, critical social education and radical social change). Such frameworks (see Butters and Newell, 1978; Hurley and Treacy, 1993; Smith, 1988) have sought to capture the diversity of youth work practices in terms of ethos, programmatic approaches and intended outcomes. They provide us with manageable ways of academically conceptualising, disaggregating and imposing order on what are complicated and eclectic youth work processes, practices and outcomes in society. While acknowledging the merits of a framework approach, the case is made in this chapter that an overreliance on traditional un-reworked models frameworks can be problematic in making sense of youth work practices and their desired outcomes in contemporary Irish society.

Youth Work and the Universal Ideal

The notion that the youth service is a universal service available to all young people is frequently reiterated. It is stated in the National Youth Work Development Plan 2003–2007 that '... youth work should be regarded as something from which all young people can benefit, rather than a remedial service for those whose needs are not being met otherwise' (Department of Education and Science, 2003*a*: 14). The National Youth Council of Ireland (2008) provides a definition of youth work that also emphasises a very distinctive universal quality: 'Youth work is for all young people, with particular focus on those aged 10 to 25 from all aspects of Irish life, urban, rural, all nationalities and social classes.' There are many realities that undermine the principle of universalism, which is supposedly at the heart of youth work philosophy and practice. Indeed it is very doubtful that youth work ever was this 'open to all' provision written about in the discourse, as historical accounts of youth work practice have drawn attention to the undisputed targeting of certain categories of youth, namely poor working-class young men and women (Davies and Gibson, 1967; Oldfield, 2001; Spence, 2001).

However, apart from its rhetorical commitment to universalism as a principle of practice, youth work has a long tradition of facilitating large groups of young people to come together for recreational purposes, giving it a genuinely strong universal character (Jeffs and Smith, 2002). It is precisely this that is threatened as the youth work agenda narrows in response to Government policy objectives and funding schemes. The allocation of State resources in the Irish context clearly favours a targeted approach where mainline and special services are distinguished and resourced substantially differently. Youth clubs, located at the least formal and more open end of youth work, have always been starved of funding and are often operated out of run-down buildings, while the more specialised projects, with the 'problem youth' tag attached, have been considerably better resourced by successive governments. Increasingly, resources have been provided for very specific interventions directed at particular categories of young people, such as drug users and young people who have come into contact with the Gardaí. The chief executive officer of Foróige (Campbell, 2007) observed that, in 2006–2007, youth club numbers fell but that the number of projects (including Garda Diversion Projects, Youth Cafés, and teen parenting and drug education programmes) increased. Youth cafés, which have the potential to be a form of 'open house' provision, tend to have a health promotion remit as when they are funded by the Health Service Executive (HSE). Presently there are a hundred Garda Youth Diversion Projects throughout the country and there are plans underway for expanding this number (Irish Youth Justice Service, 2008). No other form of youth provision has been developed at such a remarkable pace in recent years, indicating that the Government expects youth work to make a major contribution to the maintenance of law and order.

In the context of competing for limited resources, youth work organisations also target their efforts at the 'at risk' groups. In so doing, they draw on and bolster the popular discourses and feed the stereotypes that undermine the principle of universalism. They present themselves in funding applications as best positioned to target those constituencies of young people who are judged to be 'at risk' or already exhibiting the 'problems' or 'deficits' marked out as in need of targeted intervention. In the literature, the privileged access that youth workers have to the 'at risk' constituencies of young people is often highlighted. Research conducted by Spence and Devanney (2007) in Britain was designed partly for the purpose of collecting stories from youth workers about their practice. A key theme in the stories collected related to how youth interventions could be critical in changing the lives of young people. Williamson (2005: 73) recalled the difference he made as a youth worker to one young man's life, while reminding politicians and funders that there are few quick wins in youth work:

> I have often talked about one deeply alienated young man who hated all professionals but hated me slightly less than others. He was the classic focus of political attention and concern ... yet he had been largely untouched by professional intervention. I 'stood by' him for at least six years, making little difference and [being] constantly rebuffed by him. Eventually, however, while he was serving his fifth period in youth custody, he sought my support and, along with his girlfriend, we helped him to turn his life around.

When youth work is represented in these ways, youth workers tend to be constructed by themselves and others as the 'heroic agents' at a distance from the professionals whose interventions can have negative effects on young people. The impression conveyed is that youth workers' informal styles uniquely position them to relate to the most disadvantaged young people in positive ways.

The public image of the youth work relationship as being unique and special has made youth work increasingly attractive to the State as a means of managing and socialising young people who move outside the radar of other agencies. The notion of an adult who can be trusted captures to some extent what a youth worker might represent to a young person who has 'burnt bridges' with other organisations. Harland and Morgan (2006: 6–7) have written that 'One of the most powerful influences in encouraging young people to engage in potentially contentious work is the trust they have with the youth worker.' Devlin's (2006*a*) research indicated that young people viewed their relationships with the adults in their lives as fraught, with the exception of youth workers, who they viewed more positively. The youth work sector has enabled the State to focus its policy interventions on 'problem' constituencies of young people, not only in the name of education, justice or social work, but also in the name of youth work. Indeed, Williamson (2005) has suggested that 'specialist' youth work organisations in Britain have received higher levels of public sector finance than traditional youth services because they have gotten the language right. They have framed their practice in a way that strikes a chord with funding bodies. It also seems that, in the Irish context, it is also no longer wise to talk about ordinary relationships with young people because the financial resources will not be forthcoming. As acknowledged by Kearney (2007*a*: 2), the Government and the sector are both responsible for the problem focus; '... service providers have followed the funding sources which have focused on problems, we have failed to impress policy-makers, legislators and funders that all young people have the right to access services...'.

If due to the shortage of funding it is not possible to have a universal youth service, we have to consider if the values of equality and inclusiveness have any real import in Irish youth work practice. Equality and inclusiveness are not values distinctive to youth work because they are part of the lexicon of Government policy, economic interests and almost every other institution or group in Irish society. The everyday use of the language of equality and inclusiveness has led to confusion about what these concepts actually mean, as they can be interpreted and defined in diverse ways (see Lynch, 1999). In the Irish context, narrow liberal versions of these concepts[v] suffuse the discourse (see Lynch, 1999; O' Sullivan, 2005) and also dictate the terms of practice with young people. As youth work is increasingly State funded, it is likely that the areas that fit with the Government's equality agenda will also get priority. Paradoxically, because youth work is becoming more specialised and issue based, projects can be initiated with young people who find themselves excluded from or marginal to other kinds of youth work provision and, thus, these young people's sense of separateness and difference can be reinforced. For example, BelonGTo is a youth group specifically for gay, lesbian, bisexual and transgender young people and Pavee Point also has a youth work programme specifically for young Travellers. The reality is that the youth service, like other services, cannot always accommodate young people as heterogeneous groupings and indeed many young people choose not to be involved in provision that includes other young people for prejudicial reasons. The membership of youth organisations is also often stratified along class, gender, racial and other dividing lines (see Gaetz, 1993: Ronayne, 1992).

In the British context, Spence (2004: 268) fears that '... the current fate of youth work is to be colonised by a range of initiatives, which all seem relevant to its self-conception, but which constantly fail to acknowledge its central motors.' Spence was referring to the reconfiguring of youth services resulting from the policy intentions underpinning Connexions.[vi] She was arguing that concepts associated with youth work were mobilised for intentions which bore some relation to youth work but were not derived from it. Indeed, in Britain, employer-led skills-based approaches to youth work education, as well as courses serving the integrated children's workforce, are oriented towards producing a kind of generic 'youth development' professional who can practise to the momentum of any kind of policy environment (see Jeffs and Smith, 1994; Spence and Jeffs, 2007/2008). Referring to the British context, Smith (2002) has also argued that there is a notable shift away from talking about values in youth work to talking about principles of practice because this is more in keeping with a managerial culture.

Undoubtedly, increased State intervention in the Irish context will put more pressure on the sector to undergo the necessary metamorphosis required to fit Government policy imperatives. Specialisation in youth work, or what is also called 'issue based' youth work in the Irish context, developed in response to the way the State allocated resources. The implications for practice are that youth workers find themselves increasingly working with young people under the terms of reference of health, juvenile justice or education, and their associate bodies of knowledge. Increasingly, the hand of youth work is found in projects that are not funded by the Youth Affairs Section of the Department of Education and Science. Programmes and interventions targeting teenage parents, young offenders and young people who use drugs have grown in number and tend to be delivered in partnership arrangements between voluntary youth services and other statutory agencies. Health promotion initiatives and youth cafés have been provided by youth organisations in partnership with the HSE. Many youth service initiatives are now grant aided by the Department of Justice, the HSE or the National Drugs Strategy Team / Local Drugs Task Forces. To a lesser extent, partnerships or funding arrangements have also begun to be forged between youth organisations and corporate interests.[vii] Indeed, youth agencies might well take notice of how corporate interests have used school communities in the Irish context to promote market values and influence family consumption practices (see Curley, 2005).

When practised in different fields and in inter-agency practice contexts, it is more difficult to say what youth work is, what it is not and what it seeks to achieve. Values that are more in keeping with social service or control have the potential to bankrupt what is supposedly critical to the youth work relationship. As the trend towards specialisation gains momentum, it becomes an increasing challenge to nurture generic or universal youth work provision and to say what is distinctive about the knowledge base and practice of youth work. Indeed, generic work or what we have come to know as traditional youth work has increasingly become the province of the volunteers, as paid, professionally trained youth workers have gravitated towards the specialised projects concentrated overwhelmingly in poor urban areas. As Smith (2002) has observed in the British context, the principle of collective association so central to the philosophy of youth work has become increasingly displaced by youth work activities that have become more individualised and specialised. There is an undeniable push towards professionalising youth work practice in Ireland with the introduction of a quality standards framework and the increasing emphasis on qualifications and accountability (see Chapter 7). Ironically, as the context for the work changes, workers might also find that they are afforded less opportunity to put their particular expertise into practice.

Youth Work as a Nonformal, Informal or Social Educational Activity

There is a repertoire of concepts in youth work discourse, which are tossed around but which are problematic precisely because they mean all things to all people. Putting the young person at the centre of the process (what is often called 'person centredness') has also been acknowledged as an important value underpinning the practice of youth work. It has frequently been used to distinguish youth work from the business of formal education, which requires young people to fit in with a set of structures and an already prescribed curriculum, or live with the negative consequences of examination failure or school exclusion. Jenkinson (2000) advocated that youth work should be 'youth centred' so that the needs of young people drive the process, not the needs of the agency, worker or the funders, all of whom, she claimed, were of lesser importance. The ethos of person centredness was articulated by Sr Joan Bowles at a function for volunteer youth workers in Limerick in 2001 as being about 'walking beside young people' which meant for her, among other things, respecting young people, valuing their contribution and listening to them without any compulsion on their part. She identified this to be '... the importance of youth work – a curriculum much broader than any school can offer and adult volunteers provide it free' (Forde, 2003: 107–108).

In recent years, strident moves towards programme-based work and curriculum-based practice in Irish youth work seems to be at odds with the dialogue and negotiation that a person-centred approach might entail. The youth work curriculum is sold to its detractors as a way of making the art of youth work transparent to State agencies or funding bodies on the grounds that when youth organisations explain what they do, they do so in a way that is too fuzzy for the purpose of accountability (see Merton and Wylie, 2002; Sandwell's Young Peoples Service, undated). In the British context, core curricular areas in youth work are expected to tie in with Government youth policy and the work of other State agencies such as education and health. The curricular approach to youth work also propagates a managerial language, which is increasingly adopted when talking about youth work and which reduces youth work to stated goals, targets and outcomes (see Sandwell's Young Peoples Service, undated). In the contexts of the Republic of Ireland and the North, the distinction between informal and nonformal education creates a legitimate place in youth work for curricular or programme-based approaches. Nonformal education is defined as 'learning and development that takes place outside of the formal education field, but which is structured and based on learning objectives ...' – as distinct from informal education, which is defined as unstructured learning (McCready, 2006: 100). The growing emphasis on curriculum-based work undoubtedly shifts the focus of youth work towards a form of education that involves the delivery of prepackaged material and away from the learning-by-doing methods more readily associated with person-centred styles of learning.

'Starting where young people are at' is another mantra in the youth work lexicon that underpins the informal educational approach intrinsic to the work. However, it is a particularly nebulous notion. In some situations it is argued that youth workers have no agendas when they commence working with young people, unlike other professionals with whom young people come into contact. Rather they state that they listen to young people and mutually come to some agreement as to how to proceed in accordance with young people's own defined needs. Moving at a pace appropriate to young people is often emphasised in an engagement, which is presented as being more organic and process-oriented than other interventions in young people's lives. In other instances, an ability to 'start where young people are at' is used to valorise the contribution of the volunteer living in the community of the young people concerned. The volunteer is thus perceived as being more 'in touch' than the paid professional, who parachutes in to work with young people. 'Starting where young people are at' is also interpreted as respecting the knowledge each young person brings to bear when thinking and talking about his or her own personal situation.

However, detracting from youth workers' intentions to 'start where young people are at' is the proliferation of expert knowledge, which is increasingly at their disposal. Indeed it has been convincingly argued that youth work is one of many forms of practice, which involves transmitting knowledge and skills to young people, particularly those 'at risk', so that they learn to manage themselves in line with expertly and professionally prescribed norms of conduct

(Bradford, 2005). The fact that teenage pregnancy, crime prevention and drug education have become key strands of Irish youth work practice provides further validation of youth work's role in preventing 'problems' through educational-style intervention. Evaluations of the practice of peer education,[viii] which has been presented as an alternative form of education pioneered by voluntary youth work organisations, reveals that there is no significantly altered power dynamic as youth workers tend to maintain control, albeit at a distance, over the educational content and the process involved (see Milburn, 1996; Parkin and McKeganey, 2000). Rather than 'starting where young people are at' it would seem that the desired outcomes of many programmatic interventions in the youth work field are already set. Furthermore, the principle of 'starting where young people are at' is not illuminated in the definition of youth work provided in the Youth Work Act 2001, which is unequivocal when it states that youth work is 'A planned programme of education designed for the purpose of aiding and enhancing the personal and social development of young persons...'. If, as Spence (2004) has explained, 'starting where young people are at' means engaging young people in the constructive and reflective understanding in the here and now in order to create futures which cannot be preplanned and outcomes which cannot be pre-figured, it seems that this principle is increasingly endangered as youth work changes shape to fit the demands of Government policy.

The significance of the youth work relationship has also been articulated in other sources as well as the essential features required to make the relationship work (Bradford, 2005; Harland and Morgan, 2006; Spence, 2007; Young, 1999). For example, Kerry Young (1999) has identified the key principles of the youth work relationship as being acceptance, honesty, trust, respect and reciprocity. Investing in the relationship dimension of the work may become more of a challenge as agencies feel the pressure to account for their work in terms not of their own making. Spence (2007) pointed out that the concept of informal education does not appear in the policy discourses and Smith (2003) has written that when the work is framed with reference to concepts like outcome, curriculum and issue, workers face losing 'relationship' as a defining feature of their practice. In Bradford's (2005) estimation, the performance culture has impacted on youth work in Britain to the extent that it has shifted the emphasis away from expressive goals towards instrumental ones.[ix] He argues that youth organisations, in their quest for legitimacy and resources, convey their achievements in a narrative form that resonates with funding bodies. For example, quantifying the young people who complete an educational programme is seen as more important than being there, providing support for young people who are grieving the loss of a close friend. Youth work is also being managerialised in the Irish context and when organisations submit annual reports for Garda Youth Diversion Projects, they are required to identify the aims of the action, project or group, the objectives, the expected outcomes and their assessment of the degree to which the outcomes were achieved (Office of the Minister for Children, 2008). As voluntary organisations tend to be reliant on diverse State funding streams, the resulting administrative burden has clear implications for direct youth work practice. Youth workers now engage in extensive record keeping and report writing, which means a reduction in the amount of frontline work or the actual time they associate with young people. When youth workers operate in this culture of numbers, targets and achievements, it becomes increasingly difficult for them to conceptualise and develop their work in ways that have the youth work relationship as a central point of reference.

The informality that characterises youth work is constantly mentioned in policy documents and other sources, when in fact all the recent indicators are that the work is being formalised. If, as has happened in other professions, a managerial cadre is being established in the youth service comprised of persons from business rather than youth work backgrounds, this will also bring greater formality to youth work practice. Organisational policies and procedures focused on health and safety and child protection have also reduced the potential for spontaneous and creative practice. In this climate of increased regulation, doing something different or exciting is often quickly ruled out on the grounds that 'it mightn't be covered by insurance' or 'it might breach child protection guidelines.' Despite the rhetoric about volunteering, the contribution that can be made by volunteers is increasingly circumscribed as they are perceived as being subordinate to the professional workers employed in services. Youth work is also being increasingly integrated into systems and frameworks common to other areas of professional service delivery in the name of accountability for State funding. Underpinning the competence-based approaches to youth work, which were mentioned earlier in this chapter, is the reduction of youth work practice to a set of core tasks, leaving little room for creativity or ingenuity (Spence and Jeffs, 2007/2008). Working in partnership with other professionals or engagement in 'inter-agency work' further dilutes the informality and the distinctiveness that characterises the work, as its values and practices are inflected by those of other occupations.

Through interagency arrangements, there is also the danger that youth agencies take referrals and are drawn in to perform 'social youth work' without adequate resources, thus compensating for flagrant inadequacies in vital State supports for young people with difficulties. The National Education Welfare Board (NEWB) has remained underfunded for some time, as has the National Educational Psychological Service (NEPS). There is a clear lack of dedicated mental health services for young people in the Irish context. Youth work has to resist becoming the cheap surrogate for State support services that some young people need in contemporary Irish society. As Shaw (2003*a*: 225) has written, joined-up thinking can very quickly become 'stitched-up thinking' when there is failure to adequately analyse what is happening. Youth workers are now part of the professional culture that they previously castigated for oppressing many young people. In the current climate of enthusiasm for joined-up working, can youth workers retain what they argue are their more authentic relationships with young people when they are perceived as having motivations common to, or indeed influenced by other agencies? The legislation (Youth Work Act 2001) provides little solace in this regard, as youth work is identified as complementary to the work of other agencies, clearly indicating its perceived marginal status relative to these other agencies in the lives of young people. The legislation does not encourage voluntary youth organisations to take lead positions in interagency working arrangements. Given their lower status, can youth organisations and individual youth workers have the confidence to preserve what is precious about what they do and to question what others do when working interprofessionally?

The concept of social education has anchored youth work over time, yet it is a concept that is highly amorphous. In the context of youth work it can be deployed in many different ways. According to Smith (1988: 105) '... the definitional and strategic problems associated with social education in youth work are of such magnitude as to make the term useless as a theoretical and hence practical tool.' While social education is a concept and approach that has at different times been radicalised, it is largely imprinted on Irish youth work in ways consistent with individualistic and liberal values. By this I mean that the focus of social education in Irish youth work has been largely concerned with enabling young people to manage their lives as best they can in the society of which they are part. In contrast, a more radical social education approach might engage young people in a consciousness-raising exercise so that they develop the kind of sophisticated socio-political analysis of their oppressive life situations. It is intended that this would prompt young people to collectively want to act on society in a way intended to bring about structural or institutional change. The life-skills programmes that were in vogue in the 1980s, or indeed the peer education, teen pregnancy or crime prevention programmes are indicative of a long-standing tradition in youth work, which seeks to produce subjects who are sufficiently informed and skilled to live responsible lives. The radical potential is not realised in such programmes because they are conceptualised in ways that prioritise individual solutions to issues structural in origin. We have witnessed the proliferation of social education approaches in schools and other settings. Indeed the Costello Report (Department of Labour, 1984), which is seen as the landmark in the usage of the term, recommended that a space be made for social education in the formal school curriculum. As a result, social education is no longer the property of youth work alone. Furthermore, with the influence of postmodern thinking in the field of education, increasing doubt has been cast on the potential of active learning strategies and critical pedagogies to liberate (see Gore, 1993; Usher and Edwards, 1994). The intentions of those who seek to liberate the oppressed have also been subjected to interrogation. Magnuson (2005: 164), referring to work with young people, has argued that '... it is often those who seek to liberate who are the most self-deceptive about their own motives.' Weiler (1991) referred to the history of the women's movement to support her assertion that, even when there is a strong grounding in Freirian consciousness-raising and feminist pedagogy, it does not always happen that a commitment to social transformation is maintained.

Voluntary Participation

The voluntary principle has been used to distinguish youth work from other services concerned with young people. Traditionally this meant that young people freely involved themselves in youth provision and continued or ended their involvement entirely at their own behest. However, included under the mantel of the youth service in Ireland are projects that can be characterised as having more coercive kinds of participation and a greater orientation towards the surveillance and control of young people. The use of contracts more often associated with social work or probationary practices have crept into use in youth work projects and clearly compromise the notion of voluntary participation. Garda Youth Diversion Projects or what were formerly called Garda Special Projects operate on the basis of targeting and referrals from other agencies and they typically involve close working relationships with local Gardaí. Bowden's (2006) case studies of youth crime prevention initiatives demonstrate that projects can move away from what distinguishes them as youth work initiatives to function as part of a network of agencies involved in the disciplining and surveillance of young people. While one diversion project actively resisted the pressure to become crime preventionist by pursuing a 'young people's right to be on the streets' agenda, another such project charged parents with the responsibility of monitoring more closely their children's unstructured leisure time and linked the young people hanging around into more structured provision. Considering the raft of laws, policies and other measures[x] curtailing young people's access to public space in recent years, this project did not focus on asserting young people's rights in this regard (Bowden, 2006). The *National Youth Justice Strategy* (Irish Youth Justice Service, 2008) acknowledges the social context of youth offending but describes the role of Garda Youth Diversion Projects in a way that bypasses this broader context in favour of an approach focused on individual offenders and their families. The 'risk conditions' identified for the attention of these projects are young people's problematic behaviours, their personal and social deficiencies and their unstable home environments (Irish Youth Justice Service, 2008). As youth organisations are increasingly finding a niche in the crime prevention policy arena, their policies and practices are at real risk of being conceived along very narrow crime prevention lines.

The participation of young people at the decision-making levels of youth organisations is limited, as acknowledged in the *National Youth Work Development Plan* (Department of Education and Science, 2003*a*) and other sources (Galvin, 1994). Recently the Comhairle na nÓg Implementation Group (2007: 7) saw fit to distinguish between what the Group termed 'participatory work' from 'youth work' on the grounds that '... it is possible to be engaged in youth work in an organisation in which there is no involvement by children or young people in decision making.' Skott-Myhre (2005), writing about youth work in the American context, has identified the lack of democracy in youth organisations as a serious problem. He argued that this democratic deficit is evident in youth worker and young people's exclusion from decisions as to how money is raised and distributed within agencies. Indeed, voluntary youth work organisations in Ireland tend to have relatively hierarchical structures and fairly centralised control over budgets and decision-making, so that democratic decision-making, a key value of youth work, is not experienced in practice by workers employed in these organisations. If youth workers are not enfranchised or empowered in their own organisational environments, working in empowering ways with young people may well elide them.

Youth organisations have also been called upon to facilitate consultation with young people for Government and funding bodies. In so doing, the voluntary youth work sector has colluded with the State in the promotion of a new vocabulary of participation and new niches or one-off consultative events[xi] where young people are invited to participate. The Union of Secondary Students perceived Comhairle na nÓg and Dáil na nÓg to be tokenistic developments (see Murphy, 2005). The view of the union was that the production of the National Play Policy was the only recommendation from the Dáil to have been taken seriously and that any recommendations made, which might be at odds with official policy, would not be taken on board. The union argued that progress would only be made when there was a concerted move toward a young-person-led agenda. An evaluation of the Children and Young Persons Forum (Harper, 2007) revealed that it had no clear aim and objectives, no procedures guiding the forum participants in representing their peers, no rules governing the term of office and no transparency around how young people identified and linked in with the forum.

In a report identifying the barriers to children's rights in Ireland, Kilkelly (2007) recommended that it was vital to move beyond one-off consultation processes if young people's participation in mainstream decision-making structures was to be embedded. She argued that it would require legislation or financial incentives to persuade decision-making bodies to integrate children and young people's voices. Within the youth work sector there appears to be some misgivings about its role in facilitating consultation exercises with young people for Government and funding agencies. Kearney (2007*b*: 2), CEO of Youth Work Ireland, urged organisations to consider if the 'whispered comments of tokenism and manipulation' are taken seriously or if the sector is complicit in 'striving for comatose consensus'. A commitment to youth participation was attributed to youth work practice before it became significant in Government policy and rhetoric. However, despite some progress, the adjustments in power relations required in the youth service and in wider society to invest the concept of youth participation with real meaning have not yet happened.

Models of Youth Work Practice

Youth work is closely aligned to the disciplines of education, psychology, sociology and social work. According to Jeffs and Smith (1987: 2), counselling, group work, community work and social work have all been 'raided for theory and guides to [youth work] practice'. Social movements, particularly the feminist, anti-racist and gay liberation movements, have also generated a corpus of knowledge and practice, which the youth sector has drawn upon in practice over time (see Batsleer, 1996; Kampmann, 1996; Spence, 1996). As highlighted earlier in this chapter, in the Irish context, youth work organisations and practitioners have been drawn into other sectors and related fields of practice in order to develop and maintain services. The implication of this is that youth work policy and practice risks being perceived as constituting a little bit of everything else rather than as an identifiable field of policy and practice in its own right. It is hardly surprising that, over time, theoretical and models frameworks drawn from the discipline of sociology have been increasingly employed to explain and analyse the practices of youth work and to mark it out as a distinct form of social intervention.

In the Irish context, Hurley and Treacy (1993) produced a sociological framework and a set of models, which has been overwhelmingly utilised in Ireland to capture the breadth of youth work practice. This framework is comprised of four models, which could be further subdivided into two types: two models (character building and personal development) that seek to promote the status quo and are based on a deficiency perspective in terms of how young people are viewed; and two models (critical social education and radical social change) that seek to promote societal transformation and are based on a perspective that emphasises young people's potential to be engaged as agents in bringing about this transformation.

Employing a framework to make sense of youth work can have its attractions. Typologies of practice or frameworks attempt to put order on what can be very messy, fragmented and fluid. Traditionally, in some practice contexts, theory was disparaged as having no place and the business of youth work was presented as being no more ambitious than 'getting the kids off the streets'. Undoubtedly the framework approach has the potential to promote some kind of congruence between theory and practice and to promote conversation about the dialectical relationship between them. Distinctive elements of styles of practice are made explicit, as well as their outcomes, when a models framework is utilised to conceptualise what is happening. It could even be argued that typologies are needed now more than ever as the penchant towards competence-based youth work threatens to reduce youth work to a set of tasks driven by unimaginative policy imperatives, devoid of moral or analytical thinking.

However, as Meade argues in the case of community development in Chapter 3, the field of youth work practice is possibly not best served by being bracketed into types. Treacy (Chapter 8) points out that very little youth work theory has come from youth work practice and thus, in my view, the models framework can privilege what is predominantly an academic and idealised study of youth work. The possible implications are that we are not sufficiently mindful of the limits of theory-driven models to access the truth and to guide practice. For example, while there may be the possibility of youth workers and young people collaborating to bring about revolutionary change, is it possible to find youth work practice in the current field with overt revolutionary intent? Models also have the potential to be culled in a crude fashion to give legitimacy to some activity in the name of youth work practice. Similarly, a complicated theory, such as Freirian conscientization (Freire, 1971), can be reduced to assertion or slogan as if to suggest it pervades practice, when in fact it is sparsely evident in practice.

It could also be argued that there is now a theoretical incompleteness in Hurley and Treacy's models framework, considering that it was developed in the 1990s and is still being applied without due attention to key developments and debates in the sociological field of enquiry. Postmodern approaches have prompted new ways of looking at the social world and new questions relevant for any sociological theorisation of youth work. For example, the notion that there can be one transcendent programme of social change has been challenged very convincingly from a postmodern perspective (see Leonard, 1995), raising key questions about the conceptualisation of the critical social education and radical social change models of youth work practice. Furthermore, many sociological commentators (Miles, 2000) have argued that, in advanced capitalist societies characterised by risk, young people's transitions have become more complex (see Chapter 2 for more discussion). Young people have fewer reference points by which they can plot their life courses and they are exposed to a pluralisation of life opportunities (Melucci, 1992), albeit in societies where structural and social cleavages still exist (see Chapter 2). Aside from the material conditions in which young people live their lives, culture and identity have gained greater credence as significant markers and postmodern thinking has prompted us to attend more carefully to the multiple realities of young people's lives. The models framework was largely influenced by a sociological analysis that concentrated on the significance of social structures, institutions and the material circumstances governing young people's lives.

The prevailing models frameworks would need to be reworked to take account of theoretical developments and forms of practice, which are not readily accommodated in their underpinning analysis. Critical poststructuralist insights prompt alternative and useful insights into the dynamics of the relationship between youth workers and young people.[xii] For example, rather than viewing youth workers as all-powerful and young people as entirely powerless, the poststructuralist conceptualisation of power enables us to attend to the ways young people also exercise power in their interactions and negotiations with workers (see Fitzsimons, 2007). Postmodern thinking also directs our attention to strains of practice that have identity, transitions or lifestyle as a key focus of the work.[xiii] Indeed, the discussion that underpinned the *National Youth Work Development Plan* (Department of Education and Science, 2003*a*) referred to pressures, choices, complex transitions, individualism and consumerism, concepts that we have come to associate with commentaries on youth inspired by postmodernist thinking. As Devlin comments in Chapter 2, it was envisaged in the plan that youth work had to play its part in addressing the problems generated by the accelerated pace of change in Irish life and in educating young people to be critical consumers. We can indeed add models to the existing framework, but it might be more useful to consider frameworks of practice as nothing more than 'ideal-typical overviews' (O' Sullivan, 2005: 104), a central point of reference with merits as well as significant limitations.

Conclusion

In 2007, Diarmuid Kearney (2007*b*), CEO of Youth Work Ireland, posited a number of searching questions relating to whether contemporary youth work was moving in a direction that was causing it to lose touch with key aspects of its heritage. Kearney attributed the problems underlying the questions he posed to failure within the sector to achieve and articulate a clearer vision as to what youth work is precisely. He suggested that, if this clarity was achieved, then the legislation, policy and other planned developments should not present too many difficulties for the sector. Despite the obvious concern that exists,[xiv] the main voluntary youth work organisations in Ireland seem determined to stay on the path of least resistance, lest they endanger their bright, new, secure future. At last it might seem that the tide has come in for the youth work sector, which has in the past felt left out in the cold, unrecognised and unappreciated by State agencies. Pragmatism seems to have taken root in the sector as it tries desperately not to lose sight of the money and its 'rightful' place alongside the other professions, and centre stage on the Government policy agenda. Given the stance adopted by the sector in the context of recent developments, it is now more important than ever that a wider vision of youth work is projected than that circumscribed by Government policy imperatives. We might take some solace from the sector's very public and unequivocal opposition to the introduction of Anti-Social Behaviour Orders (ASBOs) in Ireland. However, the sector needs to develop and maintain a strong critical voice on behalf of young people and this will at times involve challenging Government policy unambiguously.

The values at the core of youth work can no longer be reduced to slogans. These values have to be given meaning and the ways in which they breathe life into youth work have to be made explicit. Then we can be clear about what we stand to lose when they are constrained, compromised or, indeed, impossible to practice. A vigorous independent reassertion of the concepts, values and practices is now urgent if they are not to be further mutated and appropriated in a manner that renders them meaningless.

Bowden's (2006) case studies of youth crime prevention initiatives indicate that, in responding to the State's crime prevention agenda, youth work practice can mutate into something that resembles policing rather than youth working. The Irish youth work sector might well heed Jeffs and Smith's (1994) assertion that, if youth work is to survive with integrity, it has to stay out of key State surveillance systems. It may also be time to apply their 'democratic audit' to policy and programmes in the Irish context so that any practices that do not embody democratic values can be exposed and rejected as having no place in youth work (see Jeffs and Smith, 1994). The sector must not tender for or accept funding for projects that threaten to undermine significant aspects of its practice.

Youth work agencies have to campaign for universal provision rather than settle for delivering stigmatising residual provision for certain constituencies of young people. Increasingly, a marker of the youth service's success is the extent to which it engages with 'unattached' or 'marginalised' young people as targets for particular policy initiatives. The challenge now for the service is to re-engage with young people whose lives are not defined as 'problematic' and where the scope of the intervention is open and organic rather than policy driven. In Ireland, the youth service has a mode of practice that is unique to it – the youth club. It would do well to champion and protect the club rather than see it sacrificed to the vagaries of Government policy and funding priorities, which continue to be short term and insecure. As Jeffs and Smith (2002) remind us, in youth work practice there is a clear associational alternative that has strong empirical support in terms of its long-term impact upon the lives of communities. The British Government recently acknowledged the evidence suggesting that the more unstructured the provision, the more likely it is to attract the more disadvantaged young people (see Spence, 2007). The club and other such generic youth work initiatives possibly offer the best opportunities for a relatively genuine engagement with young people and for a positive reassertion of youth work's core values.

Notes

i Traditionally, the youth work sector in Ireland was very fragmented (see Jenkinson, 2000) but in its pursuit of sectorisation and legitimacy, the youth work sector has increasingly laid claim to a small set of core values distilled out of a more complex or confused set of intentions held by the different organisations now constituted as making up the youth sector.

ii Jeffs and Smith (1994: 19) noted that '... many early youth workers unapologetically laid claim to specialist expertise in controlling working-class youth, viewing it as their duty to apply their skills in the interest of society.'

iii Sociological 'post' theories incorporate a critique of previous theoretical assumptions about a range of issues including the self, the social and the political, which I believe are useful. The value of preserving a critical impulse is that we can resist sliding into forms of 'post' thinking that may be ethically and politically regressive (for more extensive discussion see Browning *et al.*, 2000).

iv Post-structuralism is a complicated skein of thought encompassing a number of diverse intellectual currents (see Peters, 1998). There is a poststructuralist orientation in this chapter in that it seeks to critically interrogate taken-for-granted assumptions or ideas in the field of youth work.

v When liberal conceptualisations of equality prevail, the hierarchies of wealth, power and status in society remain unaffected (see Lynch, 1999).

vi The Connexions Strategy devised by the British Labour Government in 2000 brought together a number of already established and new initiatives in England and was designed to work across Government departments and agencies. The rationale for the strategy was that it would enhance participation and attainment at school and in turn participation in the labour market, thus providing a ladder out of social exclusion for underachieving young people aged between 13 and 19. It is essentially a careers, counselling and advice service. Connexions Partnerships throughout England bring together all the youth support services in each area. The negative implications of the Connexions Strategy for the youth service in England have been explored by many commentators, including Smith (2002) and Spence (2004).

vii Youth organisations compete for the Allied Irish Bank Better Ireland Awards and Permanent TSB supports Foróige's youth citizenship programme.

viii There are many definitions of peer education, but a key characteristic or principle of peer education is that those of the same societal group or social standing educate each other about a variety of issues or a specific concern (see Parkin and McKeganey 2000 for further discussion of peer education approaches).

ix According to Bradford (2005), the notion of the youth work relationship as an intrinsic good in itself and the emphasis on emotional engagement (the expressive goals of youth work) associated with traditional forms of practice are losing ground to a focus on narrow goals, on task performance and on efficiency and effectiveness (the instrumental goals of youth work).

x Some retailers use a mosquito device, which emits a sound only heard by children and young people and is designed to prevent them from congregating close to their outlets. Increasingly, architectural designs of public places and housing estates have sought to prevent young people from engaging in such activities as skateboarding. A survey undertaken by the National Children's Office in December 2002 found that there were 168 playgrounds in the State, compared to 405 golf courses (National Children's Office, 2004). Young people are subject to criminal justice public order legislation and can also be administered behaviour orders and anti-social behaviour orders as a result of their introduction into Irish law in 2006.

xi Dáil na nÓg is the annual national parliament for children and young people (aged 12–18 years). Delegates are elected to the parliament through their local Comhairle na nÓg. This was set up under the National Children's Strategy in City and County Development Boards throughout the country to give children and young people a voice in the development of local services and policies. The Children and Young People's Forum (CYPF) was established to advise the Minister for Children on issues of concern to children and young people. The forum is comprised of young people (aged between 12 and 18) from different parts of the country. The Office of the Minister for Children has conducted consultations with children and young people on a range of legislative and policy issues which concern them.

xii Critical post theories provide a useful resource for analysing issues relating to context, power relations, identity and change in the practice of youth work.

xiii Examples might include youth work projects specifically for young people who identify as gay, lesbian, etc. or projects assisting young people with independent living. Environmental or Internet-based projects might be other examples.

xiv In an editorial in *Irish Youth Work Scene*, Diarmuid Kearney welcomed the '... flurry of activity' or the developments designed to increasingly professionalise the sector. However he also pointed out the need to be vigilant in ensuring that young people remain the primary and exclusive service focus and that the core principles youth work hold dear are being preserved (see Kearney, 2007*c*).

2

Theorising 'Youth'

Maurice Devlin

Introduction

Theory is something that is often not highly valued by youth workers and others who work with young people. 'I'm not a great one for theory. I prefer to get on with doing the job,' is a not uncommon opinion. Such a view is based on a misunderstanding of the nature of theory and of the relationship between theory and practice. Specifically, it reflects the misguided notion that theory is necessarily both abstract and abstruse, something 'academic' and impractical. But in fact, as Kurt Lewin once wrote, 'there is nothing as practical as a good theory' (Lewin, 1952: 346). Theory is essentially concerned with *explanation* and *understanding* of why things are the way they are; of why things work the way they do. It is therefore utterly indispensable to good practice, whether the practice in question is car mechanics, brain surgery or youth work.

Theory of youth work provides an explanation and understanding of what makes for effective and appropriate youth work practice, in different settings and contexts and with different groups of young people. It critically examines the values and assumptions that underpin practice, and it throws light on how youth work and youth workers relate to the State, social policy and the economy; to other professions and stakeholders; to local communities; and to young people themselves. Other contributions to this volume explore some of the key dimensions of youth work theory.

Also of fundamental importance to practitioners is theory that is concerned with an explanation and understanding of the *youth* in 'youth work'. Theory of youth addresses a wide range of topics and questions. What is distinctive about youth as a stage in the lifecycle or the life course, and how does it relate to other stages? To what extent does it overlap with the concept of adolescence? What is the lived experience of young people, or of different groups of young people, for example, young people in different classes or cultures, or with different identities or circumstances? In what ways is the experience of 'youth' different for young men and young women? How have young people's lives changed over time, and what has caused such change? What factors are shaping the experiences of young people and the nature of youth in today's society, and how is it likely that relations between the generations will change in the future?

Answers to questions such as these are far from straightforward, and there are often differences of opinion from one theorist to another, or one academic discipline to another, as we will see. However, such answers are also far from abstract. The nature of any youth work practice will depend crucially on the understanding of 'youth' on which such practice rests. Therefore different responses to these 'theoretical' questions will lead to different types of practice. This is why practitioners who say 'I'm not a great one for theory. I prefer to get on with doing the job' (or a variation on this theme) are actually betraying the fact that they simply do not recognise or understand the theoretical assumptions on which their practice rests. This means that they may not be in a position to explain their practice, either to themselves or others. They may not be in a position to reflect consciously or creatively on it (for example, by exploring *alternative* assumptions) and therefore may not be in a position to improve it.

Youth and Adolescence in History

Adults – particularly of course adult intellectuals, whose views tend to be highly influential in shaping the way 'lay' people think – have been 'theorising' about youth for generations, even for millennia. In *Ars Rhetorica (Rhetoric)*, Aristotle (384–322 BC) gave an account of the 'youthful type of character', which he distinguished from adulthood and old age. He had a decidedly gendered understanding of such a character, holding certain views that remain widespread in our own society today (reflected for instance in the fact that in English the singular noun 'a youth' is almost exclusively used to refer to young men). In other ways too his perspective on youth foreshadowed many of today's stereotypical images of young people:

> Young men have strong passions, and tend to gratify them indiscriminately. Of the bodily desires, it is the sexual by which they are most swayed and in which they show absence of self-control. They are changeable and fickle in their desires, which are violent while they last, but quickly over: their impulses are keen but not deep-rooted.... They think they know everything, and are always quite sure about it; this, in fact, is why they overdo everything ...

As regards the boundaries between youth and other stages, a similarly gendered example from the ancient Western world is the fourfold categorisation put forward by the Roman philosopher and statesman Cicero (106–43BC) in the treatise *De Senectute (On Old Age)*. He distinguished between 'boyhood' (*pueritia*), 'adolescence' (*adulescentia*), 'settled or middle age' (*aetas constans* or *media*) and 'old age' (*senectus*). However, in practice, age gradations were not carefully applied, and apart from certain specific instances – such as age of enrolment in the army (which sometimes had lower and upper age limits), liability for taxation (which may have had age bands), and perhaps the holding of political office – in general 'a simple binary was applied', as Barclay (2007) points out:

> After childhood and a loosely defined 'youth' (for men until their mid-twenties), the free population (both male and female) was divided into two categories, the 'young(er)' and 'old(er)', with no clearly defined boundary between them, or rather, only such demarcation as fitted the rhetorical or political interests of those who created it. (Barclay, 2007: 230)

This appears to have been the case for much of the intervening period in the Western World (and is true in many 'traditional' societies even today). Insofar as a clear demarcation between the generations *did* exist, it was provided by the onset of puberty and physical signs of 'adult' reproductive capacity (and associated capacities and responsibilities); the idea of a protracted 'transition' into adulthood had not taken hold. This is the thesis of Philippe Aries (1962), who argues that Europeans made no significant distinction between childhood and adolescence before the end of the eighteenth century. People had 'no idea of what we call adolescence' because effectively there was 'no room for adolescence' (Aries, 1962: 23, 27) by which he meant that the institutional arrangements and provisions that set young people apart from young children and from adults, such as an extended period of formal education, were not yet needed and had not yet developed.

Others have taken issue with this view, a notable example being Natalie Zemon Davis (1975) who analyses the sixteenth-century French 'youth abbeys' or 'youth kingdoms': groups of young people in towns and villages who played a key part in carnivals, festivities and other important communal events and who helped to regulate or sanction aspects of community members' behaviour through a variety of (often uproarious) methods. Davis suggests that, not just in France but 'throughout rural Europe', such groups fulfilled some of the functions attributed to contemporary adolescence:

> They gave the youth rituals to help control their sexual instincts and also to allow them some limited sphere of jurisdiction or 'autonomy' in the interval before they were married. They socialized them to the conscience of the community by making them the raucous voice of that conscience. (Davis, 1975: 108–9)

Nonetheless, whatever the precise configuration of age relations in the past, and whatever echoes we can find of today's age-related assumptions in the literature, art and philosophy of other times and places, it is still safe to say that conceptions of 'youth' and 'adolescence' and their relationship to other stages in life are much more complex and multifaceted (some would say much more ambivalent) in contemporary society than they have ever been heretofore. Such conceptions – and the *practices* associated with them, the lived realities of young people's lives – have, in particular, undergone a dramatic shift since the onset of the industrial era. Industrialisation and the attendant processes of urbanisation and modernisation transformed all aspects of social life, including age relations, the lifecycle and the life course (concepts which will be explained further below). As part of the process of transformation, new academic disciplines emerged (including sociology, psychology and education), which provided new ways of understanding, responding to and perhaps even shaping the changes taking place.

These disciplines remain crucial in providing us with sets of (often contrasting) 'lenses' through which to apprehend and understand the experiences of young people in today's society. As will be suggested again later in this chapter, it is very important that we do not accept any of their theoretical accounts unquestioningly or at face value. We should continuously subject them to scrutiny and test them against our own personal experience and against the views and voices of the young people with whom our work brings us into direct contact. Only then can we assess the extent to which any or all of these theories can live up to Kurt Lewin's touchstone of 'practicality'.

The rest of this chapter will present a range of theoretical perspectives on youth under five main headings. The five categories are neither exhaustive nor mutually exclusive, and in some cases individual theorists and researchers can be seen to straddle different perspectives at the same time, or to have moved from one to another in the course of their careers. The perspectives are briefly summarised below and described in more detail in the sections that follow.

Developmental perspectives are rooted in mainstream psychology and are principally concerned with the processes of change which individual young people go through – physical change, cognitive and intellectual change, and socio-emotional change – during their *adolescence* (which is the central concept employed).

Generational perspectives are highly complementary to developmental accounts and emphasise the ways in which young people, as they undergo shared processes of individual development (and to a large extent because they have this in common), also engage in collective forms of expression and activity through a distinctive *youth culture*, which marks them out in a very public way as a separate generation.

Structural conflict perspectives reject what they regard as a homogenising approach to 'youth culture' (and indeed 'youth work') and focus instead on the ways in which the lives and experiences of different groups of young people (often in different subcultures) systematically reflect broader structures of social inequality (relating particularly to class, gender, culture and ethnicity, sexuality, dis/ability).

Transitional perspectives began with a specific focus on the 'transition from school to work' (TSW) in the late 1970s and early 1980s but have broadened to accommodate a more recent postmodernist concern with the complexity and contingency of young people's *transitions* (plural) in both their personal and public lives, and with the increasing need for young people to manage risk and negotiate their own 'biographical projects'.

Constructionist perspectives overlap to some extent with transitional ones and place an emphasis on the ways in which youth, both as a social category and as a stage in the lives of individual young people, is actively constructed and 'constituted' within a variety of *discourses* and related *practices* – discourses and practices which are often incompatible or contradictory (youth as a troublesome social problem; as a vulnerable or turbulent 'phase'; as an idealistic and energetic social resource, and so on).

Developmental Perspectives

As already noted, developmental perspectives tend to be associated with the discipline of psychology, and for the most part they start by recognising the biological and physiological aspects of adolescence: the most obvious way in which it is a 'developmental' stage is that, physically, girls become young women and boys become young men. As well as a generalised 'growth spurt', the key physical changes include menarche (the onset of menstruation) and breast development for females; and sperm production and 'voice breaking' (the growth of the larynx) for males. Both sexes also experience hair growth, particularly in the pubic area, which is why the stage of early adolescence is also called 'puberty' (which ultimately comes from the Latin for 'growing hairy'). Boys begin to mature physically on average two years later than girls, while both sexes are maturing earlier today than ever before due to the influence of socio-cultural factors such as diet and nutrition. Brain size, structure and function also change significantly during the adolescent years. Accompanying all of these transformations, and directly inducing some of them, is a dramatic increase in hormonal activity in the body: adolescence is the most 'hormonally active' stage in the lifecycle.

However, what is of most interest from a psychological (and certainly from a youth work) point of view is the impact of these physical changes on other aspects of young people's experience and development. The physical changes in the brain are clearly related to young people's *cognitive development*, which refers to 'all those abilities associated with thinking and knowing' (Birch, 1997: 63). The best known and most influential account of developments in cognition from infancy to adolescence is that of Jean Piaget (1926), who identified four intellectual stages, culminating in the *formal operational* stage, beginning at about eleven years of age and therefore closely associated with development during adolescence. This is when more complex and abstract thought becomes possible:

> [Adolescents] are more aware than the younger child that events can be interpreted in many ways and that there is no final version of truth ... This mature system of thought allows the mastery of complex systems of literature, mathematics and science. It also enables the development of abilities necessary for adult socio-emotional

> adjustment, such as the planning of future goals and the integration of past and present into a realistic self-identity. (Bourne and Ekstrand, 1979: 309–310)

Piaget also argued that changes in cognition were necessary (but not sufficient) for *moral development* to take place. Building further on Piaget's work, Lawrence Kohlberg (1963) identified three levels of moral development (each of which was in turn broken down into two stages, which need not concern us here). The first level he called *pre-conventional*, when 'morality is shaped by the standards of adults and the consequences of following or breaking their rules' (McIlveen and Gross, 1997: 87). This applies up to about ten years of age and is followed by *conventional* morality, when the sense of right and wrong is further internalised, shaped by the desire to help and please others and to maintain social order. Kohlberg believed that only a minority of people progress beyond this to *post-conventional* morality, and those who do tend to do so well into their adulthood. At the post-conventional level it is recognised that moral and legal precepts are sometimes in conflict, and people come to be guided by their own ethical principles. Kohlberg was criticised by Gilligan (1982) for not recognising gender differences, specifically the contrasting 'moral orientations' of 'justice' and 'care' into which boys and girls are, respectively, more likely to be socialised. His work can also be criticised on a number of other grounds but the conceptual framework he presented remains useful as a point of departure in the study of moral development.

Cognitive development is closely related not just to moral reasoning but – as the quotation above makes clear – to young people's overall *personal, social and emotional development*, because among the things they are capable of 'thinking and knowing' about in new ways are their own personalities and their relationships with others and with the world at large. Much of the psychological investigation of such matters has focused on the concept of identity, and most studies of identity are influenced in one way or another by Erik Erikson's (1963) theory of psychosocial development, which was further elaborated upon by James Marcia (1980). Within Erikson's framework, adolescence is one of eight universal psychosocial stages in the lifecycle, each of which has a particular 'crisis' associated with it (by 'crisis' is meant a key issue to be resolved). In adolescence the crisis relates to identity formation, to the formulation of a coherent answer to questions such as: 'Who am I?' 'What are my beliefs and attitudes?' 'Who or what do I want to be in the future?'

While Erikson's claim that his psychosocial stages are universally applicable is highly questionable, the notion that during their adolescence young people begin the process of grappling with substantial questions about their identity is certainly very persuasive. What is less convincing (or in tune with the experience of most adults and young people in today's society) is the idea that identity is 'resolved' or fully formed by the end of adolescence. A further criticism of Erikson's approach is that it was unduly influenced by his clinical work with troubled adolescents and therefore serves to reinforce the widespread stereotypical image of youth as inherently 'problematic'. For recent discussions of such stereotyping in the Irish context, see Devlin (2005, 2006*a*).

An alternative and more balanced view of young people's social and psychological development is provided by Coleman and Hendry (1999), who argue that what is needed is a theory of adolescent *normality* rather than abnormality. There are certainly a lot of developmental tasks and challenges confronting young people during the adolescent years, including relations with peers and parents, the discovery and development of sexuality, and issues related to education, (un)employment, leisure and lifestyle; but for most young people concerns about the different issues reach a peak at different ages or stages, so the pressures are not simultaneous or overwhelming. Based on an empirical investigation, Coleman (and later his collaborator Hendry) developed 'focal theory' to explain how and why most young people move through their adolescence without undue difficulty (in other words without experiencing 'storm and stress'), while acknowledging that some do have a need for special support and intervention.

Coleman and Hendry also stress the role of individual young people as 'active agents' who play a significant part in shaping or determining their own development (rather than being helplessly swept along by unseen hormonal, biological or psychological forces). Furthermore, they support the argument of writers like Bronfenbenner (1979) that human development has an 'ecology', meaning that it is shaped by and interacts with its environment: 'for children and young people, the context of development is not just the family, but the geographical, historical, social and political setting in which the family is living' (Coleman and Hendry, 1999: 12). This raises questions more usually dealt with by the discipline of sociology, which is the principal source of the theoretical and empirical work discussed in the following sections.

Generational Perspectives

As already suggested, 'generational' perspectives within the sociology of youth are highly complementary to developmental psychological accounts of adolescence. What we are here calling generational theory accepts that young people, by virtue of their age alone, are inherently different from children on the one hand and adults on the other; that these differences are in themselves of great significance for individuals and for society; and that they manifest themselves in a distinctive *youth culture* with its own roles, values and behaviour patterns. Generational accounts are most typically presented within an overall approach to sociological analysis called 'functionalism', which explains all major social phenomena with reference to the positive functions they fulfil in terms of promoting social order and stability. From this perspective, youth culture – despite its frequent apparent 'unruliness' and 'rebelliousness' – serves a number of 'important positive functions' both for young people and for society as a whole (Parsons, 1972: 146).

Youth culture's positive functions, even when it appears problematic or troublesome from many adults' point of view, includes the fact that it encourages young people to be creative and innovative rather than accepting unquestioningly the values and norms of their elders, and such a willingness to innovate is vital if society is to remain progressive, flexible and capable of responding to the complex demands of a changing environment. Paradoxically, however, it is through the very same 'problematic' or 'troublesome' peer groups that young people learn to *conform* (because of the influence of peer pressure), and conformity also is necessary for social stability. They may be more concerned in the short term with conforming to the expectations of their friends than those of their parents or teachers, but the important thing in the longer term is that they learn what conformity is, and they come to value it. Most rebellious young people, the thinking goes, 'return to the fold' having had the chance to experiment and innovate, and they are better equipped to be active and committed members of society having had such a chance (if they were denied it they might feel frustrated or resentful). In the meantime, their individual psychological need for a delay on assuming adult responsibilities (a 'moratorium', as Erikson called it), so as to facilitate their identity development, has also been fulfilled.

Generational accounts of youth dominated sociology throughout Europe and the United States in the 1950s and 1960s (although important earlier essays on the theme of generation included those by Ortega y Gasset, 1923, and Mannheim, 1927). The most systematic treatment came from S.N. Eisenstadt in *From Generation to Generation* (1956). Starting from the position that 'age and age relations are among the most basic aspects of life and the determinants of human destiny' (1956: 26), Eisenstadt argued that youth is a stage of particular importance in modern industrial societies. This is because there is a pronounced structural gap between the family of origin within which children spend their early years and the economic and social system in which they must eventually take their place. The family has become concentrated on emotional and sexual (rather than economic) functions, so new institutions are necessary to manage the transition out of the family. These include education, youth services and the media. They also include youth culture itself, whose key function relates to identity and autonomy:

> Youth's tendency to coalesce ... is rooted in the fact that participation in the family became insufficient for developing full identity or full social maturity, and that the roles learned in the family did not constitute an adequate basis for developing such identity and participation. In the youth groups the adolescent seeks some framework for the development and crystallization of his identity, for the attainment of personal autonomy, and for his effective transition into the adult world. (Eisenstadt 1963: 31–2)

Youth culture therefore has to be understood by reference to 'the process in which industrial society detaches children from their families and places them in/prepares them for the wider social system' (Frith, 1984: 20); this preparation being its key social function. While functionalism no longer commands the dominant position it once did within sociology, an emphasis on the central importance of age and generation continues to be found in much 'common sense' thinking about young people, youth culture and youth work, and indeed continues to characterise much social policy on youth in Ireland and elsewhere, the most obvious example being the age-based structure of the formal education system, a point to which we will return below. Media reports or casual discourse that generalise about 'young people today' are common. The 'needs of young people' or 'young people's experiences and opinions' (the suggestion being that young people are inherently different from children and from adults) are usually regarded as a starting point for youth work policy and practice; and of course the very idea of 'youth work' and other forms of youth service provision are rooted in the assumption that 'youth' itself has its own empirical and conceptual integrity. Much of the relevant recent research does, in fact, continue to sustain such a view; but it also suggests that the generational perspective should be tempered with an appreciation of the significance of factors other than age alone (Devlin, 2006*b*; Lalor *et al.*, 2007).

Structural Conflict Perspectives

We have seen that generational perspectives on youth are associated with functionalist sociology, which in turn is usually regarded as part of a broader approach to the study of modern society called 'consensus theory'. It is so called because it assumes that societies such as ours are built on a broad value consensus (basic agreement among their members on the things that matter), which helps to provide a sense of fundamental order and stability, even though there may be problems or challenges to be confronted from time to time. Closely related to its assumption about value consensus, this theoretical perspective adopts a generally benign view of contemporary western societies, regarding them as the enlightened product of centuries of progress and therefore as examples of the kind of social organisation to which other, less 'developed' societies, should aspire.

This view, which dominated sociology in Europe and North America for much of the twentieth century, came to be increasingly challenged by an alternative approach which can be termed 'structural conflict theory' (sometimes just one of the two words 'structural' or 'conflict' is used on its own). From this point of view the striking thing about contemporary societies is not their value consensus or social order but the fact that the entire social structure reflects (and sustains) pervasive conflict and inequality.

Whereas a generational or functionalist sociologist would begin the analysis of youth and youth culture by asking 'what positive functions does it serve for individuals and society?' a structural conflict approach assesses any social phenomenon by asking: 'in what ways is it related to major conflicts of interest and inequalities of circumstance and position?' Such major conflicts and inequalities, according to these theorists (most of whom have been influenced to a greater or lesser degree by the thinking of Karl Marx, 1818–1883) have little to do with age or generation, and therefore these concepts are of limited interest to them. Of far more interest is the way in which people's lives and experiences are systematically structured by such factors as class, gender, 'race', ethnicity and culture, sexuality and dis/ability. These are all significant forms of social stratification and inequality, whereas 'the generation gap' is not.

> We would argue, in the sense that it is [conventionally] aimed at ... that there can be no 'sociology of youth' – it is a misleading quest for a holy grail that does not exist. Youth as a concept is unthinkable. Even Youth as a social category does not make much empirical sense. Youth as a single, homogeneous group does not exist. (Hall, Jefferson and Clarke 1976: 18)

This is a statement from the authors of what is perhaps the best-known and most influential book dealing with youth from a structural conflict perspective. It emerged from the work of the Centre for Contemporary Cultural Studies (CCCS) at the University of Birmingham in the 1970s, and was called *Resistance Through Rituals* (Hall and Jefferson, 1975). It presents a broadly Marxist analysis of youth in society. Clearly, when the authors say that youth is 'unthinkable' they do not mean it literally, because it is obvious from the earlier part of this chapter that the concept of youth has been 'thought' (and acted upon) for centuries, at least in some parts of the world. What they mean is that youth as a concept is *not worth* thinking, that thinking it has little sociological value; or, worse, that it serves the ideological purpose of distracting attention from more important matters, specifically analysis and action in relation to major social inequalities, particularly those relating to class (Devlin, 2006*b*: 2). From a Marxist perspective (and even from the point of view of many contemporary theorists who recognise material and economic inequalities as fundamental but do not define themselves as Marxists), the most significant groups in society are the social classes, and all other major 'cultural configurations' will relate in one way or another to class.

For this reason Hall and his colleagues were interested not in a homogeneous 'youth culture' (which they did not believe existed) but rather in class-based youth subcultures, which at the time they were writing (or shortly beforehand) included the Teddy Boys, Rockers and Skinheads. It was certainly true that the particular dress, style, musical tastes, *argot* (slang), 'focal concerns and milieux' of such subcultures seemed to set them apart as different from both their parents and from 'ordinary' working-class boys and girls, but from Hall's point of view these differences were relatively trivial:

> Through dress, activities, leisure pursuits and lifestyle, they may project a different cultural response or 'solution' to the problems

> posed for them by their material and social class position and experience. But ...[e]specially in relation to the dominant culture, their sub-culture remains like other elements in their class culture – subordinate and subordinated. (Hall and Jefferson, 1975: 15)

The subordination of these young people is perpetuated, paradoxically, by the very subcultural activity and expression which to them seems so autonomous and 'self-controlled', and this key point is captured in the title of *Resistance Through Rituals*: forms of opposition and resistance that are 'ritualistic' and symbolic, operating at the level of dress, music, language and so on but not going beyond this, cannot provide a solution to 'working-class unemployment, educational disadvantage, compulsory miseducation, dead-end jobs, the routinisation and specialisation of labour, low pay and the loss of skills' (Hall and Jefferson, 1975: 47).

The analysis of Hall and the CCCS team remains enormously influential today, even if the particular forms of subcultural expression among young people have changed. From a class-based structural conflict perspective, even if the numbers of young people participating in second or third-level education have increased in the intervening decades, and the numbers of severely 'disadvantaged' (educationally and materially) have declined, the fundamentally unequal economic relationships on which the class structure rests have not changed at all (in other words the owners of wealth and the political elite are still largely the same individuals and families).

Because of its explicit focus on class and economic inequalities, the CCCS approach could be accused of being insensitive to (almost blind to) other significant inequalities, particularly gender. *Resistance Through Rituals* contained a chapter on 'girls and subcultures' followed by one on the 'marginality of girls', but these amounted to twenty pages in a book almost three hundred pages long. The deficit was remedied somewhat in later years by authors such as Angela McRobbie (herself co-author of the 'Girls and Subcultures' chapter), who provided an analysis in which the concepts of patriarchy and gender inequality are at least as significant as class (see, for example, McRobbie, 2000). As the title suggests, *Young Femininity: Girlhood, Power and Social Change* (Aapola *et al.*, 2005) also provides a recent feminist analysis, although its authors do also address the significance of class, 'race', disability and sexuality. These factors have themselves been prioritised in a range of studies which argue that a 'neat' developmental or generational model of adolescence and youth cannot sufficiently take account of the diversity of young people's lives and lifestyles (for example, Back, 1997; French and Swain, 1997; Monro, 2006; Robinson, 1997).

In Ireland, research studies of youth subcultures that draw on (at least elements of) the structural conflict approach and that are based substantially on ethnography (sustained participant observation) among young people include that by Jenkins (1983), who studied Protestant working-class young people very much from a class-conflict perspective, leading to criticism from Bell (1990), for whom the 'all embracing sectarian habitus' among young people (and older people) in Northern Ireland was at least as significant. Gaetz (1997) highlights both class differences and geographical divisions among young people in Cork, while Fagan's study (1995) of early school leavers adopts a 'post-structuralist and post-Marxist' framework which aims at contributing to the development of a radical democracy in Ireland. Fagan advocates a 'critical pedagogy' in which 'cultural workers' (which might include youth workers) would engage collaboratively with early school-leavers and together 'examine the specific contexts and constraints of the social and cultural practices that relate to their material location' (1995: 167).

Even when an avowed conflict perspective is not adopted, it is now largely accepted among youth studies scholars and researchers that an overemphasis on factors related to age and generation in shaping the lives and circumstances of young people can be simplistic and unrealistic. A recently published textbook on young people in contemporary Ireland (Lalor *et al.*, 2007) not only includes consideration throughout of the influence of gender and socio-economic background on young people's experiences of (for example) family life, the education system and leisure opportunities, but also devotes specific attention to the position of young LGBT (lesbian, gay, bisexual and transgender) people, young people with disabilities, young Travellers and other ethnic minorities, young people who are in care or homeless, and young people in rural areas.

Transitional Perspectives

Transitional perspectives can be dated back to the concern throughout the EC (or European Community, as the EU then was) in the 1970s and early 1980s with policy relating to youth unemployment and youth training, resulting in numerous studies focusing specifically on the 'transition from school to work' (TSW). The emphasis in youth policy at that time on matters relating to employment and unemployment (or 'employability and unemployability'), in Ireland as elsewhere, can be gauged from the fact that, for a period in the early 1980s, the Youth Affairs Section was attached to the Department of Labour rather than the Department of Education, its usual home. Transitional accounts are the most empirically orientated of all accounts of youth, in that they are often based on the detailed results of surveys and other quantitative research, and they are not as obviously aligned with a particular macro-sociological worldview as are generational and conflict perspectives.

More recent research from this perspective has moved beyond a concern with the transition from school to work alone to explore a variety of other aspects of young people's progression into adulthood, and particularly the relationship between the two principal 'axes' of transition, the public and the private (Galland, 1995). In the transitional pattern that came to dominate the industrial era, the public and private transitions of young people – from education into employment and from living at home to living independently with a partner – were relatively predictable and unidirectional, and also relatively irreversible (in the sense that having left the education system for the workplace, people did not normally return to it; and having left the parental home to marry and set up an independent household, they did not go back). There were of course some differences in the experience of transition, both public and private, based on factors such as class and gender (young working-class people moving into the workplace earlier; young women much more likely to move out of the workplace and into home duties after a few years), but overall the framework was relatively stable and predictable, like two parallel lines along which young people made the public and private transitions into adulthood. This 'traditional' model of access to adulthood in the industrial age is represented diagrammatically in Figure 2.1.

It now seems that this 'traditional' model may have been historically specific to industrial society and is being progressively redefined as we move into the 'post-industrial' era. Increasingly today, transitions are much less unidirectional and definitive and much more reversible and provisional. This is because adulthood itself – the supposed 'endpoint' of young people's transitions – is being redefined: 'Life trajectories have lost their predictability, values are irredeemably pluralized ... The very criteria upon which adult recognition rests are not static' (Blatterer, 2007: 787–8). Elsewhere it has been suggested that transitions previously associated with 'youth' are no longer so limited in scope: at all ages, 'backtracking, re-visiting, revising and the reversing of earlier decisions regarding life style and content are a growing feature of life' (Jeffs and Smith, 1998/99: 54). To take an obvious example of how things have changed, many more people in Ireland – both young

Figure 2.1: Traditional Model of Access to Adulthood

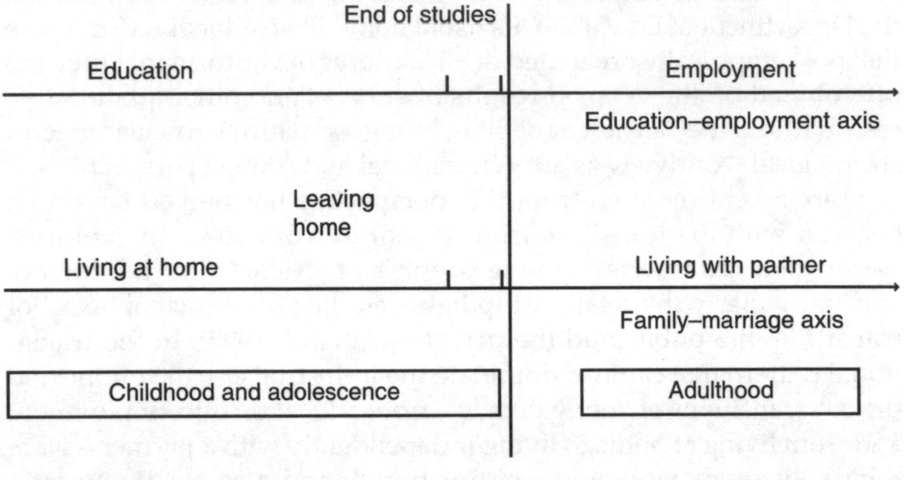

Source: Galland, O. (1995), `What Is Youth?' in A. Cavalli and O. Galland (eds.), *Youth in Europe*, London: Pinter, 3. Reproduced by kind permission of Continuum International Publishing Group.

people and adults – are today likely to be both in education (of one kind or another) and employment (of one kind or another) simultaneously, and the idea of being educated (or trained) at an early age for a job that will last a lifetime is increasingly becoming a thing of the past. Such blurring of 'traditional' generational boundaries has resulted in the development of concepts such as 'emergent adulthood' (Arnett, 2007; Bynner, 2005) and 'extended youth' (see Lalor *et al.*, 2007, Chapter 12) and has also led to a move away from the linear notion of a 'life-cycle' with predetermined stages towards the more historical and sociological concept of the 'life course' (Hunt, 2005).

In terms of the private sphere (or 'axis'), even in the 1980s an empirical study in Britain by Claire Wallace (1987) suggested that young people's transitions had become much more complex and contingent than was suggested by the traditional model, and the process of change is likely to have accelerated in the intervening years. Some of the 'flexibility' and 'reversibility' involved in contemporary personal transitions is reflected graphically in Figure 2.2.

In Ireland, the *National Youth Work Development Plan* (Department of Education and Science, 2003*a*) also noted changes in young people's personal transitions:

> ... the picture is more complex than in the past, when it was overwhelmingly the norm for young people to progress (or at least to

Figure 2.2: Transitions in the Lifecycle: the 1980s

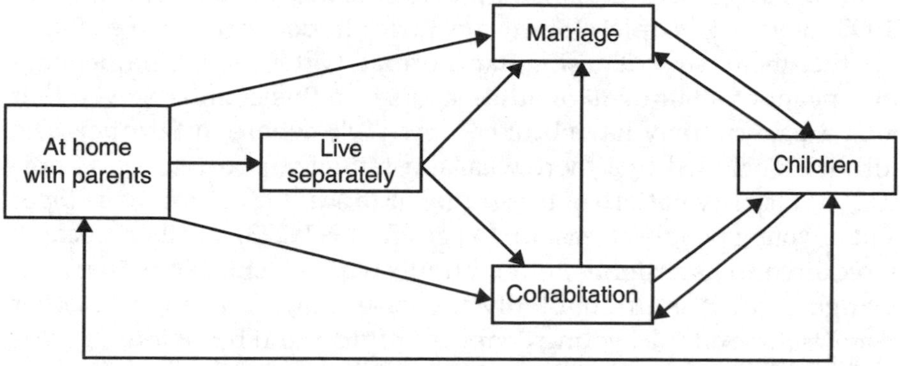

Source: Wallace, C. (1987), *For Richer, For Poorer: Growing Up In and Out of Work*, London: Tavistock, 130.

> want to progress) sequentially, and at a relatively early stage, through heterosexual courtship, marriage and parenthood. While this is of course still a prevailing norm, young people are today exercising a greater variety of choices about lifestyle, relationships and sexuality, and in particular about the sequence and timing of significant life events. (Department of Education and Science, 2003*a*: 3)

It is important to remember, however, that, while there may indeed be a 'greater variety of choices' for young people in contemporary society, significant structural *constraints* also remain in place and the choices are by no means evenly divided across different social groups. Moreover, such 'choices' may actually be experienced by many young people as increased pressures or problems (Department of Education and Science, 2003*a*). This paradoxical state of affairs is part of a more general process of cultural change, which has been described by Beck (1992) in terms of such concepts as individualisation and 'risk', with life as a 'biographical project' which each individual has to manage (in much the same way as the manager of any project has to make assessments and decisions about strategies, 'investments', developments and risks).

The international literature on transitions takes little account of the ways in which specific cultural, historical and economic factors – such as the experience of emigration in twentieth-century Ireland – can have a decisive impact on young people's experience of transition in a given national or regional context; while in Ireland itself there has been little research drawing explicitly on transitional perspectives. Some years ago an important empirical study by Hannan and Ó Riain (1993) of young people's 'pathways to adulthood' set out to examine whether there was still a singular 'normal' pattern in the sequencing and means of attainment of adult statuses in this country (given that such a pattern 'may have broken down' elsewhere in Europe). The authors concluded that there was 'substantial support … for a "normal" or majority pattern of integration into adult life ... for over 90 per cent of young people at least up to age 22' (1993: 223). Further research is required to ascertain whether and to what extent this pattern has changed, but it is undoubtedly the case that, in a range of other respects (for example, young people's attitudes and behaviour in areas such as relationships, family, sexuality, religion, leisure pursuits and popular culture), the Irish situation has converged with our European neighbours in the intervening years (see Lalor *et al.*, 2007, Chapters 3, 4, 7 and 8).

Constructionist Perspectives

The British sociologist Frank Musgrove (1964: 33) quirkily expressed one key tenet of the constructionist approach to youth studies when he stated that 'the adolescent was invented at the same time as the steam engine'! What he meant was that a new stage in life had effectively been created (constructed) by the process of social and economic change. Peter Berger, one of whose co-authored works helped to give 'social constructionism' its name (Berger and Luckmann, 1967), similarly argued that the 'basic causal factor' of modern youth was 'industrial society and its institutional dynamics':

> [T]he deepening of the division of labour, brought about by the industrial revolution ... separated the family (and thus childhood) from the process of modern production and administration. Modern youth is a further extension of the same process of institutional separation or differentiation ... [T]he industrial revolution has produced an institutional structure which 'allows room' for youth. (Berger and Berger, 1976: 240–1)

The reader may note that this reference to 'allowing room' recalls the views of Philippe Aries, cited earlier. What emerged to fill the room, from a constructionist viewpoint, was not just youth itself but a range of professions concerned with young people's education, welfare and development (for example, teachers, youth workers, social workers and care workers), drawing on the theories and concepts being developed within the new disciplines of psychology, sociology and education. For example, Hendrick (1990) charts the emergence and institutionalisation of the key elements of adolescent psychology in the late nineteenth and early twentieth centuries. He questions the widely accepted interpretation provided by Gillis (1974) to the effect that adolescence was 'discovered' (or 'invented') in public schools (that is, elite fee paying schools) between 1870 and 1900 – that, in effect, it was a middle-class creation which was gradually 'democratised' to include the working class. Instead, Hendrick argues that the concept of adolescence was at first 'principally concerned with working-class youth' and related to the emerging social problem of urbanism:

> The concept of adolescence as the social psychologists developed it and as other social scientists and educationalists adopted it, was important for categorising knowledge of youth: it delineated reference points; it established norms; and, moreover, it facilitated a more precise age-structuring of the urban population at a time when commentators were eager to know as much as possible about what they regarded as the pathology of urbanism. (Hendrick, 1990: 88)

Ultimately concerns about working-class young males became concerns about adolescence and youth in general, and a pattern emerged of regular 'moral panics' (Cohen, 2002) about young people's problematic behaviour, fuelled as time went on by a burgeoning mass media for whom the combination of 'youth' with 'sex and drugs and rock'n'roll' (and variations on the theme) was to become – and remain – a staple of news and feature coverage, often with a distinctively gendered character (Devlin, 2003; Griffin, 1997). The continuing prevalence of stereotypical images of young people, and the fact that young people take heed of and care about such images, has been the subject of recent research which places the Irish experience in a comparative international context. Devlin (2006*a*) found that dominant media images of young people in Ireland tend to correspond to those in countries such as Britain, the United States and Australia, whereby young people are represented overwhelmingly – particularly in the news media – either as 'being problems or having problems'. Even the more 'positive' images of young people in other media such as teenage magazines or TV 'soaps' also tend to be stereotypical and distorted, focusing predominantly on certain types of young people, or certain aspects of being young. The research also found that young people – while they did not tend to use the term themselves – are highly sensitive to the ways in which such images and representations are 'social constructs'.

An important constructionist analysis with a pan-European dimension is provided by Wallace and Kovatcheva (1998), who argue that youth was just one of a number of essentialist categories like 'race' and 'gender' which emerged and – at least for a time – became entrenched during modernity, when there was a 'need to divide people into strongly distinguished groups ... with the elaboration of theories to sustain and justify this division' (Wallace and Kovatcheva, 1998: 6). In particular, youth was the creation of State systems through which age became 'bureaucratically calibrated'. Without a comprehensive State, such precise definitions would not have been possible. The authors go further and suggest that, just as modernisation constructed youth as a social category, so too 'postmodernisation is deconstructing youth' (209); an idea which clearly complements some of the thinking on youth transitions outlined in the previous section (and in fact you may have noticed that Wallace's work features in both sections). Table 2.1 summarises Wallace and Kovatcheva's view of the contrasting implications of modernisation and postmodernisation for youth.

As well as referring to the process whereby social structures and institutions (including institutionalised age relations) can undergo evolution or even transformation, the term 'constructionism' can also be used to refer to the capacity of individuals to construct their own identities through exercising 'agency', making choices about the kind of life they want to live (this point was also touched on in the previous section). In contemporary society, such 'choices' are often essentially about *consumption* patterns, a process that has been termed 'shopping for subjectivities' (Langman, 1992). This concept has a lot of resonance in the Irish context, where the shopping mall has become a key element of urban and suburban culture for both young people and adults. Frost (2003) notes that for both boys and girls 'shopping' need not simply be a case of passive consumerism – 'the context of shopping may allow for a sense of choice, action and agency' (2003: 58) – but also cautions that it carries the risk of being experienced as excluding or disempowering: a case of 'conform or else' (2003: 59). One way or the other, the individual as consumer, and the lifestyle(s) that can be actively constructed through consumption, are at the heart of many analyses of young people's (and indeed adults') experiences

Table 2.1: Contrasts between Modernisation and Postmodernisation for Youth

Modernisation	Postmodernisation
Youth defined by precisely calibrated age	Youth as an age group dissolves
Work-achievement ethic	Leisure-expressive ethic
Distinguishing youth by male and female (separate schooling, youth provision, etc.)	Mixed provision
Ethnic groups defined as 'immigrants', assimilationist model through social policies	Range of ethnic hybridisation and differentiation through youth cultures; multicultural models
Separations by class/education linked to levels of the labour market – more education for some and work or training for others	More and more education and training for everyone
Youth culture associated with specific 'courting period'	Youth culture associated with all periods of life
Youth as a period between family of origin and family of destination	No clear division between family of origin and family of destination – perhaps no family of destination
Working class most disadvantaged youth	Non-working class (those without jobs) most disadvantaged youth
Politicisation of youth movements and youth as the bearer of the bright new future	De-politicisation of youth
Conventional right–left politics	New social movements

Source: Wallace, C. and Kovatcheva, S. (1998), *Youth in Society: The Construction and Deconstruction of Youth in East and West Europe*, London: Macmillan, 216. Reproduced with permission of Palgrave Macmillan.

in the postindustrial and postmodern age. Indeed, concepts such as 'taste', 'fashion' and 'lifestyle' have been described as 'the key sources of [contemporary] social differentiation' (Pakulski and Waters, 1996: 121–2).

While longer established forms of social differentiation may persist (including class and gender), consumerism is certainly a core value in contemporary society. The *National Youth Work Development Plan* (Department of Education and Science, 2003*a*) has suggested that, while consumerism in itself is probably irreversible, forms of 'critical consumption' can be encouraged and enhanced through effective educational programmes both in schools and through youth work, which would better prepare young people to make positive use of the increasing consumer choices open to them, including the opportunities for self-expression and socialising provided by information technologies. (Of course, these are not new arguments – see, for example, Henriksson, 1983; see also Chapter 1 in this volume.) Without support, information and guidance, consumption and lifestyle choices 'may be exercised to harmful effect, whether for the individual him/herself or for others, and often with consequences for the wider community or for society as a whole' (Department of Education and Science, 2003*a*: 4).

Conclusion

This chapter has provided an overview of five major theoretical perspectives on young people drawn principally from the academic disciplines of psychology and sociology. There are some direct points of conflict or contradiction to be found, and many points of tension and differences of philosophy or ethos across the five. There are certainly considerable differences of emphasis from one to the other, and this is what makes it meaningful to present them separately. To repeat the image presented earlier, each is like a set of lenses through which we can apprehend and understand 'youth' in contemporary society, and, depending on which set we choose, our attention will be drawn to some features rather than others. Indeed, some features will remain virtually hidden unless a particular set of lenses is chosen.

How do these lenses relate to Irish youth work policy and practice? Certainly we can say that, historically, social policy on young people in Ireland has, for the most part, reflected a generational approach, one that places an emphasis on the way in which young people *in general* are different from other sections of the population. Thus, youth policy documents have tended to start with a focus on such matters as 'the needs of young people' and 'the social situation of young people'; in fact these were the exact titles of chapters or sections in two significant documents, the O'Sullivan Report (Department of Education, 1980) and the Costello Report (National Youth Policy Committee, 1984). Devlin (1989) explored the ways in which this generational emphasis could be interpreted as serving the *ideological* purpose of emphasising a 'consensual' vision of Irish society and playing down possible sites or sources of conflict, including those relating to class, gender and sexuality (although other writers, including Kiely and McMahon in Chapters 1 and 5, highlight the fact that the Costello Report was the first important Irish youth policy document to emphasise young people's potential role in bringing about social change). By contrast, more recent youth policy, including the *National Youth Work Development Plan* (Department of Education and Science, 2003*a*), explicitly addresses at least some of the ways in which young people have different - indeed *unequal* - experiences and circumstances, identities and opportunities, and in doing so appears to reflect a greater awareness of the insights provided by a structuralist analysis.

As will be clear from the previous two sections of this chapter (and as Kiely suggests in Chapter 1), the *Development Plan* also includes some observations about young people in contemporary Ireland which are very much in tune with the transitional and constructionist perspectives, indicating that an unquestioning acceptance of the generational approach may be a thing of the past. However, it is important not to overstate the change. Formal education is a central element of 'youth policy', broadly defined (accounting for a huge proportion of public spending as compared with nonformal or informal education), and it remains firmly generational in orientation, both in policy and practice, reflected most obviously in the continuing use of an age-calibrated approach to entry into, and progression through, the primary and secondary systems.

It is important to remember that all of the theoretical perspectives outlined in this chapter emerged and developed in a predominantly Anglo–North American environment and that, whichever perspective is at issue, the 'theory' needs to be tempered with an awareness of the ways in which a given social and cultural context will have an impact on lived experience. For example, as touched on already, in twentieth-century Ireland (and indeed before) the experience of emigration was an important part of the transition into adulthood for a very large proportion of Irish young people, with obvious implications for their own families, for local community life throughout the country and for social and demographic systems in general. Yet the conventional transitional model takes no account of this.

It is also important to reiterate the fact that - while they have been presented separately for the sake of analysis, and while there are certainly points of tension and contradiction - the five perspectives outlined above are *not* mutually exclusive, and neither are they exhaustive. In practice - including youth work practice - human experience is too complex to capture in a single theoretical lens. The point therefore is not to *choose* one of these perspectives, but rather to weigh their arguments one against the other (in the light of our own experience and that of the young people we work with) and draw on them as appropriate in different settings and contexts. As was said at the outset, all practice with young people reflects underlying assumptions, whether consciously or not, which are likely to be based on theoretical frameworks such as those presented here. Making sure that these assumptions *do* become conscious puts workers in a much stronger position to place them in context and to explore alternatives, thereby interrogating and hopefully improving their practice.

3

Community Development: A Critical Analysis of Its 'Keywords' and Values

Rosie Meade

Introduction

This chapter does not evaluate the real-life failures and successes of the many different community organisations currently active in Ireland. Nor does it offer a general diagnosis of the health of community development: what it can or cannot do for social policy; its status à la the State, the market or the 'people'; what's hot and what's not in terms of practice methods or issues on the ground. Instead this chapter is preoccupied with some of community development's 'keywords' (Williams, 1983), by which I mean those concepts and values that are invoked in order to cultivate, legitimate and advance its public image. Community development is a curiously polygamous idea. It is coupled with the most beguiling and worthy concepts in the English language - democracy, participation and empowerment - and assumes relationships between the concepts that are often represented as rock solid, regardless of what is actually happening on the ground. This chapter starts from the premise that community development *can* generate actions, initiatives and opportunities that challenge oppressive or unequal social relationships, but that it does not always or inevitably do so. If there is progressive potential, then there are also countervailing tendencies: community development that is politically pragmatic, manipulative of or irrelevant to people's needs. You could put this down to the inevitable gap between theory and practice, the strong probability that we academics begin our analysis with inflated and abstracted expectations that could never be realised in the cold hard reality of the field. Theory or social science thus appears to be a useless encumbrance, adding nothing and devaluing everything.

While there is a real risk of overstatement when it comes to community work, the problem is more suggestive of a theoretical deficit than theoretical surfeit. Firstly, terminology and theory are not the same. Simply juxtaposing community development with highly suggestive keywords offers little in the way of detailed understanding or analytical depth, and the pretence of definitional clarity deflects important questions about those words. As Raymond Williams (1983: 16) explains, those questions are not 'only about meaning; in most cases, inevitably, they are about *meanings*' (my italics): plural, disputed and evasive *meanings*. This chapter focuses on the keywords, or, as they are more usually described, 'core values' of *process*, *participation* and *empowerment*. It emphasises and demonstrates that their meanings are fundamentally contested, that they can be co-opted for contradictory political ends and that, ultimately, rather than guiding values they are obscure scratches on community development's moral compass.

Secondly, critical sociological analysis destabilises certainties, unearths relations of domination and illuminates the connections between the personal and the public, the local and the global. It also helps us to trace the limits and intersections of 'out there' structures and 'in here' agency. For community activists and workers, this knowledge is useful, not as a set of alternative truth claims, but as an intellectual armoury that protects against the ideological onslaughts of political, business, academic, media and community leaders. Furthermore, theory helps us to clarify our intentions and maybe even our methods. For example, to claim that communities need empowerment demands a nuanced analysis of the different dimensions and forms of power, a consideration of what power communities already have and recognition of how and why vested interests may resist meaningful change. With his emphasis on 'praxis', Paolo Freire (1972*a*; 1972*b*) reminds us that social enquiry and social action are mutually rewarding, that they should never be detached and that both are central to the purpose of community work. I believe that community development's value base is an appropriate focus for such enquiry and this article draws on useful sociological concepts and literature in order to explore its dialectical potential.

Community Work or Community Development?

The first step in any critical analysis of the discourse and values of community development is to clarify what it is we are talking about, a more challenging task than it initially seems.[i] Some textbooks represent *community work* as *the* generic term, incorporating a range of approaches or models, among which can be found *community development, social planning, community education, feminist community work* and *community action* (Dominelli, 2006; Popple, 1995; Twelvetrees, 1991). Here community development signifies a distinctive praxis – that is, its core values and modus operandi are recognisably different from those applied in alternative models of community work. In other instances the terms *community work* and *community development* appear to be synonymous (Commins, 1985; Ó Cinnéide and Walsh, 1990), and community development itself is represented as a potentially variegated field of practice.

Keith Popple (1995: 65–66) typifies the Community Action model as 'conflict' and 'direct action' oriented, whereby groups contest the limitations, excesses or misadventures of State and market intervention in their communities. The 'Shell to Sea' campaign in Mayo might serve as a contemporary example. In contrast with what he terms Community Action's 'radical' or 'socialist approaches' (Popple, 1995: 72), community development is concerned with self-help in neighbourhood contexts and is more consensus orientated. Rather than 'fight the power', groups attempt to become players in the broader field of power relations, perhaps through involvement in local State-partnership structures. Patrick Commins (1985: 166–168) distinguishes a 'Classical Model' of Irish community development, emphasising community as a 'harmonious entity' and where issues 'are reconcilable in the "common good"', from a Social or Community Action model that adopts a structural analysis of inequality. Chris Curtin and Tony Varley (1995) have used a somewhat looser but complementary categorisation to differentiate 'integrationist' from 'oppositional' tendencies in Irish community action. Whatever their preferred terminology, authors agree that community-based activism and interventions take a variety of organisational forms, are oriented towards a diversity of social outcomes and are led by a complex range and combination of actors. Furthermore, activity is underpinned by contrasting political claims and expectations; whether in terms of the composition and role of the community or in terms of that community's relationships with the State, market, mainstream political processes and other sites of power (Commins, 1985; Dominelli, 2006; Ife, 2002; Ó Cinnéide and Walsh, 1990; Popple, 1995; Powell and Geoghegan, 2004; Twelvetrees, 1991).

This chapter uses the concepts of community work and community development interchangeably, partly for convenience and partly because I am unconvinced that this field can or should be carved up into precise or definitive models. Firstly, since the 1990s a consensus-driven conception of community development has become hegemonic in Ireland and Britain (see Chapter 6; Meade, 2005; Popple, 2005; Shaw, 2006). This is neither to deny the possibility or actuality of dissent and resistance on the ground. Rather it is to recognise the current marginal status of protest strategies in 'mainstreamed' community work. By mainstreamed I refer to community development that is core-funded, and in some cases initiated, by the State. Furthermore, a rigid classification of models may be of limited utility in the practice context, not least because of its potential to reify what are, to use the sociological parlance, 'ideal types'. Within the Weberian social scientific tradition, ideal types are academic constructs rather than descriptions of reality; they 'portray in heightened, indeed sometimes caricatured, form characteristic social relationships' (Callinicos, 2007*b*: 157) so that those relationships might be more easily subject to academic analysis or comparison. By emphasising too strongly the distinctiveness of particular models, we are liable to forget that community work is probably messier or more contradictory in practice. Ultimately, the boundaries between approaches are permeable. Groups may oscillate between oppositional and conciliatory tactics or they might adopt different organisational structures at particular points in their history. Community education or community care strategies may be subsumed within the work plans of an individual community development project. Depending on the issues or crises that emerge in communities, projects may shift from advocacy to service provision to information giving and back again.

Despite its fungibility, community development boasts a disparate range of advocates and supporters, including Shell Nigeria, the World Bank, the W.K. Kellogg Foundation, New Labour, former Taoiseach Bertie Ahern, the Combat Poverty Agency[ii] and a host of locality based and identity groupings in Ireland. Among State and non-governmental organisations, it has become official shorthand for a more participatory and socially inclusive approach to planning (Department of Social, Community and Family Affairs, 2000*a*). Community development is credited with offering potential solutions to the most entrenched problems of Irish society: racism, inequalities in health, criminality, poverty and social atomisation. Fusing two of the most desired yet elusive goals of contemporary living, our hankering after community and our insatiable pursuit of development, it links the best bits of traditional life to the promise of the modern. When it presents past and future in perfect symmetry, who could be 'against community development'? And what is the alternative? Barbarism, unbridled individualism and the death knell for all that is social.

It is precisely because it is so universally popular that we need to be on our guard when community development is invoked. For one thing, it trades on our long-standing but nonetheless problematic affection for 'community', a concept that magically confers democratic properties upon all words paired with it. As the US-based political scientist and left-wing activist Adolph Reed Jr (2000: 10) has observed:

> [A]ssertion of links to, roots in, messages from, or the wisdom of 'the community' is more of a way to end a conversation about politics than to begin one. It is often the big trump in a game of one-upmanship, an attempt to validate one's position or self by alleging privileged connection to the well-spring of authenticity, to preempt or curtail dissent by invoking the authority of that unassailable, primordial source of legitimacy.

In Chapter 4 Hilary Tovey explores the sociological claims and counterclaims surrounding the idea of community. The concept of development deserves equally rigorous assessment. Theorists including Gustavo Esteva (1992) and Arturo Escobar (1992; 1995) argue that development is an 'ideology'; that we must learn to deconstruct the truth-claims and value judgments that it masks. When US President Truman launched the 'era of development' in 1949, progress came to be understood internationally as unidirectional and evolutionary, with all roads leading towards the standards of consumption, growth and wastefulness normalised by the 'modern' countries of the West. New scientific practices of development were invented – along with an associated lingua franca – that were framed as neutral, expert led and rational (Escobar, 1995; Esteva, 1992). Economic and cultural inequalities were redefined in technical terms, as glitches in the machine that could be repaired without any significant reordering of overarching systems of power and domination.

The Irish State's discursive commitment to community development and more recently to sustainable development implies that it is willing to accommodate diverse and pluralised perspectives on the best way forward for its citizens. But, in my view, a rigidly economistic vision of development still dominates the public sphere. It is articulated through the actions and pronouncements of Government, and elevated to the status of *the* truth in mainstream newspapers. Just think how regularly the bottom line of money and jobs is invoked to disparage alternative visions; be they May Day protesters in Dublin or community activists in Mayo (Meade, 2008; Rossport 5, 2006). As O'Dalaigh (2006: 144) wryly observes, with reference to the ongoing dispute over the location of the motorway in the Tara/Skryne Valley, ours is a public culture that finds 'scholars dismissed as tree huggers, environmental scientists damned as romantics'. This is because a genuinely open conversation about development demands searching questions about the role and legitimacy of the State's own actions, and those of the business and corporate sectors. It may even elicit troubling questions about the cohesiveness and democracy of communities themselves.

The Progressive Values of Community Development

Notwithstanding the academic ruminations about what to call or how best to define community development, there is general agreement that it is underpinned by a socially progressive value base. Values associated with community work typically include *collective action, participation*, a commitment to *process, social inclusion, equality, empowerment, anti-discrimination, mutual aid* and *bottom-up development*. Fred Powell and Martin Geoghegan's (2004) research suggests that 'humanistic' and 'liberal' values strongly influence the practice of community organisations in Ireland. Writing in Australia, Jim Ife (2002: 269–70) rejects technocratic accounts of community work that construct it as a neutral or politically disinterested practice; inevitably it embodies the values of 'community itself', 'democracy, participation, self-determination'. In 2004 a gathering of policy-makers, researchers, academics and practitioners endorsed what has become known as the Budapest Declaration on 'Building European Civil Society through Community Development'. A vision of how community development might be supported by EU and national governments, it identified priorities in terms of research, training, sustainable development, justice and economic growth. It also explicitly referenced community development's 'core values/social principles' as 'covering human rights, social inclusion, equality and respect for diversity' (http://www.iacdglobal.org).

Accepting that community development is value driven, that people's intentions impact on their worlds, means recognising that social change is not delivered from on high through the intercession of governments or great leaders alone. Nor is change crudely determined by the onward march of historical or economic forces. With regard to the perennial debate about the sociological significance of structure and agency, community development comes down on the side of agency: that we can – and must – *actively* and *knowingly* participate in the construction of social reality. By coming together in communities, by purposefully interacting, negotiating and endlessly making demands, we can fundamentally shape the texture and content of our political, cultural and social lives. To find evidence of this agency we must reinterpret what might otherwise appear to be local or mundane experiences. For example, the building of a community resource centre is significant not only for the physical act of construction, the suitability of its design or for the services it provides, but also potentially for the new visions of possibility that it engenders. It may transform relationships between neighbours, lead to a renegotiation of roles between communities and State agencies, challenge the norm of private ownership by expanding communal or public space, and it may generate a new spirit of efficacy among those who work towards its completion. All of this can be seen as desirable social change, microscopic perhaps, but real in its consequences for particular communities. It can also be seen as public enactment of the kind of values to which community development lays claim. If similar kinds of collective agency are unleashed in other places, among other groups, micro-experiments in community development might merge to become national, even international, movements for change.

Except, of course, for the fact that they might not. We should not get too carried away with either the promise of our own agency or our conviction that values can change the world. In *The Eighteenth Brumaire of Louis Bonaparte*, Karl Marx (trans. 1973: 146) warned that '[M]en make their own history, but not of their own free will; not under circumstances they themselves have chosen, but under the given and inherited circumstances with which they are directly confronted.' Community workers and activists practise in complex political, economic and cultural contexts, where local, national and global forces intersect and interact. Their actions are shaped, and often constrained, by new trends in social policy, legislation, the availability of funding and resources, community power dynamics, moral panics, unforeseen crises or the waxing and waning of voluntary effort. Because communities are rarely homogenous and most community development projects are answerable to a range of what are increasingly referred to as stakeholders, pragmatism, rather than values, may be the final determinant of outcomes. Moreover, the State plays a decisive role in defining community development's character. Mae Shaw (2006) distinguishes between 'provided/invited spaces' and 'claimed/demanded spaces' as sites of practice (see also Chapters 6 and 9). She argues that priorities are predominantly defined in relation to issues, structures and policies determined by Government – the 'invited spaces'. 'Demanded spaces', where communities call the shots with reference to their own values, are all too rare by comparison.

When community development activists or workers identify their values, they engage in a process of reflexivity – a kind of 'rational "monitoring" of their own conduct' (Giddens, 1995: 235) – whereby they admit to the aspirations and assumptions that underpin their actions. They also seek to demonstrate the 'uniqueness' of community development, how it differs from social work, for example, because it is concerned more with the autonomous organisation of people than it is with intervention in their private lives or with 'working' on them. There is, however, a fundamental and irresolvable paradox in these claims of uniqueness. Alan Twelvetrees (1991: 15) finds that the 'uniqueness of community work derives from a value system which emphasises the importance of people discovering what they want to do, doing it, and not having it imposed on them.' Surely then, we must allow for the possibility that people will pursue agendas that are out of step with other putative community work values. To assume that communities will ultimately act in honourable or mutually beneficial ways is to be guilty of populism. In some obviously extreme cases, exploitative or abusive employment practices, financial irregularity, corruption, nepotism and unreasonable demands are the realities of community development irrespective of the high-minded claims that groups insert in their mission statements. In the 1970s, Jo Freeman's classic feminist text *The Tyranny of Structurelessness* (c.1972) railed against the tendency of activist groups to give lip service to progressive values. She argued that, once named, values were frequently abandoned, the inevitable consequences being frustration, cynicism, power struggles, burnout and new unaccountable forms of hierarchy.

The problems with values are more apparent when we take an internationalist and historical perspective. Marj Mayo (1975) has demonstrated how, in the early to middle decades of the twentieth century, the UK Colonial Office actively promoted community development as a bulwark against anticolonialist movements in the British Empire. Reminiscent of the 'Killing Home Rule with Kindness' approach that had been adopted in Ireland in the early twentieth century, this was effectively a last-ditch strategy to stave off or, at the very least, to shape the postcolonial futures of the emergent nations. In a similar vein, James Midgley (1986: 18) notes that, during the 1950s and 1960s, US Aid programmes provided significant ideological and financial resources to community development programmes in 'Third World' countries, most notably Thailand and Vietnam, in order to 'contain subversive influences'. This was community development in anti-communist mode. More recently Liam Kane (2006) has criticised the World Bank's peddling of a neoliberal-friendly model of community development in the Global South. In urban USA, Randy Stoecker (2003) finds the dominant model of community development, typically delivered through Community Development Corporations (CDCs), to be pragmatic, largely focused on building construction, a narrowly framed model of economic development and the gentrification of poor neighbourhoods. On both sides of the Atlantic, Bush and Blair lauded and increased public expenditure on faith-based community development initiatives, through the White House Faith-Based and Community Initiative, for example, thus raising serious concerns about the comparative influence of religious and secular values in community work.

> [W]hat are espoused as 'community development values' are more truthfully a rather muddled accretion of well-intentioned and often passionately held aspirations drawn from its rather disparate and complex provenance. (Shaw, 2006: no page no. available)

It is difficult to reconcile the idea of community development as an organic expression of popular expectation with an insistence that it has an *a priori* value system. This chapter suggests that we treat community development's values with a fair degree of scepticism. This does not mean dispensing with optimism or denying any role for community development in the making of a better society. We should recognise, however, that the discourse of community development *can* be dishonoured by its practice. It also invites a more profound enquiry: whether it is merely in the application of that discourse or in its very construction that the roots of those anomalies lie.

Locating the Importance of Process

'[T]he community development approach is generally described as an educational *process* through which communities achieve personal and social change' (Shaw, 2006: no page no. available, my italics). Here 'process' suggests a singular concern with the *means* by which development is to be achieved: an admission that the building of active and socially engaged communities requires slow and deliberate steps. Where people feel isolated, fearful, apathetic or deskilled, it is a task in itself to mobilise the collective will and spirit of optimism that community development demands.[iii] It is a further challenge to find some grounds for consensus regarding mutually beneficial actions, particularly where conflict or distrust bubble below the surface of daily encounters. In a sense, workers and activists must become evangelists for community development, and when the pace of change is slow or tedious it is often the most modest indicators of personal growth or new-found assertiveness that become the hooks on which more long-term commitment is secured.

For Margaret Ledwith, the community development process begins with 'listening, valuing and understanding people's particular experiences' (Ledwith, 2005: 32). Across the literature, this core idea is repeated; that local wisdom has its own inherent value but that it is also the raw material for more sustainable and effective public policy (Ife, 2002; Twelvetrees, 1991; Wates, 2000). Even when State agencies, outside NGOs or established interest groups initiate community development, it is underwritten by the populist claim that ultimately it will and should be owned by the people. For example, the Department of Community, Rural and Gaeltacht Affairs (2005: 2) claims its role is 'to provide support to communities in the most appropriate way as they work to shape their own futures, address their common goals and achieve their full potential'. However, in order to make the transition from objects to subjects of development, community members may be judged as needing 'capacity building': the refining of skills, knowledge, values and attitudes so that they are better equipped to participate in the processes of change. Consequently, community workers often devote considerable time to management training, group work and introductory courses in community development. The underlying assumption is that community development requires community development and that ultimately it begets more community development; method and outcomes are indistinguishable in a process without end.

The sanctity of the process is moderated by projects' actual dependency on State funding for their material welfare. They operate in a policy context whereby increasingly ambitious claims are made about community development's capacity to respond to and resolve social contradictions. It is commonly assumed that community organisations will serve as a conduit for ordinary citizens to shape public policy. However, policy-making is a highly complex business, with political and institutional factors each playing their part and with power formations often disguised or indistinguishable (Hill, 2005).

Furthermore, because projects' greatest achievements generally occur in the more amorphous and localised zones of capacity building, they may find it easier to articulate successes and failures in qualitative rather than quantitative terms (Lee, 2006; Motherway, 2006). Nonetheless, accountability and budgeting conventions typically stipulate the kind of hard and incontrovertible data that demonstrates efficient use of taxpayers' money, for example, services provided, working groups established, courses organised or matching funds raised. The time frames within which projects return annual reports or develop strategic plans are usually determined centrally and can be out of sync with the needs and pace of community living. More ominously, the State may construct accountability in punitive terms. In spring 2003, a quite positive evaluation of the Community Development Programme (CDP)[iv] that had been commissioned by the Department of Community, Rural and Gaeltacht Affairs was followed by a controversial suspension of the department's commitment to tri-annual funding of projects. In an exercise that seemed primarily concerned with tightening the department's control over the programme, a 'review' of the CDP was instituted. Projects were plunged into a period of uncertainty regarding their futures, as organisations were required to resubmit their work plans in line with the new funding regime. Although business as usual has been restored, this episode serves as salutary reminder of how the State may use its power arbitrarily to override the processes of community development (Meade, 2005).

Community development's privileging of 'process' reflects the influence of Paolo Freire's concept of 'critical pedagogy': 'a democratic process of education that takes place in community groups and forms the basis of transformation' (Ledwith, 2005: 95). Recognising that oppression is sustained through the interaction of coercion from above and consent from below, Freire (1972*a*; 1972*b*) was concerned with how the 'oppressed' might develop the kind of consciousness that permits ruthless critique of things as they are, yet also nurtures the imagination of alternatives. His was a radical vision of a society transformed, where education ceases to service dominant economic and social relations, becoming recast as 'cultural action for freedom'. The role of the worker, activist and educator is to create spaces for and bring momentum to dialogues that allow the issues, fears and aspirations of communities to be laid bare. This role demands problem posers not problem solvers, with workers asking why, how and where to next? It also requires new forms of leadership that are founded upon an unequivocal commitment to radical change, but that are not doctrinaire about the route to achieving it.

Henry Giroux (2000) argues that Freire's ideas are often applied in superficial ways, and thus he reveals some of the risks posed by the fetishisation of process. Freire championed more participatory educational methods, emphasising interaction over didactic instruction, deconstructing the hidden hierarchies of the classroom. So, it can look as if we are following his intellectual lead when we purposefully democratise the spaces in which we work. Arranging the chairs in a circle, faithfully committing all opinions to the flip chart, discussing issues in detail, ensuring that everyone has their say – these are typical aspects of day-to-day community work. Stephen Duncombe (2007: 171) explains the concept of prefigurative politics, where 'the vision of the future is prefigured in the practices of the present, thereby erasing the distinction between means and ends.' In other words, if community development means working towards the creation of a more discursive, open and respectful society, why not start as we mean to go on by, quite literally, practising change in the resource centre or the community forum. Often though, the process stops there. Giroux (2002) reminds us that Freire wanted to radically reframe education's social role by asserting its place in the battle against oppression, a battle that calls us to recognise that society is conflict ridden and requires us to confront the roots of injustice. When Freire's methods are detached from their revolutionary purpose, his vision of the educational process is reduced to feel-good encounter sessions. Even if we do not accept that community development has a higher calling in terms of social transformation, the absence of tangible outcomes can be demoralising. If people get involved because they lack services, jobs or facilities, there is probably a limit to how long they will be buoyed along by a process. 'Things' need to change, not just feelings or mindsets but 'things as they are' in the real worlds of community and society, otherwise momentum is lost and solidarity dissolves.

The Limits of Participation

Perhaps more than any other value, community development stands for participation. This can mean that otherwise disengaged individuals become actively involved in the management of projects or, at the very least, that they are consulted about the course of development as it impacts on their daily lives. It can, however, mean much more; that citizens begin to play a more central role in the definition of public policy. Here participation is orientated towards local, national and, increasingly, global sites of influence and decision-making. It may involve making better use of the structures and processes of liberal democracy, running as candidates in elections or getting the vote out in support of community campaigns. Going even further, it might signal a richer and broader conception of democracy itself.

Liberal democracy is a compromise between individual liberty, political participation and State control, based on the assumption that the masses must be allowed speak, but only through carefully managed processes and at clearly defined times. Effectively it offers democracy 'lite'. Elections are crude instruments for accessing popular opinion, particularly in light of deficiencies in voter registration, a general trend towards reduced voter turnout – albeit one reversed in the most recent Irish general election – and declining membership of political parties (see Hughes *et al.*, 2007). Rhetorically we accept that democracy is government of the people, for the people, by the people; calls for participation concentrate our attention on the final fragment of that hackneyed phrase, asking what else can 'by the people' mean? They ask us to envision and create a participatory democracy, the kind of society in which 'all collective decisions involve active participation by some of the people that they affect and nearly everyone participates in some of the decisions that affect them' (Baker *et al.*, 2004: 99).

In Ireland and internationally, social movements and community groups have attempted to renegotiate the terms of really existing democracy, in order to move towards such a vision (see also Chapter 9). The Community Workers Co-operative had framed its own involvement in national social partnership as a form of participative democracy, one that, according to the CWC, allowed it and the other social partners to enter discussions with Government on a variety of social and economic issues and to reach a consensus on policy. The World Social Forum, an international gathering of civil society organisations and social movements, has since 2001 converged on Porte Alegre and other regions in order to explore and demand new configurations of democracy (Mestrum, 2004). Its charter of principles 'upholds respect for Human Rights, the practices of real democracy, participatory democracy' and 'peaceful relations, in equality and solidarity' (World Social Forum, 2002). More surprisingly, the Irish Government has also joined the chorus. Drawing inspiration from developments in the EU Commission, its White Paper *Supporting Voluntary Activity* (2000*a*: 14) endorsed the concept of active citizenship, meaning the 'active role of people, communities and voluntary organisations in decision-making which directly affects them'. It further agreed that 'the concept of formal citizenship and democratic society' must be extended to incorporate direct forms of 'participation' and 'responsibility'. Of course, we should be wary of the political expediency and cynicism that is masked when governments adopt the rhetoric of active citizenship. As Zygmunt Bauman (2007: 145–146) has witheringly observed with reference to Britain, official discourses on 'responsible' communities define new 'sites' where the problems abandoned by the 'great society' can be 'tackled in cottage industry mode' thus allowing the State to disengage from public provision.

Obviously the implications of participatory democracy are far-reaching. The political landscape could be transformed by the creation of new forums for negotiation and decision-making and, ultimately, through the erosion of the centrality and status of the parliamentary system (for interesting critiques, see Ó Cinnéide, 1998; see also Furedi, available at: http://www.geser.net/furedi.html). This vision requires the equalisation of access to economic, social and cultural resources, the absence of which skews political influence towards already privileged groups (Baker *et al.* 2004; Hughes *et al.*, 2007). In the current political climate, however, egalitarian politics has lost its lustre. Nancy Fraser (2000; 2003) observes that, with the global ascendance of the neoliberal paradigm, political interest in the contentious idea of economic redistribution has been decentred and diluted (see also Chapter 8). Justice is now framed primarily in terms of 'recognition', whereby minority or oppressed groups seek visibility and respect for their cultural identities and pursue 'participatory parity' in political life (Fraser, 2000; 2003). Often these are vital struggles, not only for the well-being of those minorities, but also for the health of democracy itself. For example, in Ireland the ritual demonisation of Travellers and Traveller culture has real material consequences, impacting negatively on their health, welfare and social standing (see Lentin and McVeigh, 2006). By challenging dominant ideologies of sedentarism and possessive individualism and by confronting institutionalised forms of oppression, Travellers' demands for recognition invigorate the broader struggle for equality on this island. However, if community development's politics is reduced solely to questions of recognition, if our sensitivity to cultural or social inequality is shorn of an awareness of economics[v] and specifically neoliberal economics – how it liberates some but constrains most – then opportunities for genuine participatory parity will be diminished.[vi]

Some non-governamental organisations have made the leap to broader political participation through their membership of the Social Pillar in national partnership negotiations. By securing a place at the table and effectively forcing the State to concede that many groupings – including women, Travellers, young people, the poor – were inadequately represented by mainstream political parties or the other partners, the Social Pillar won a significant victory in terms of official recognition. The community sector has used the processes and forums of social partnership to challenge dominant representations of minority communities and to lobby for progressive reforms. Whether these achievements amount to a new era of 'participatory democracy' is dubious, especially since the State has abdicated little in the way of real influence to the Social Pillar (see Chapter 6, also Kirby, 2002; Meade, 2005; Meade and O'Donovan, 2002; Murphy, 2002). Youth, community and voluntary sector organisations are widely regarded as junior partners who lack the muscle of both the employer and trade union sectors. Furthermore, the Social Pillar organisations are not unanimous in their commitment to partnership or in their estimation of its usefulness. Individual members are ambivalent about the effort, compromises and lost opportunities for protest that participation entails (Meade, 2005; Murphy, 2002). Finally, social partnership is a highly institutionalised process of decision-making. It engages a select group of negotiators from organisations that have been picked by the Government and not freely chosen by the majority of citizens. Irrespective of the progressive and insightful contributions of those involved, partnership is insufficiently transparent, accountable and broad based to constitute a genuinely participatory model of democratic life.

Aside from its democratising potential, participation may address other, more existential needs. In recent years, a range of sociological, philosophical and popularising texts have diagnosed profound levels of alienation within contemporary Western society. Among the most famous is possibly the US best seller *Bowling Alone* (2000; also Putnam *et al.*, 2003) in which Robert Putnam records the decline of active community in the US. He explains that citizens have retreated into privatised realms of TV viewing, travelling by car or workplace ambition, thus sacrificing the social networks, bonds of trust and norms of reciprocity that otherwise give life meaning. His book demonstrates that human interaction and connectivity - or, in a phrase, 'social capital' - significantly enhances health, wealth and happiness, while their absence generates tremendous costs in terms of criminality, suspicion and social breakdown.

There is much that is vague and analytically lightweight about this discussion of social capital (see Navarro, 2002; Mowbray, 2005; Smyth and Kulynych, 2002). Problematically, it is underwritten by a benign view of market and state. Putnam fails to interrogate how the political and economic structures of advanced capitalism have contributed to the processes of atomisation and alienation that he describes. Nonetheless, his work is notable because it encapsulates a mood of popular disquiet regarding modernisation's collateral damage. In Ireland, it has informed the public statements of former Taoiseach Bertie Ahern, the research agenda of the National Economic and Social

Forum (NESF) (2003) and the establishment of a Government Task Force on Active Citizenship in 2006.[vii] Discussions on social capital tend to focus on two questions: how can we maintain and extend existing levels of voluntary action *and* how can we re-energise a 'spirit' of community so that trust and neighbourliness are once again normalised in Ireland? Participation, it seems, builds community and community builds participation. If we are to reveal and evaluate community participation's ultimate purpose, we need to raise some additional questions. What vision of power, and power relations, is participation expected to serve? Can all interests and agendas be reconciled so that everyone participates as equals? How can we distinguish the healthy and unhealthy, the acceptable and unacceptable forms of participation? And, finally, who makes those distinctions and, in doing so, whose interests do they serve?

Empowering the Concept of Empowerment

Empowerment still has some radical cachet. The concept is rooted in Freire's educational philosophy and the progressive discourses of the New Social Movements (Cleaver, 2001). Empowerment implies that community development is an inherently political process with an inherently political purpose (for definitions, see Community Workers Co-operative, 2007; Ife, 2002; Ledwith, 2005; Lee, 2006). It promises that community power can be unleashed and redistributed, that social relationships will be reconfigured in favour of the poor or dispossessed. Unfortunately, overuse has left the concept almost threadbare. Marketeers and the market, Government and international governmental organisations have appropriated the word, effectively erasing its unsettling connotations of power, inequality and politics. Adolph Reed Jr (2000: 116) dismisses it as a 'negative keyword' representing everything from 'self-help psychobabble to bootstrap alternatives to public action, to vague evocations of political mobilisation'. Now it serves 'technical' and 'project-dictated imperatives' in the fields of local and international development (Cleaver, 2001: 37) or as a byword for individualised voyages of self-discovery that have no broader political or public importance.

Maybe there is a case for abandoning empowerment to its fate, for using better or more robust concepts to define the purpose of community work. Maybe it is possible to reclaim the concept for the Left, to anchor it more securely in discourses of solidarity, democracy and equality. Either way, an analysis of power must remain central to the theory and practice of community development. Of course this in itself is no easy task, because 'power' is a much contested sociological concept (see Crossley, 2005) and there are ongoing debates regarding the primacy of conflict or consensus approaches; whether power is 'something' that others have 'over' us and at our expense or an inexhaustible resource that can service all social interests simultaneously. Marxist and Weberian sociologists typically adopt the former construction, with the latter, somewhat benign understanding associated with the functionalism of Talcott Parsons (see Giddens, 1995).

Saul Alinsky, the infamous community organiser from Chicago, was a committed advocate of the conflict perspective on power. As a self-styled political realist, he believed the world to be 'an arena of power politics' (1971/1989: 12) in which communities must get down and dirty in the battle for influence. He argued that community workers 'must rub raw the resentments of the people of the community; fan the latent hostilities of many of the people to the point of overt expression' (1971/1989: 116). To contemporary readers these might seem brazen and alarming sentiments, particularly in Ireland where partnership and consensus approaches to community development are elevated above all others. Scenes from Bellanaboy in Mayo, where activists resist the combined forces of Gardaí, Shell and Government in order to renegotiate the terms of the Corrib Gas Project, remind us that vital undercurrents of opposition still survive in this country (see Rossport 5, 2006). In contrast, mainstream or State-resourced community development organisations may fear – with some legitimacy – that resistance or confrontation will provoke a backlash from authorities, endanger future funding or diminish public approval.

In 2007, then Minister for Justice Brian Lenihan asked department officials to report on the conduct of Travellers' rights organisation Pavee Point in supporting a group of Roma who camped on a roundabout on the M50 (Lally and Healy, 2007). His comments suggested that Government is less than tolerant of the social justice demands of community organisations, even when they are not framed in overtly conflictual terms. Justifying his intervention, he is reported as saying:

> If their [Pavee Point's] involvement was simply to provide humanitarian assistance to these individuals, then I do understand their position. But if their position was that these individuals should be permitted to stay here and that we should set aside the whole immigration law of the State, and have a back-door entry policy, then that would be wrong. (Lenihan in Lally and Healy, 2007)

Given that the Irish Government poses as friend and enabler of community development organisations (Department of Social, Community and Family Affairs, 2000*b*), this is an extraordinary statement. The Minister suggests that organisations should stick to service provision – note the echo of charity in his reference to 'humanitarian assistance' – and that matters of policy or procedure pertaining to the immigration system are beyond their ken. Furthermore, his statement reveals the hierarchical nature of State–community relationships, a hierarchy that is often obscured by the dominant rhetoric of consensus. He therefore sends out a pre-emptive warning to community groups that might otherwise seek to defy or re-imagine the unwritten codes of their relationships with the State.

If we accept that power is a capacity for action or a resource that is shared unequally, then we need to consider how power is divided out and used in communities. The classic 'Community Power Debate' (Crossley, 2005; Gaventa, 1980; Lukes, 1974, 2005) focused on these questions with particular reference to political life in the US. Pluralist contributors asserted that the public sphere was relatively open and responsive to a wide range of interests, while critics such as Stephen Lukes (1974; 2005) portrayed more insidious and subtle expressions of power that bolstered the fortunes of dominant social groups. A detailed discussion of the terms of this debate is beyond the scope of this chapter but collectively its chief disputants produced a three-dimensional conceptualisation of power that still is of great relevance for our analysis of Irish community development.

The first dimension of power is revealed when we get our 'opponents' to do things they would otherwise not do; they concede to our might and act against their interests. A community organisation that is battling a county council over the location of a dump might, due to the force of its counterargument or its recourse to legal measures, convince its opponents to drop their plans. Empowerment in this instance involves mobilising local people and resources to fight for the cause; a cause that is presumed to have some hope of success in a relatively pluralistic political system. The second dimension of power relates to the parameters of public debate, how some issues are ignored, deemed non-negotiable or rendered invisible, despite their serious implications for minority or disadvantaged groups. It calls into question the pluralism of the political, social and cultural spheres and draws our attention to a 'behind the scenes' operation of power that reinforces existing hierarchies. As Bacharach and Baratz (1962: 948) explain, power holders or elites protect their own interests or world view by devoting their energies 'to creating or reinforcing social and political values and institutional practices that limit the scope of the political process to the public consideration of only those issues which are comparatively innocuous.'

For arts activists who are committed to a multidimensional conception of cultural democracy that embraces participation in the consumption, production and distribution of the arts, this second dimension of power is an ongoing site of struggle. Declan McGonagle (2007: 425), former director of the Irish Museum of Modern Art, argues that community arts, such as are practised in or by community development projects, are generally perceived as occupying a 'marginal' status in 'the culture' of Ireland and are disregarded or disrespected as second rate by mainstream cultural commentators and institutions. Established selection and validation procedures ensure that most museums and galleries neither engage with these artforms nor with the communities that make them. McGonagle (2007: 426), therefore, asserts that '[D]evelopment requires a connection to power but to redistribute and to refocus that power, not to destroy it', and so activists must contest and remake the institutional, policy and cultural processes that define what art is and what it is not.

The third dimension reflects what Lukes (1974: 23) calls 'the supreme exercise of power'. There are strong parallels between this theorisation of power and those of Paolo Freire (1972*a*) and Antonio Gramsci (1971) insofar as all three emphasise the distorting effects of ideology on the behaviour of ordinary people. Complex and unseen, power robs us of insight into our objective circumstances; we interpret the world through false or alien frames of reference and our compliance with the status quo is secured as dominant interests control our 'thoughts and desires' (Lukes, 1974: 23). In other words, many communities appear to have real and legitimate reasons for protest but their apparent apathy, acquiescence or fixation with irrelevant concerns is a regular source of disappointment to politically committed activists who dream of change. Contrast the vivid and highly charged exchanges that surrounded the Roy Keane–Mick McCarthy imbroglio with the impoverished debate associated with the Citizenship Referendum of 2004. Worse, the high level of electoral support for that constitutional amendment suggests that public opinion *was* decisively shaped by the negative constructions of migrants and migration that had been a feature of Government and media discourses for almost a decade. Of course, it is both discomfiting and impolite to say that 'other people' get it wrong because they are duped by power; at the very least it invites the charge of arrogance or cultural imperialism. In the world of community development, where so much emphasis is placed on the wisdom of communities and the importance of listening to people's voices, it might appear to be the ultimate betrayal of practice values.

Nonetheless, Lukes' critical theorisation of power raises fundamental questions for community activists and workers who are driven by progressive political aspirations. It suggests that argumentation towards what communities don't know rather than facilitation of what they already presume may be the true vocation of the community worker. Maybe projects should attempt to mould rather than mirror community expectations. More worryingly, it implies that there may be tensions between the participatory ethos of community development and its commitment to citizen empowerment; the seamless connection between one value and the other may be more rhetorical than real.

Community groups can pursue empowerment on any or all of the three power dimensions, and in doing so they will face active, institutionalised or even unwitting resistance from established power blocks. Frances Fox Piven and Richard A. Cloward (2002) remind us that even when poor people's movements win critical victories in terms of welfare, labour or social rights, those victories can be reversed; that governments, employers or institutions can and will claw back concessions unless they are jealously guarded.[viii] Consequently, empowerment should never be classed as a technical exercise or as a deliverable that can be quantified to universal satisfaction. If groups struggle to win campaigns, to publicise their concerns outside their own communities or to rouse the masses from their willing acceptance of the status quo, they might, out of sheer frustration, conclude that they have no real power. A key problem with the 'Community Power Debate' is that it treats power as 'something' that is 'out there', a kind of end-point that signals either ultimate success or ultimate failure. There are, however, other useful ways of understanding power such as approaches that treat it as relational rather than as a fixed capacity or approaches that recognise how power is negotiated continuously in all human encounters.

Although acutely conscious of oppression, Michel Foucault (1994) also emphasised that some forms of power are socially dispersed, that power is more than repressive capacity, that it is 'the means whereby all things happened', including the production of pleasure and knowledge (Giddens, 1995: 263). He recognised that power is expressed not only in the obvious arenas of decision-making, but also in everyday routines, institutional arrangements, cultural practices, and in dominant and subaltern discourses (Foucault, 1994). For example, Colin Cameron (2007) describes how the Disability Arts Movement has consciously subverted mainstream discourses about disability by representing and celebrating positive, boisterous and creative images of the disabled subject. In doing so, the Disability Arts Movement has rejected the established canon of the arts world and asserted its own power to cultivate alternative ways of being, knowing and expressing. In Cameron's analysis, interestingly, 'non' or 'anti' participation is a manifestation of power. By supporting and validating resistant forms of living, talking, organising and imagining, community groups may subvert or inflect dominant relations of power. This resistance will not by itself radically transform overall patterns of inequality or oppression, but it does at least reveal a capacity for contrariness and altered thinking that is immensely valuable in a homogenising world.

Conclusion

Sometimes I think that the words participation, process and empowerment could easily be replaced by a 'there, there, there now' – those vaguely encouraging noises our mammies made to calm us down when they thought we were too stirred up. Participation, process and empowerment should be meaningful concepts, but all too often they are not. Often this is because the crucial responsibility of explanation is evaded when they are named as community development's values; explanation regarding what it is we might hope to achieve by pursuing them, who or what stands in their way and what are the kinds of sacrifices we might be forced to make in their honour. It is also because community development has become all things to all people: simultaneously attractive to the international and national architects of neoliberalism and to activists with a deeply felt commitment to egalitarian politics.

Community development groups do useful, even essential work. They provide basic services, share information about welfare and entitlements, support people who are distressed, lonely or isolated and they create much needed spaces for sociability. They show that people have potential power, power that can be expressed as resistance, outright opposition, acquiescence and co-operation. Our agency is expressed both individually *and* collectively, often through community organisations, so that we leave discernible imprints upon the social, political and cultural spheres we inhabit. Adult literacy classes, community parades or lively public meetings can enrich and improve our society. At a time when the desires of the individual consumer almost invariably trump the needs of the collectively minded citizen, community organisations that claim a value for solidarity, mutuality and creativity are actively subverting dominant cultural and political discourses. They remind us that the 'self' is always social and so are our interests, so are our needs.

It is, however, more difficult to distinguish what kind of imprint community organisations are leaving locally, nationally and internationally in terms of decisions made, policies followed through or progressive legislation enacted. William Gamson (1995) notes that, for collective forms of action to be possible, people need to develop new 'frames' or frameworks of thinking through which we can re-appraise our worlds. Specifically, we must develop 'injustice' frames that support the kind of moral indignation or anger that will fuel our desire for change; 'agency' frames that engender self-belief that *our* alternatives are possible; and 'identity' frames, that position our 'we' in opposition to a 'they' who 'have different interests or values' (Gamson, 1995: 90). In contemporary Ireland, the official narrative of community development presents a perpetual and all-encompassing 'we', but no 'they'. This ideology of consensus has been institutionalised both locally and nationally, in the form of partnerships. Many community activists and development workers believe that participation in these structures and processes offers the only viable route to empowerment; therefore they are strategically, if not ontologically, committed to partnership. Often this is articulated as 'we have no choice but to be involved.'

There are choices, however, albeit uncomfortable and potentially painful ones. The consequences of alternative choices may be a community development that is less well funded, that has less status in policy discourses or a community development that embarrasses and alienates powerful interest groups. Protest is a gamble. It brings no guarantee of success and every likelihood of reprisal, but it does at least force our attention to the impoverished scope, form and processes of Irish political debate. It reminds us of hierarchies of access, opportunity and outcome that partnership obscures. If community organisations are determined to stick with partnership, then they must demonstrate its effectiveness with more conviction. We need to hear and read about the tangible successes they have secured through partnership: if and how it incorporates good quality and rewarding process; evidence that their participation is not merely tokenistic, but that community groups can actually win out in instances of serious controversy; that the many rather than the few are engaged; that it supports new sources of power and a new spirit of efficacy within them. Sounds like a tall order? Of course it does, because it is precisely these kinds of expectations that are raised when community development becomes associated with words such as empowerment, process and participation.

Notes

i During 2009 Community Workers Co-op organised a very timely and welcome series of workshops in various locations around Ireland. These workshops created a valuable space within which participants could discuss and reflect upon the values and meaning of community development in the current practice and policy context.

ii Since 1986, the Combat Poverty Agency has been centrally involved in the measurement of poverty in Ireland. As a State body, it has played a significant role in supporting and celebrating anti-poverty work, in particular acting as a strong advocate for community development. In summer 2008 its future seemed uncertain as Minister Mary Hanafin at the Department of Social and Family Affairs was reported as 'giving strong indications that she wants to abolish the organisation' (*Irish Examiner*, 28 July, 2008).

iii In using the term community worker, I do not necessarily suggest that this worker is either paid or a 'professional'. I am referring instead to any individuals - activists, volunteers, paid workers - who attempt to activate and support community organisation based on a conscious commitment to the improvement of those communities. Dilemmas associated with professionalisation of community development are discussed by Seamus Bane in this volume (see Chapter 7).

iv The Community Development Programme is core funded by the Department of Community, Rural and Gaeltacht Affairs and it is, perhaps, the most high profile and extensive programme of community development in the history of the southern Irish State. According to the department, projects are 'designed to mobilize the capacity of disadvantaged communities to participate in mainstream local development, training, education and employment opportunities'.

v According to the Equality Authority (http://www.equality.ie), '[T]he Employment Equality Act, 1998 and the Equal Status Act, 2000 outlaw discrimination in employment, vocational training, advertising, collective agreements, the provision of goods and services and other opportunities to which the public generally have access on nine distinct grounds. These are: gender; marital status; family status; age; disability; race; sexual orientation; religious belief; and membership of the Traveller Community.' Notably class and economic status do not feature as grounds for discrimination and exclusion.

vi The primacy of economic and material considerations in the Irish policy-making sphere has been crudely illustrated by recent proposals to merge the State's key equality bodies: The Equality Tribunal, National Disability Authority, Equality Authority, Irish Human Rights Commission and the Office of the Data Protection Commissioner. According to the *Irish Times* (De Bréadún, 2008) the plans have been criticised by Labour Party Spokesman on Human Rights Joe Costello: 'It now seems that the tightened Exchequer situation is going to be used to neuter organisations like the Human Rights Commission and the Equality Authority that have been critical of the Government.'

vii Interestingly, the report of the Task Force suggested that there is no obvious decline in rates of volunteering but that voting trends should give more cause for concern. It did also acknowledge the difficulty in measuring qualitative experiences of community life. Its report suggested that it is these dimensions of social capital that give most concern.

viii Two examples from summer 2008 illustrate this point. The Small Firms Association has called for a decrease in the minimum wage (Small Firms Association, 15 July 2008), claiming that 'Ireland has "lost the plot" in terms of having a competitive labour market' and arguing for a €1 cut in the already paltry hourly rate. Meanwhile, Minister for Social and Family Affairs christened the recession with the inevitable 'Crackdown on Jobless Benefits Claims' (Radio Telefís Éireann, 2008), signalling the return of weekly 'signing on' for new applicants and increasing checks on the bona fides of existing recipients.

4

Theorising 'Community'

Hilary Tovey

Introduction

The story of community which is most familiar to sociologists, and probably also to most members of Irish society today, is that 'community' and 'modernity' are antithetical ideas. As modernisation progresses, community weakens its hold and starts to be seen as regressive, particularistic, and an obstacle to the emergence of an open, cosmopolitan society founded on universalistic individual rights and citizenship.

We can trace this story back in particular to the work of Emile Durkheim, a classical social theorist whose ideas continue to shape contemporary theorising in profound ways. In his book *The Division of Labour in Society* (1893), Durkheim argued that the emergence of modern industrial society depends on a transformation in the nature of the social solidarity that allows individuals to feel part of the larger collectivity in which they live. In the premodern era, he suggested, most people lived within 'mechanical' forms of solidarity, that is, they lived with others who were very similar to themselves in their economic activities and their cultural beliefs. Living in such groups called out a sense of collective identity in a 'mechanical' or unreflective sort of way, through simple recognition of sameness; the appearance of deviance or difference in some individual or household would be experienced as a great affront, and punished as a threat to the whole group's way of life.

Modernisation brings with it a change to a different form of solidarity, which Durkheim called 'organic', to emphasise how it is based on expectations of difference and complementarity in social relationships. Organic solidarity is the form appropriate, Durkheim says, to a type of society where there has been a dramatic growth in the division and specialisation of economic activities and work tasks, such as we find in highly industrialised and urbanised societies. Industrialisation, occupational differentiation, and social and spatial mobility detach people from their local geographical loyalties; thus the process of modernisation prepares people to shift their allegiance to larger collectivities such as the nation-state. In a world where nearly everyone has become occupationally specialised, individual difference is highly valued and the key issue for those in charge of social organisation and order is to ensure that differences complement each other and work together to produce an integrated economic and social system. Modernisation also brings increasing 'moral density', that is, increasing social interaction between different social groups, which enables people to develop insights into perspectives, knowledge and values that are different from their own. We can see how easily this account can be assimilated into assumptions that rural 'communities' are traditional, unreflexive and an obstacle to development, whereas densely populated urban 'societies' with advanced divisions of labour are modern, flexible and universalistic in outlook.

This is not the only story Durkheim tells us about 'community', as I discuss further in Section III below. But it is one which, in various guises, permeates much contemporary understanding of our world. In this chapter I raise some questions about its usefulness. It is evident that, as I have interpreted him here, Durkheim seems to make a series of assumptions about the 'community' form of social belonging, which can be questioned. Did this take a 'mechanical' form? Is it essentially linked to rural and agricultural economies, or can it be found in urban and industrial settings as well? Is it, indeed, 'pre-modern' at all or better seen as an enduring dimension of social organisation and social relationships in all historical settings? What have more recent discussions of community added to the picture? Discussion of such issues in the chapter is organised into two main sections, each addressing a distinctive perspective on 'community': one which understands community as local and relates it to 'place' as a source of collective identity and a site for collective action (Section II), and another which focuses on community primarily as a form of social 'bonding' or social relationship (Section III). The conclusion discusses some overlaps and differences between the ideas of community and civil society as a way of pulling together and reflecting on the earlier sections.

To start, however, we need to disentangle some of the different meanings that have become caught up in the complex concept of 'community'.

I. Community as a Contested Concept

'Community' is a good example of what the philosopher William Gallie (1968) called 'an essentially contested concept'. In this respect it is like many other ideas that social and political theorists address: democracy or sustainable development, for instance. These are concepts for which we tend to believe, initially at least, we all share an agreed meaning, but as soon as we start to try to itemise the components, and, particularly, to suggest ways of implementing or strengthening specific elements, we discover that there is considerable disagreement and debate. In part, this arises from the fact that such concepts are used evaluatively as well as descriptively, and people develop ethical commitments to one or other version of their meaning; in part, too, it arises from the very general nature of the concept which is what gives it much of its discursive force. Essentially contested concepts tend to be simultaneously deeply ambiguous and deeply interesting, and this is certainly true of how social theorists have responded to the term 'community' over the past hundred and more years.

Bell and Newby (1976) identified four different dimensions of meaning for community, which tend to be systematically run together when people use the term, and their analysis is still very useful. Community, they point out, is often used in a 'topographical' sense to refer to a specific place and to imagine it as a small self-contained society. Second, it often connotes a 'local social system', or the suggestion that in such boundaried settlements there is a high level of interaction and interconnectedness between individuals, which helps to sustain a degree of independence and autonomy - or isolation - from outside actors. Third, and perhaps most commonly, it is used to mean 'communion' or 'communality' - a particular way of relating to others characterised by personal ties, familiarity or warmth. And, finally, it can be used in an 'ideological' sense, when efforts are made to attach communality to locations and places in ways that mystify or conceal the actual relationships present there. Slippage between these meanings is a familiar phenomenon to us in Ireland, given the widespread discourse of community that still characterises Irish society (see Tovey and Share, 2003, Chapter 5).

Debates around each dimension of meaning have continued in the period since Bell and Newby's work, and new concepts have emerged that pick up or transform our understanding of community. My discussion in this chapter focuses on debates around community as locality and as communality, picking up some issues around community as social system as we go. Community as ideology is probably better treated not as a dimension of the meaning of the term, but rather as a warning to us to be on our guard whenever we hear it used. When someone speaks through a discourse of community, what vision of social relations, what assumptions about consensus and collective identity is the speaker trying to seduce us into accepting? As a warning, it applies to all the uses of the word 'community' we may encounter.

II. Community as Place

The most popular everyday use of 'community' is in terms of the topographical (among sociologists, the idea of community as place has not been popular at all, for most of the recent past). Topographical uses suggest that if a place is of a specific kind, or has particular spatial features, it also exhibits the sorts of social relations which Bell and Newby call 'communality'. But why should features of physical space affect social relations between people? It seems an implausible claim, yet it has a long history in social theory.

Durkheim's account of modernisation, as we saw at the start, associates changing forms of social solidarity with changes in the material form of space, particularly changes in population density. Simmel (1997) also thought population density changed our social relationships; he celebrated the arrival of the city as a place that produces very distinctive ways of relating to others. City dwellers, he said, are constantly exposed to rich and diverse sets of stimuli, and to cope with this they develop an attitude of reserve and insensitivity to others. They cultivate a self-presentation which is detached, reserved and world-weary or blasé, even while they are constantly alert to the transient impressions they make on others and are obsessed with fashion and appearance. Thus, cities give individuals a distinctive type of personal freedom that is not found in the small-scale community; they allow space for individual differences and for the cultivation of internal and external uniqueness.

From these and similar arguments emerged a thesis that preoccupied many social theorists in the first half of the twentieth century – that contemporary societies exhibit two distinct 'ways of life', urban and rural, which reflect differences in their size, population density and the extent of homogeneity or heterogeneity found within them. Modernity, in other words, does not transform everything all at once; it is a spatially uneven process in which the more peripheral locations (equated with rural areas) 'lag behind' and the people living within them remain attached to their geographical location as the main source of their identity. At the same time, in more central (i.e. urban) areas, people are significantly detached from a sense of place and form their collective identities along other, less particularistic lines of division (class, status, occupational, civic). Eventually, as even these collective identities lose their grip on our understanding of ourselves (Bauman, 2000; Beck and Beck-Gernsheim, 2002), urban people come to be seen as highly individualised, isolated from collective norms, and autonomous in their behaviour.

Much sociological research emerged first to support this 'two ways of life' thesis and then to question it. Communities (neighbourhoods stable over several generations, marked by personalised relations with familiar others and a strong self-identification in terms of locality) were discovered alive and well in the heart of great capital cities such as London. Then studies began to challenge the picture of rural life the thesis evoked: as homogeneous communities where people know each other and each others' friends, where people are mutually connected in diverse and overlapping ways. Newby *et al.* (1978) revealed the strength of occupational identities and class divisions within the British farming area of East Essex, between capitalist farmers, their farm labourers, and a large non-agricultural middle class, and the presence of conflicts around social status, access to housing and land. Ironically, they suggest, many of the middle-class residents were attracted to live in these rural villages in the first place because they believed them to be repositories of community and an escape from the anomie and divisions of city life. The 'community' they themselves created, however, was one that largely excluded the original occupants, the agricultural workers, and they tended to collude with the large landowners to keep out developments (council housing estates, supermarkets, new industries) that could have benefited that group.

Some social theorists also argued that it is not features of local space (such as population density) that structure our relations with each other, but rather changes in technologies for spatial mobility. These are generally seen as progressively detaching us from place. For example, automobilisation – the penetration of the car as a private means of transport into every aspect of daily living – has been said to both foster the sort of blasé relations to others Simmel identified with city living and to diffuse these across space, thus destroying the distinctiveness of rural 'community' as against urban 'society'. Arguents prioritising the impact of technological change also permeate much globalisation theory. This generally starts by identifying the role of new information, transport and communication technologies in enabling the 'stretching' of social relations across time and space, and then goes on to show how that is creating new modes of social relationships in contemporary society (see Chapter 10). The 'distanciation' (Giddens, 1990) of social relationships, which follows from our increasing use of information technology, is said to make a profound contribution to the 'de-traditionalisation' of society: we live in a world of anonymous others with whom we have to find a way to do business, and we must develop new modes of trust which no longer rely on face-to-face observation, or personal or reputational knowledge. Increasingly, we must put our trust in 'expert systems' rather than specific experts in order to get on with our lives, and that form of trust is based more on individualised rational and instrumental appraisals than on traditional expectations of how particular types of actors (professionals, service providers, public officials) will act. Globalisation, understood in this way, simultaneously erodes any lingering vestiges of attachment to place and promotes increasing individualisation among ordinary actors.

Place as a Source of Collective Identity and an Appropriate Site for Collective Action

Against visions of globalisation as the creation of homogenised space and a landscape of stretched, anonymous, individualised and instrumentalised social relations, we find accounts that emphasise the renewed importance in a globalised world of communal forms of solidarity and collectivity. These new communities are understood less as a hangover from the past than as a product of global 'high modernity' itself. Some theorists argue that the spatial diffusion of capitalist economic relations and the new possibilities for communication and interaction across space encourage the emergence of 'differentiated publics' (Blau, 2001) rather than isolated and homogenised individuals. These range from post-national formations (fundamentalist ethnic, racial and religious groups) reacting against the threats from global markets to their identities and social organisation, to groups engaged in liberation struggles who draw on global ties in their fight for self-determination, to 'alternative globalisation' groups such as Fair Trade activists and consumers. 'Globalising economic processes encounter tenacious community solidarities' (Blau, 2001: 59), or provide the conditions under which new community solidarities arise and seek to establish themselves.

Place is also re-emerging in social theory, both as a hoped-for source of *difference* (against the feared homogenising effects of globalisation) and as the site for social *action* (against what are thought to be the disempowering effects of globalisation). Discussions of the complex relations between globalisation and community have not ignored communities based on place. The term 'glocalisation' is commonly used to identify how global economic processes create new relationships between local places and global systems, bringing new economic opportunities and a renewed interest in local distinctiveness to some, even while bypassing and marginalising others. The spatial inequalities that were a feature of earlier modernisation (or capitalist development) persist rather than disappear under globalisation, and provide a continuing basis for local identification. The important divisions are no longer between 'rural' and 'urban' – many rural locations are tied more tightly into global economic systems through their involvement in the production of food for world markets, for example, than are many urban ones – but between 'glocalised' and 'peripheralised' locations. In turn, this has re-animated an interest among sociologists in studying how people in local places respond to and engage with globalising processes and systems, politically and culturally as well as economically (see also Chapter 10).

One theorist whose work opens up interesting issues around this topic is Castells (1997), whose account of globalisation as the construction of a global 'network society' incorporates a discussion of two competing 'spatial logics', which he labels the 'space of flows' and the 'space of places'. The 'space of flows' is where telecommunications and information systems organise social and economic practices to operate simultaneously over great distances. This is the space where power, wealth and information flows are concentrated, and it is hostile to place: 'For power to be free to flow, the world must be free of fences, barriers, fortified borders and checkpoints' Bauman (2000: 14) says, and later adds that 'the might of the global elite rests on its ability to escape local commitments and globalisation is meant precisely to avoid such commitments' (188). Castells, however, wants to bring identity, networks and social movements into his account of globalisation as well as economic flows, and this is addressed by the 'space of places'. Most human experience and the meanings we use to interpret it are still locally based: the space of places 'privileges social interaction and institutional organisation on the basis of physical contiguity' (Castells, 1997: 123). The gap between the spatial logic of economic development and that of human social development is, for Castells, a key mechanism of domination in the contemporary world, because it moves powerful economic and political processes away from the realm within which social meanings are constructed and political control might be exercised, i.e. the level of local place. Globalisation processes overlie a fundamental conflict between controlling and managing development across space, and doing so within local places. An oppositional 'politics of place' arising at the local level (often derided as NIMBYism) thus appears inherent to life in the contemporary globalised world.

Community and Environment

One source that has fed into the regrowth of sociological interest in place and place-based communities is the growing body of work on the sociology of the environment. Environmental practices and policies provide, in fact, a fascinating site within which to explore Castells' two competing spatial logics. On one hand, ecology is local and locally specific and should therefore be addressed within the 'space of places'; on the other, environmental policy is increasingly part of and articulated within the 'space of flows'. Emphasising the local nature of nature, and the right of local people to control over their own living spaces, inevitably challenges the bases of power in the global system.

The environmental policy of choice of most states across the world today, including the European Union, is *ecological modernisation* (usually expressed in the discourse of sustainable development). Ecological modernisation sees no incompatibility between economic development and environmental preservation, because the modernisation of industry requires the application of advanced technologies for cleaner industrial processes and the minimisation of waste and 'externalities' in production. Ecological modernisation is largely uninterested in locality. It focuses the attention of decision makers and environmental managers on what are supposedly universal, all-encompassing and trans-local processes, ignoring the differentiated ways in which these impact on local societies and local natures. 'The impacts of environmental degradation are always socially and spatially differentiated. They may end up affecting the global environment, but first they damage small parts of it.' (Low and Gleeson, 1998: 19). A policy discourse that favours ongoing economic and technological development and the adaptation to this of local lives is better suited to the interests of the powerful, which dominate the 'flow of spaces', than one that locates sustainability in the socio-natural practices of local places.

Yet, as environmental sociology shows, we can find many examples of resistance to top-down environmental policies by local groups and communities. Often what starts as resistance to the imposition from outside of some new enterprise, or an attempt to change old practices underpinning access to and use of land and other natural resources (sometimes called 'ecological marginalisation' or 'environmental injustice') develops into 'campaigns for autonomous, sustainable and equitable communities rooted in local natural, social, cultural and financial assets' (Pena, 2003: 163). Pena's study of the mobilisation of local groups living in the Rio Culebra watershed in Colorado's San Luis Valley, who farm using a centuries-old snow-fed irrigation system and resisted take-over of their lands by capitalist 'ranchers', shows how their campaign developed into a new understanding of 'sustainability', which combines principles of self-determination with those of environmental justice. Local place becomes 'an anchor for their identity' (Pena, 2003: 163) and local agricultural practices the basis for an ethic of production oriented to 'inhabiting' rather than 'developing' their local environment; in turn followed claims to communal ownership of the local biophysical resources (land and water) on which their livelihoods depend. Pena (2003: 163) concludes that a defining quality of place-based identity is the immediate connections that are made between material livelihood (economy) and the natural conditions of existence (ecology), and that it offers a good prospect for the 'multigenerational reproduction of ecosystem knowledge and management values'.

We might assume that this version of sustainable development as 'livelihood sustainability' – very different to ecological modernisation – can only emerge in underdeveloped areas of the world where economic survival still depends on a close relationship with nature. But we can find that it resonates with many environmental conflicts in Ireland in recent decades (Tovey, 1993). European researchers have found evidence of similar moves towards a 'new paradigm' of rural development widespread across farming communities in Europe, involving the mobilisation of local networks and communities to reclaim control over local natural resources and the incomes generated from use of these, and drawing on local as well as scientific ecological knowledge to maintain them in a sustainable way (van der Ploeg *et al.*, 2000; Marsden, 2003).

It may well be asked, of course, whether 'local communities' are fit entities to be given the charge of managing their local environments, even if they are often invoked as the appropriate bodies to implement and practice good environmental policies laid down elsewhere. Recent work in environmental sociology draws attention to some reasons why communities' control over place should be enhanced. The revival of interest in 'local knowledge' (see Chapter 3) as a resource for environmental management provides one. Scientific experts themselves are starting to recognise that natural processes are unpredictable and that scientific knowledge of ecology is uncertain, and they are becoming more willing to regard the management of local environments as an open experiment in which the shared knowledge of those who live within them can be an essential resource. The resulting blend of 'expert' and 'lay' knowledge has been called 'transdisciplinarity' (Rist *et al.*, 2006) and it could usefully be applied in other areas of life besides the ecological. A second is the growing acceptance that managing the environment must be compatible with the principles of democracy, in particular democratic governance, which requires that those most closely affected by a policy should be brought into the governance process, that is, not just consulted through 'community surveys' and so on, but given a real role in the identification of problems and the design and implementation of solutions. This is often referred to as the principle of 'community governance' and is claimed (for example, under the UN's Agenda 21) to be a core element of sustainable development.

Of course we need to exercise caution about such claims, which may be 'ideological'. Creating 'community' governance can often mean no more than identifying a few local elites and well-known volunteers and inviting them to participate in decision-making, regardless of whether they represent a 'community' or not; the 'affected community' may not coincide with the 'local community'; and anyway the local place may lack much community in the sense of strong face-to-face relationships and developed collective identity and concerns (see Chapters 3 and 9). These are not new problems, however, even if the context in which they arise is relatively novel, and political arrangements to address them can, with knowledge of and care for the local situation, be worked out, just as they have been in the past for entities such as 'the nation' and are gradually being for new entities such as the European Union.

Re-evaluating the Place-based Community

This brief overview of discussions of 'local community', and the fall and rise of 'place' in sociological theory as an interesting and important dimension of social organisation, suggests some conclusions. First, not all communities are place-based communities, and there is some evidence that the modernisation of society has weakened collective attachments based on place, if not in any simple way. 'Communality' (Bell and Newby, 1976) or 'solidarity' (Durkheim, 1893) has no necessary link to place or space, and many people's most deeply held attachments may be rather to what have been called – in order to indicate that they are not place-based – 'communities of choice', that is, groupings of people who share the same professional, political, aesthetic (and so on) interests and sentiments. Today, such communities of choice may be entirely 'virtual', created through the use of the Internet or other technologies for communicating at a distance. At the same time, we should not oppose 'communities of place' to 'communities of choice' as if the former were simply inherited or given in an unreflexive way – attachment to place is as likely to be a reflexive choice as any other communal attachment. Bonds between the members of any community can be 'modern' or can be 'traditional', based on either ascribed or acquired traits, activated through different types of symbols and screening strategies. Wherever they are found, they do not have to take the form of 'mechanical solidarity', but can simply refer to 'a wide range of reasons and ways of grouping together with others with whom we share some part of our identity, expectations and interests' (Storper, 2005: 203).

Second, clearly not all places contain communities, and some societies seem to do better at transforming residential locations into places of collective engagement than others (Putnam, 2000). The Irish habit of referring to places, especially if they are small in scale, as 'communities' needs some decoding. Sometimes it seems to express a generalised expectation that localities are sites for sociability, sometimes – more problematically – it is an ideological overlay on the fact that Irish national politics and delivery of public services are spatially organised, with the effect of concealing the class, gender and other forms of inequality that this may generate.

Nevertheless, there are some reasons to expect that place will continue to underpin important collective identities and solidarities in Ireland and elsewhere in the future, and that groups will continue to mobilise and act politically on the basis of a sense of shared place. A renewed rationale for 'acting locally' comes not only from the ongoing experiences of spatial inequality and differentiation under economic globalisation processes, but also from the introduction of new concerns – ecological, 'quality of life' – into public debates. As I will suggest in the next section, community remains essential to the well-being of societies and the fact that it often comes in a place-based form is no reason for opposing it. But place-based solidarities are highly particularistic, and need to be complemented by a recognition of other, more 'universalising' forms of attachment to class, gender, human-rights-based or even non-species-based solidarities (for example, animal rights movements or other solidarities with non-human species). Those who live within local places are often well able to manage such a complex hierarchy of connectivities; problems are more likely to come from those who seek to intervene in or manage 'the local community' and, in doing so, forget that where we live does not encapsulate all the dimensions of humanity that we are capable of.

III. Community as Bonding

Looking at community as 'communality' also engages with some interesting debates in modern social theory. A starting point here is Tönnies' (1957) distinction between two different modes through which we engage with other people: 'community' (*Gemeinshaft*), where mutual relationships are based on face-to-face interaction over a long period of time, with the deep and intense personal knowledge of 'the other' that this implies; and 'association' (*Gesellshaft*), where interaction is impersonal, organised through rules and laws, and oriented in an instrumental way to only those features of the other that are relevant for the purposes of the encounter. His distinction resurfaces in a range of guises in later social theories, some of which I touch on below. It is often translated as 'belonging to a group' versus 'being a member of a society'.

The Importance of Group Belonging

For many early social theorists, belonging to a group was an essential part of the process that empowers individuals to participate – as individuals – in society. Community, in this sense, is central to the assemblage of ideas that help us to understand what it is to be a human person, and to recognise the contradictions and tensions that this involves. Durkheim, for example, believed that people cannot be fully social, or indeed fully human, without participating in group relationships. It is from our relationships in groups that we acquire all of those things that equip us to become autonomous actors within our society, for example, shared language, shared ideas and culture, a sense of self and of others, a sense of the worth and value of life, and, above all, a sense of morality and a capacity for self-regulation. Group membership is so important to us, he argues (Durkheim,

1912), that the 'real' goal of many of our social rituals, even if they describe themselves differently - perhaps as religious rituals, national celebrations, civilised dinner parties and so on - is to affirm this. We need periodically to perform group membership to ourselves and our group, as Peace's (2001) account of the performance of community in his study of the annual concert in 'Clontarf' vividly illustrates. Durkheim called the experience of participating in group rituals 'collective effervescence': an emotional heightening of the sense of group membership, a feeling that we are merged with and dissolved as individuals into the collective. But in valorising group belonging in these ways, he still remained aware that we are not, in fact, simply components of groups - we remain stubbornly individual, and if our group membership is what enables us to regulate ourselves and to adopt the normative constraints of our groups, it also provides us with the shared meanings through which we are able to construct our individual actions and lives.

Durkheim's vision of human persons as 'duplex' - double beings, at once social and individual - was later elaborated through George Herbert Mead's (1934) famous distinction between the 'I' and the 'me'. These two dimensions of 'the self' try to capture how we are simultaneously capable of autonomous action (the 'I') and constantly aware of and concerned about how we appear to others and how they evaluate us (the 'me'). For Mead, as for Durkheim, both dimensions spring out of our relations with others in smaller or larger groups and each writer tried to find a way to express the problem of finding a balance in the individual between conformity and autonomy.

Why has this issue interested sociologists from the classical period on? Primarily because sociologists find themselves constantly engaged in argument against a very different conception of the human person, sometimes called the *Utilitarian Model* (neoliberalism) and sometimes *Rational Action Theory*. These models see human individuals as rational and self-interested actors from whose individual choices of action arise the institutions - the market, property rights, government and the rule of law - that together make up 'society'. Society is the outcome of a myriad of individual choices made by actors who are engaged in realising their own individual interests. Even participation in primary networks should be explainable, in these models, as perfectly rational, which denies that primary networks could be even partially dependent on group membership, or that the participants could be 'socially embedded' in ways important to the functioning of such networks. Some versions of neoliberal thought go further and argue that society should support only those institutions that enforce the laws of competition and a free market in order to limit the attachments arising from particularistic group memberships, which are seen as capable of distorting rational self-interest.

Against such perspectives, sociology claims that the social is irreducible. The patterns of action and forms of organisation found in human societies cannot be fully understood if we ignore or erase the level of social interactions and relationships. Neither political nor economic institutions and processes, nor indeed attempts to read human development as expressions of natural scientific 'laws' (such as evolution or the laws of genetics) are adequate on their own, from the perspective of social theorists, to explain human societies. Durkheim used the concept of 'collective conscience' to illustrate this, while Weber, explaining the growth of modern capitalism out of the transformations of religious meaning within some early Protestant sects, also argued that we cannot reduce the micro-social webs of interaction within specific social groups to intentional instrumental acts by individuals. To these early theorists it was clear that individuals are socially formed, and that they possess interests, needs and wants that are complex and socially given. Individual actors incorporate ethical considerations into their actions and decisions – displaying, for example, a 'need' to undertake responsibility and to find reciprocity in relations with others – and their 'happiness' or well-being is inherently relational, interpersonal and 'intergroup' in nature. More recent versions of the same argument appear in Polanyi's (1966) emphasis on the 'social embeddedness' of what appear to be purely rational economic transactions, which are maintained through the use of 'tacit knowledge' and interpersonal trust; and Amartya Sen's (1987) claim that societal institutions and practices should be assessed in terms of their impact not just on individuals but on interpersonal and intergroup relations, such as their effects on the distribution of social equality or inequality.

Sociological interest in community, then, has always been part of a concern to establish that the 'social' is different from and not reducible to individual self-interest or political or economic institutions. Community or 'communality' expresses the idea that we are 'co-dependent' (Blau, 2001) with others, and our lives and actions cannot be fully explained as the outcomes of our individual needs, desires and purposes. From this point of view, community directs our attention to some of the social ways in which we are integrated into and shaped by our relations with others. Or, as Storper (2005: 200) puts it, '[S]ociologists invented the analytical distinction between community and society as a way of considering different forms of social integration.'

Coming at 'community' from this direction offers us a different way of reading the Durkheimian story outlined at the start of this chapter. Instead of seeing community as a historical phenomenon, which disappears and re-emerges according to specific socio-historical conditions – for example, here we can place both the thesis that community was part of a premodern world which virtually vanished in late modern society, and the argument that communities re-emerge with globalisation – we start to see it as one of two main ways in which the social lives of individuals are organised and social order is achieved, the other way being society. As a mode of social organisation and integration, 'community' is both as permanent and as significant as 'society'. Each refers to a different kind of bond between people: to borrow from Putnam (2000), communities 'bond' while societies 'bridge'. 'Community' refers to forms of collective life in which people are held together by tradition, interpersonal contacts, informal relationships, particularistic interests and similarities. 'Society' refers to collectivities held together through anonymous, rule-bound, more transparent, formal and universalistic principles (Storper, 2005). The key question for social theorists has become whether or how it is possible to achieve some complementarity between them in the contemporary world.

Reworking Tönnies on 'Community' and 'Association'

The claim that we relate to others in at least two different sorts of way – 'society' and 'community' – recurs constantly in contemporary social theory. It is evident in Castells' distinction between 'space of flows' and 'space of places', discussed above. Another writer to whose work it has been central is the German social theorist Jürgen Habermas (1984), whose distinction between the world of 'system' and the 'lifeworld', based on characteristically different types of action ('instrumental' and 'communicative'), reads like an enriched version of Tönnies 'association' and 'community'. The system world is organised around management and technical control. It uses an instrumental form of rationality, realised in 'empirical-analytical' or 'expert' forms of knowledge. Scott (1995: 232) explains this as 'information that can be organised into "explanations" and "predictions"... technically utilisable knowledge that has the capacity to expand human powers of technical control and manipulation.' The lifeworld is the world of culture and interaction; it is organised around gaining practical understanding of others, and trying to achieve and expand 'mutual understanding, consensus and community in social relations' (Scott, 1995: 232). The lifeworld expresses a type of rationality that is oriented to understanding and interaction, which Habermas calls 'communicative' rationality. This is to distinguish it from the instrumental rationality that is oriented to control of the system world. The process of modernisation, for Habermas (1984), is one in which the system increasingly tries to colonise and direct the lifeworld; introducing more rational managerial procedures into everyday social relations, as in 'community development' or 'nutritional advice', for example. However, while the lifeworld is vulnerable to colonisation, it cannot be eradicated: its own distinctive knowledge and rationality are continually reproduced through social interaction. Any enterprise or project of social action, Habermas says, necessarily combines aspects of both purposive and communicative rationality; or, in other words, social worlds are totalities that combine lifeworld and system characteristics in an irreducible way. The world of work, for example, requires instrumental rationality for the management and co-ordination of tasks, but it cannot operate without co-operation between people, which in turn relies on communicative rationality and mutual willingness to understand each other.

A more popular, if less rich, reworking of Tönnies' ideas can be found in Putnam (2000). Putnam's concepts of 'bonding' and 'bridging' also echo classic discussions of community and society: social networks found within communities 'bond' individuals together in ways that encourage strong in-group solidarity but cause difficulties in relating to the larger social world, while social networks of the 'bridging' type encourage and enable the formation of relations across group boundaries. Putnam (2000) suggests that bonding is more widely available than bridging in contemporary society, and is a more effective source of 'social capital', defined as a mutual trust, which comes from actors having a common cultural background, shared values, and good knowledge of each other by experience or reputation because of engagement in dense interpersonal networks over a long period of time. Bridging is about how diverse individuals and groups can reconcile their different interests to engage in common projects, and is thus essential for societal development; but the more diverse the actors involved, the more unstable the social capital generated by a bridging network.

The introduction of concepts like 'social capital' and 'network' into debates around community, popularised in Putnam's work, has shifted those debates in some interesting directions. In particular, they indicate an increasing preoccupation with the contribution of community to economic development rather than human development. For much of the last century, social scientists saw bonding primarily as an obstacle to modernisation: it obstructed expansion of the formal, distanced, transparent social linkages necessary to the achievement of a successful market economy and industrial society. The assumption was that community-type groups, given the opportunity, will engage in what Marx called 'rent-seeking' and Weber called, 'social closure' strategies. That is, they will try to monopolise opportunities and resources, make excessive profits from their control of these, and devise strategies to prevent as far as possible any access to them by outsiders (see Chapter 7). For those interested in economic development, this reduces efficiency as well as curtailing entrepreneurial freedom. But more recent research (see Storper and Scott eds., 1992) suggests that the economic success enjoyed by districts and regions of small-firm-based industrial clusters in Italy, Taiwan, Mexico and elsewhere depends critically on the pre-existence of communal relationships, shared norms and expectations, and interpersonal knowledge, which regulate and support complex economic exchanges between firms and workers. Community bonds or the attachments formed at 'intermediate' levels of social organisation can improve the functioning of labour markets, generate and support entrepreneurship, and contribute to organising the provision of public goods in ways that reduce the burdens on the State and on private enterprise. Putnam (2000) similarly argues that social capital is good for economic development and social integration – in societies where its levels are high, it gives rise to a sort of 'positive externality', whereby even those who do not participate in creating it still benefit from its existence, experiencing less economic fraud, less neighbourhood crime, more volunteering in social care work and so on (see Chapter 3).

These are interesting findings, but replacing the term 'community' with the more 'operationalised' term 'social capital' could be an example of system colonising the lifeworld, if local communities are evaluated only in terms of how well they can achieve economic growth, for themselves or larger others (for example, 'the nation'); the deeply interesting issues about balancing group belonging and individual autonomy, which have been a part of sociological discussions of community from the beginning, are in danger of being lost. Moreover, much contemporary use of 'social capital' represents it purely as a resource, to which people may get access by meeting others, forging connections with them, and developing joint projects of action. Bourdieu (1984), from whom the term originated, understood it as a relational condition: like the other forms of capital he discusses (economic, cultural, symbolic), possession of social capital by one group is generally at the expense of other groups. It empowers some as it excludes others; it is not a neutral resource that can be increased or diminished without social consequences, and the social capital enjoyed by elites is always likely to be more effective than that of less advantaged groups.

Social capital is defined as something generated and possessed by social networks, and the move to treating communities as 'social networks' also has some interesting implications. 'Network' helps us to avoid the older assumption that a community is a type of small-scale, boundaried 'social system' (see Bell and Newby, 1976). It opens up the possibility that different community members have different patterns of relationships with their fellow members, and may even have little or no relation with some others, even in a very small, placed-based settlement; a single 'community' can incorporate a number of different networks, which may have stronger or weaker links to each other, and a single network may encompass a range of different types of links, weak and strong, between members. Granovetter's (1995) phrase 'the strength of weak ties' indicates that ties between individuals, which seem weak, may actually be the stronger because they link otherwise separated people who have different resources to share. At first sight another version of Putnam's 'bridging–bonding' distinction, Granovetter's point is that a single network can feature both strong and weak ties, whereas, for Putnam, bonding and bridging occur in different networks. 'Network' is primarily a descriptive term, a device to trace the patterns of interaction and communication between individuals. Compared to 'community', its advantages lie in not assuming consensus, similarity or equality within a group in advance of research, but it offers less insight into issues of solidarity and collective identity. But for those interested in mobilising a community for action, whether of political, developmental or social movement kinds, locating and understanding the different networks that are present within it is an essential means of entry.

The Community–Society Relations Problem – Encouraging Bonding, Preventing Social Closure?

Debate has re-emerged within social theory, then, around the role of community as a necessary basis for a healthy economy – but also for a healthy society, stimulated by concerns about the ways in which modern society is developing, either 'over-dominating' the individual or dissolving into 'liquid modernity' (Bauman 2000). Durkheim feared that 'organic solidarity', the form of solidarity peculiar to developed societies, would give rise to two types of problem for individuals – 'over-integration', when the pressure for conformity is so strong that we lose our sense of self as an autonomous individual, and 'under-integration', when the individual is given no clear guide for living by society, and feels detached and adrift, capable of everything or nothing. Both can end in suicide, he thought, or at least in more or less serious forms of criminal behaviour.

Most later theorists suggest that 'underintegration' or 'dissolution' is the more serious problem. They ask whether the increasing organisation of society along large-scale, rational, bureaucratic principles, and the individualisation, mobility and ephemerality which seem to be associated with this, has terminally damaged the small group and face-to-face relationships necessary to social order and a meaningful individual life (Beck and Beck-Gernsheim, 2002; Bell, 1976; Bellah *et al.*, 1985; Etzioni, 1995; Putnam, 2000). In the 'hypermodernity' described by Giddens (1990), we can only respond to loss of trust in the expert systems to whose direction our lives are perforce consigned by constructing our own lonely 'life projects' to which we commit ourselves by an existential leap of faith. Perhaps the strongest exposition of the 'dissolution' thesis is found in Bauman (2000), for whom modernity itself has always been a project of 'melting the solids'. First to be lost are those of tradition and custom, and he describes modernity as 'shredding the "irrelevant" obligations standing in the way of rational calculation of effects…liberating business from the shackles of family-household duties and from the dense tissue of ethical obligations' (Bauman, 2000: 4). Later come those of collective solidarities, i.e. 'the bonds which interlock individual choices in collective projects and actions – the patterns of communications and co-ordinations between individually conducted life policies on the one hand and the political actions of human collectivities on the other' (2000: 6). The 'liquidising powers' of modernity have moved progressively from 'system' to 'society' to the 'micro-level of human co-habitation' and we are now in a condition where we must construct ourselves, but the materials we need to do this are 'endemically and incurably underdetermined' (2000: 7). If Durkheim suggested that too much society and too little community is problematic for the individual (although not for societal development), Bauman brings us to a point where we have little, if any, of either.

Some social theorists (for example, Etzioni, 1997) turn to strengthenin community as a possible cure for these ills. Often called Communitarians, their views have been widely criticised as conservative, unrealistic and gender-blind, among other things. They are accused of trying to reinvent the patriarchal, hierarchical and consensual collectivities of the past – or of the past when imagined as 'mechanical solidarity'– and of trying to engineer the production of conforming, 'over-socialised' individuals. Therefore, they are accused of not recognising that the goal of social formation is to produce individuals who can balance a sense of autonomous self with a recognition of mutual obligations to and dependence on others. Bauman's chapter on 'Community' in *Liquid Modernity* is an especially savage attack on Communitarian thought. Communitarians are against choice, he claims, and their preferred model of community is the type of community we are born into – particularly the ethnic type, which, more than any other, 'naturalises history… presenting the cultural as a fact of nature, freedom as … necessity' (2000: 173). Communities, Bauman says, are inevitably 'gated', metaphorically or literally: they can only survive by drawing boundaries and excluding difference. Like the nation-state, their history is one of suppressing internal and magnifying external differences. In trying to revive them, Communitarianism undermines alternative models of democratic citizenship, which value social collectivity as a negotiated outcome, not a precondition, of shared social life.

Yet Bauman does recognise the dilemma that Communitarianism tries to confront. Late modernity contains a deepening imbalance between individual freedom and security, and a new fragility of social bonds: 'The brittleness and transience of bonds may be an unavoidable price for individuals' right to pursue their individual goals, and yet it cannot but be, simultaneously, a most formidable obstacle to pursue them *effectively*, and to the courage needed to pursue them' (2000: 170). We value our individual freedom intensely, but without relations and attachments to others we cannot recognise or realise our own interests, and in the absence of collective supports we feel fearful and exposed if we try to act in individual or autonomous ways. Contemporary social theory, Bauman says, must therefore privilege 'individual self-awareness, understanding and *responsibility*' (2000: 213). But where or how can we can learn these attributes, if not from growing up in communities?

Conclusion: Community or Civil Society?

If we need both society and community to lead lives that are fulfilled and creative, how can we ensure a useful balance between them? Can modern societies, which are complex, highly specialised, and individualised, encourage co-operation and co-dependency between individuals without presupposing and enforcing some framework of shared norms and meanings?

Many contemporary theorists who reject the Communitarian solution to this question have turned instead to the idea of civil society as the arena that holds the answers. Strengthening civil society has been promoted as a 'third way' (Gouldner, 1980; Giddens, 1998) between 'the atomisation of competitive market societies and a State-dominated existence' (Gouldner, 1980: 370). Civil society is represented both as the realm of freedom and citizen association outside, and often against, the State, and as the realm of solidarity, sociability and everyday civility, which is the essential underpinning to modern democratic life. It recognises the importance of citizenship as a universalistic guarantee of individual freedom, but also that, on its own, securing citizen rights expands neither collective solidarity nor civic engagement in the public sphere; citizenship needs to be surrounded by a strong network of associations and institutions 'below the State' which intermediate between State agencies and our private lives, and provide citizens with opportunities to learn how 'to co-operate in their own affairs' (de Tocqueville, 1856: 107). Just as Communitarians have done with community, '[T]he new studies of civil society tend to furnish this concept with many desirable qualities and to see it as the crucial antidote to all social problems' (Misztal, 2001: 75).

Civil society is as much a 'contested concept' as community is; as Misztal shows, it is ambiguous in definition and conflicting in uses. Some theorists (for example, Keane, 1988) use it to emphasise the importance of 'associational' life in modern societies, or what we have seen Putnam calling 'bridging' social networks; for others (for example, Alexander, 1998), the 'project of civil society' is to restore social bonds and reintroduce emotional dimensions into participation in public life. It is sometimes depicted as an arena of social interaction in which the particularities of others and their difference from ourselves are appreciated and respected, and sometimes as an arena in which difference is ignored in favour of exercising universal civic virtues.

Debates about community and civil society have tended, given the antipathy between Civil Society theorists and Communitarians, to be conducted in separate theoretical sites; but there is much they could usefully learn from each other. Civil Society theorists could learn, perhaps, not to equate 'community' automatically with the particularistic, mechanical forms of collective solidarity identified by Durkheim with small-scale, isolated and primarily rural settlements.

Thinkers about 'community' could pick up useful ideas from the civil society debates. Primary among these, perhaps, is the realisation that collective attachments and group memberships are not an automatic by-products of social arrangements but need to be understood as active political accomplishments. As Peace (2001) shows, we 'perform' and 'accomplish' our communities, sometimes but not always in response to outside interventions. Communities exist in their mobilisation, and the conditions under which and means through which mobilisation comes about need to be carefully understood if we are to avoid creating the sort of community that 'over-dominates' the lives of its members and engages in the sort of social closure practices noted above. At the same time, community mobilisations are an essential element in democratic civic engagement and societal arrangements need to enable their continuance.

The 'civil society' debates also suggest that many approaches to community, whether in sociological research or in managerial interventions, are too narrow: they identify community with nonpolitical interactions between individual members or at best with 'volunteering' in local self-help and caring associations, but rarely include the local manifestations of social movements and other strategic networks through which community actors seek to create both solidarity and social change. And both civil society and community debates often tend to expect too much from these arenas of social relationships; neither can, on their own, resolve problems of limited resources or of societal forms of inequality, discrimination or prejudice. Ultimately, though, both bodies of theory are addressing the same problematic: how do we ensure that private, particularistic interests can be translated into public, universal solidarities, without losing the group belonging which seems essential to our formation as full human persons? In the contemporary globalised world, this is probably the most pressing problem that we face.

II

Context

5

The Voluntary Youth Work Sector's Engagement with the State: Implications for Policy and Practice

Sinéad McMahon

Introduction

Much of what is currently written about State involvement in Irish youth work tends to provide descriptive outlines of implementing the Youth Work Act 2001 and the *National Youth Work Development Plan 2003–2007*. Commentaries seem to generally infer that the State's increased role is a good thing for Irish youth work and any critical observations relate to slow progress and lack of commitment and resourcing by the State to implement policy agreements. Given the excitement and optimism expressed by the voluntary youth sector in the rolling out of the Act and plan, there are seemingly few opportunities to problematise the growth of State intervention in Irish youth work or the nature of the relationship evolving between the youth work sector and the State.

In this chapter the focus is on the relationship between the youth work sector and the State, which has become increasingly formalised over the years, most starkly through the Youth Work Act 2001. The perspective taken here is to consider the evolving relationship between youth work and the State as having served the interests of both the State and the youth work 'sector' – each influencing and mutually addressing the interests of the other in various ways. It will attempt to problematise the issue of whether the needs and rights of young people are served adequately within this relationship. It is suggested in this chapter that, within the context of the current State–sector relationship, young people are treated primarily as passive consumers of youth services. The discourse of youth policy, when examined, illustrates that the emphasis is clearly on the provision of services for young people, as opposed to youth work as a social movement for youth rights. But even within the dominant discourse of service provision, a rights based analysis, one that puts young people central to that service provision, seems virtually absent from both sector and State contributions.

For the purposes of this chapter the term the 'State' is used to refer to the political institutions of national and local Government as well as State administrative agencies that exist at national and local level. There is sociological discussion about the complex nature of the State, its relationship to society and interest groups (Peillon, 1995; Share *et al.*, 2007). These issues of complexity can be applied to considerations of the youth work sector's role as an interest group in Irish society. But what is meant by the term 'youth work sector' and whose interests does it represent? Generally, the term 'youth work sector' is used to refer to the amalgam of all youth work organisations and groups that exist at national, regional and local level[i] and this chapter uses this meaning. But discussions of a youth work sector can suggest a unity that does not exist and simplifies the complex array of different organisations that exist within the 'youth' sphere. These organisations differ from each other in relation to function, mission, profile of youth participants and geographical boundary.[ii] There has been a long history of tension and competition between youth organisations at national and local level, and we could ask about whose interests are then represented by such a diverse youth work sector? One would expect the simple answer to be the interests of young people. The view taken here challenges this straightforward assumption and includes the self-interest of the sector itself when analysing the relationship between the sector and State. As such, the 'sectorisation' of youth work is discussed and refers to the attempted creation and continuing development of a collective identity, status and structures for youth work in Ireland. Alongside this, the State's agenda for increasing its involvement in youth work is considered against a backdrop of a corporatist framework and a mixed economy of welfare provision, as well as a general desire to shape youth work to fit broader social and economic policy objectives.

Sector–State Relationships in Youth Policy

The beginnings of State involvement in youth work can be located in the legislation of the Vocational Education Act 1930 (Hurley, 1992*a*). From the 1970s onwards, there have been quite a number of youth policy documents contributed by both the youth sector and the State (see Table 5.1).

Table 5.1: Key Youth Policy Contributions Made by Sector and State

1930	*Vocational Education Act*
1971	*A National Youth Policy*, NYCI
1973	*The Development of Youth Services*, NYCI
1977	*A Policy for Youth and Sport*, Bruton Report, Government publication
1978	*A Policy on Youth Work Services*, NYCI, submission to Bruton Report
1980	*The Development of Youth Work Services in Ireland*, O'Sullivan Report, Government publication
1983	*Youth Services 2000*, the Federation of Youth Clubs in Ireland (now Youth Work Ireland)
1984	*Final Report of the National Youth Policy Committee*, Costello Report, Government publication
1985	*In Partnership with Youth: The National Youth Policy*, Government Publication
1990	*Youth Services Bill*, Private Members Bill, defeated in Dáil
1992	*Education for a Changing World: Green Paper on Education*, Government publication
1993	*Report of the Consultative Group on the Development of Youth Work*, Response to the Green Paper
1995	*Charting our Education Future: White Paper on Education*, Government Publication
1997	*Youth Work Act*, enacted but not implemented, Government publication
2001	*A New Impetus for European Youth*, European Commission White Paper on Youth
2001	*Youth Work Act*, Government publication
2003	*National Youth Work Development Plan*, NYWDP, 2003–2007, National Youth Work Advisory Committee

Analysis of these youth policy documents reveals an increasing and more interventionist role for the State in Irish youth work. Policy developments also highlight the changing nature of the relationship between the youth work sector and State over the last 30 years. Policy contributions from sector and State supported the view that youth work ought to be provided by the voluntary sector. The sector aimed to preserve youth work activity as a voluntary-based service and guard against the development of a statutory youth service by indicating the advantages of voluntary organisations over statutory provision and by asserting belief in the voluntary nature of youth work, whilst also expressing the view that the State should have ultimate responsibility for ensuring the provision of youth work (National Youth Council of Ireland, 1978; Consultative Group on the Development of Youth Work, 1993). Policy commitments from the 1980s indicated a growing acceptance by the State that it had an active role to play in youth work (Department of Education, 1980, 1985). For the most part, Government policy proposals avoided committing the State to direct involvement in the delivery of youth work services. Instead, the State defined its role in terms of supporting youth work by providing local and national administrative structures and improving financial assistance. Eventually, the State came to accept the need for a legislative duty to be imposed on its responsibility for youth work and the *White Paper on Education* paved the way for this legislation (Department of Education, 1984, 1985, 1995). Speaking in the Dáil on the Youth Work Bill 2000, then Minister of State at the Department of Education Willie O'Dea noted:

> Ever since the report of the national youth policy committee in 1984 the issue of youth work legislation has been on the agenda. The long progress to this point has been with Governments of differing complexions and, sometimes, with opposing views of the structures which should be in place to facilitate good practice and the effective administration of the youth service. There has always been, however, common ground that the youth work service, mainly of a voluntary nature, should have a legislative basis on which to function and operate. (Dáil Éireann, 2000)

In the Youth Work Act 2001 the role of the State as a youth work actor is carefully laid out. The role encompasses responsibilities for essentially 'managing' youth work in Ireland, including functions such as policy-making, assessing, monitoring, planning, budgeting, co-ordinating, evaluating and funding youth services. Under the Act, the State also has the power to recognise the status of youth organisations as prescribed, approved, designated and authorised, as well as power to revoke such recognition. The Act 'is significant in that overall responsibility for the delivery of Youth Work is vested in the Minister for Education and Science' (Breen, 2003: 16). The State's responsibility for youth work is shared with local State actors in the form of Vocational Education Committees (VECs). Speaking on the Youth Work

Bill 2000, Dr Mary Upton, Labour TD, summarised the proposed legislation as a:

> …formalising of the partnership approach to youth work with the State, its agents and the voluntary youth groups all involved in the process….with the State taking overall managerial responsibility for youth work and existing youth work organisations being the deliverers of the product. (Dáil Éireann, 2000)

Youth Work Structures and Funding

Hurley (1992*a*) identifies the first official recognition of the need for the State to support the work of voluntary youth organisations when the Department of Education called a meeting of all voluntary youth organisations in April of 1966. The meeting decided on the establishment of a co-ordinating and policy-making body for youth work. Following from this decision, the National Youth Council of Ireland (NYCI) was established in 1968 and was core funded by the State. The Youth Work Act 2001 prescribes for a national youth organisation to act as the sector's representative and to function as a key liaison point between the sector and the State. The NYCI is currently conferred with this status. The State has also created specific structures for partnership between the youth work sector and State. The National Youth Work Advisory Committee (NYWAC), provided for under the Act, 'epitomises the spirit of co-operation and partnership between statutory and voluntary sectors in the provision of youth work in Ireland' (Breen, 2003: 17). The composition of the committee is made up of fifty per cent statutory representatives and 50 per cent voluntary youth sector representatives. At local level, new structures for sector–State partnership were also provided for in the Act. Youth Work Committees are to be established as sub-committees of the VECs, again the composition of which will be made up of half statutory and half voluntary representatives. The youth work sector has also been brought into the broader social partnership bodies by the State. As early as 1985, the Government outlined 'the objective of making youth an effective social partner' through consulting the NYCI in national partnership arrangements, though it clearly warned that, 'This major role of articulating youth needs and interests to Government goes far beyond simply looking for grant-aid for youth organisations' (Department of Education, 1985: 57). The NYCI was made a full social partner in 1996 and has been involved in the negotiations for new national development programmes as part of the Community and Voluntary Pillar (NYCI, 2006*a*: 9). At local level, youth service organisations have been involved in local social partnership structures such as the County Development Boards.

The State has also supported the building of internal structures and capacity within youth service organisations. The Youth Service Grant Scheme provides for the organisational and administrative support of national and regional youth services and has been in place for many years. In the 1980s other grant schemes included the Organisational Development Grant, the In-Service Training Grant and the Facelift Grant Scheme. In earlier times, the State was also called to support the capacity building of paid and voluntary youth workers and even considered establishing a Youth Service Training Unit within the Department of Education (Department of Education, 1985: 32). Under the National Youth Work Development Plan (NYWDP) a proposal to set up a new structure, a National Development Unit for youth work, is under consideration. Alongside this, the State has created its own internal administrative structures for youth work. Until 2008 youth work issues were dealt with by the Department of Education and Science with a minister of state with special responsibility for Youth Affairs (a section within the department). However, in a surprise move, the Cabinet reshuffle by the new Taoiseach Brian Cowen in 2008 brought about the relocation of Youth Affairs to the Department of Health and Children.[iii]

The implementation of the Youth Work Act 2001 marks a new era in creating statutory structures and roles to support youth work, at both national and local level. The Act provides for the ministerial appointment of an Assessor of Youth Work and this appointment was made in 2006. At local level, VECs are required to 'ensure that there is adequate provision of youth work programmes and services' and they are to be 'enabled to grant, withdraw or reduce financial assistance to Youth Work Organisations' (Breen, 2003: 16). In order to perform these functions, youth officers have been appointed to all VECs and new Youth Work Committees are to be set up within each VEC.

Since the first youth service grants were given in the late 1960s, the State remains the main funding body for youth work in Ireland. As such, funding is a key issue in shaping the relationship between the sector and the State. A constant theme in policy contributions, debates and commentaries on youth work in Ireland relates to the sector's need for more financial assistance and simpler funding arrangements. Over a period of 40 years, the State has moved from ad hoc provision of relatively small amounts of money to investments of large, though still insufficient, amounts of money for a range of Department of Education and Science (DES) youth work grant schemes.[iv] Apart from DES funding for youth work, the State provides funding for other Government initiatives featuring the use of a youth work approach.[v]

However, the way in which youth work is funded by the State has been criticised, prompting an independent external review of the issue by the DES. Uncertainty around annual budget allocations, 'grant-in-aid' status and the limited availability of budget lines to fund various types of work have all been criticised. Grant-in-aid is a form of financial assistance rather than funding per se, with some suggestion that this model of funding 'could be described as a euphemism for Government having the sector delivering services "on the cheap!"' (Kearney, 2006*a*: 2). The limited availability of funding has also led to a competitive tendering process between youth organisations at local level and transparency in the selection of one organisation over another is seriously lacking, as criteria for selection are very loosely defined. 'Tendering' for contracts to deliver Government-devised youth work initiatives is fast becoming a dominant feature of the funding landscape. Under the Youth Work Act 2001, VECs were given the responsibility to arrange for the provision of youth work services where they are not being provided and to invite local youth organisations to 'submit a proposal' for selection (i.e. tender). In particular, there is limited funding for mainline work and vastly more schemes and amounts available for targeted work with specific sections of 'problematic' youth.[vi] The State's preference for youth work intervention with disadvantaged youth is clear in the ways in which it makes money available for youth work and this has implications for youth service providers. When the vast bulk of funding that is made available by the State is for work with disadvantaged youth, youth organisations engage in a process where they seek out and label certain sections of young people they work with as 'at risk' or 'disadvantaged' to access the funding.

There has been a distinct change in the way the State is funding youth work, characterised by a movement away from innocuous patron towards hard-nosed purchaser; a move from 'here is some support to help you do what you do' to 'here is what we are in the market to buy'. While youth organisations battle it out in tendering processes, the State is in the powerful position to act as 'purchaser' and exercise its 'consumer choice' in selecting which organisation to fund. As purchaser, the State now offers a substantial amount of its funding for youth work in prepackaged format,[vii] giving it a powerful reach into shaping actual service delivery, challenging the independence of the voluntary youth sector to innovate, devise and respond to young peoples' real and changing needs on the ground, and lending to the general commodification of youth work. Doorley (2003: 5) suggests that 'As a consequence of funding shortages, some organisations are being lured into contracts that bind them to implement policies of the State rather than meet the needs of the group they are working with and for.' There is awareness within the sector of the problems of overreliance on State funding in youth work. In a submission to the European Youth Forum, the National Youth Council of Ireland (2002: 4) identified the need to explore other sources of funding, saying, 'We must ensure we do not become solely reliant on public funding with all the implications that would have for the independence and legitimacy of the sector.' The position of the State as primary funder of youth work enables it to have an indirect influence on the design and delivery of youth work. A more insidious proposition for State influence in the delivery of youth work is a provision in the Youth Work Act, section 8.6, which states that the Minister may, following assessment, 'give directions to the organisation in relation to the manner in which the programme or service is provided, and the organisation shall comply with the directions.'

The Sector's Pursuit of State Involvement

Undoubtedly, one of the factors behind increasing State intervention in youth work is the success of the youth work sector's campaign to achieve this very thing, the pinnacle of which was to establish a legal and statutory footing for youth work provision. The assumption is that formalised State commitment to youth work implies recognition of the value of youth work and a secure future for the sector. The desire for security is understandable for a sector that has barely survived financially over the years; security of status will confer security of funding and a secure youth service will be able to focus on meeting the needs of young people, so the logic goes.

So, are there other, more self-serving motivations behind the sector's move toward formalising relationships with the State? The 'Cinderella' comparisons with the formal education sector and the worrying realisation that youth work still struggles to make its identity visible in Irish society is bound to affect sector morale. As the NYCI indicated, 'The introduction of the Youth Work Act 2001 and the preparation of the draft Development Plan heralded a climate of optimism, confidence and self-belief among youth organisations. This is in contrast to an earlier suspicion that youth work was the "Cinderella" of the Irish education system.' (National Youth Council of Ireland, 2003*a*: 2). But in the years since achieving a legislative basis for youth work, the battle for adequate funding continues.[viii] It is questionable just how much more secure the sector feels especially in light of, as yet, undetermined implications arising from the likely new evaluation and assessment arrangements and devolved decision-making to local VECs. Indeed, the security of the sector has been deeply undermined by the recent shock removal of Youth Affairs from the Department of Education and Science, which took place without any consultation between Government and the youth work sector, despite notions of strong social partnership relations. The move left a vacuum, with the sector simply unable to predict what the implications are for the status of youth work or for the implementation of the Youth Work Act 2001, including the anticipated central role of VECs. The sector is particularly concerned that 'any diminution of the link with education doesn't undermine the principles that have underpinned youth work for decades' (Cunningham, 2008: 1).

It is increasingly challenging for youth work to remain relevant to young people in the face of competition with commercial leisure activities and home-based entertainment technologies (Department of Education and Science, 2003*a*: 11–12; Sweeney and Dunne 2003). Other professions and statutory agencies have attracted youth workers into their employment and have adopted features typically associated with youth work in their own modes of intervention.[ix] Put these things together and it is understandable that there might be some self-interest among those in the youth work sector in pursuing the 'sectorisation' of youth work. To retain the institution of youth work and to gain improved status for the sector and its workers requires: enhancing the professional status of youth work; legislation that defines the activity as a separate sector; and the creation of a sophisticated infrastructure to support youth work. The pursuit of 'sectorisation' for youth work is clear throughout youth policy developments. Ireland, it is argued, employs a 'static' youth policy concept, meaning 'there is no distinction between youth work and youth policy, and the major youth work providers are also seen as the major youth policy actors … youth policy is identical with the state of youth work' (Istituto de Ricera, 2001: 59).[x]

As is evidenced by even a cursory glance at the titles of many policy documents, the nature of youth policy in Ireland has become synonymous with the institution of youth work itself. The core focus of the Youth Work Act 2001 is on developing the arrangements, structures and functional roles that will enable future youth work provision. The Act scopes out the authority of various statutory actors and defines their 'right' to carry out functions, such as withdrawing financial assistance from organisations. It protects the status of the voluntary youth sector as 'primary provider' of youth work and defines the 'right' of providers to appeal decisions made against them. But there is no mention of the rights of young people in the legislation. Youth policy and legislation has tended to be 'sector' centred rather than youth centred, with the starting point for policy interventions focused on the youth service sector and its needs, such as: more volunteers, training for workers, professionalisation, legislative framework, more funding, better evaluation systems and the need for a close relationship with the State via partnership. The focus has been on building a quality youth service in Ireland and a well-defined youth work sector. With this in place, the needs of young people, it is assumed, can then be met.

The sector's desire for developing increasingly formal structures to support 'sectorisation' is clear. For example, the NYCI welcomed the appointment of the Youth Work Assessor, stating that this appointment would 'serve to improve the professionalism, accountability and standing of youth work through a recognised assessment process accountable to the Minister for Youth Affairs', would help 'build a world class planned and strategic Youth Work service' and would 'provide the public with a mechanism for ensuring that funds spent on the youth work sector provide value for money and that the sector is accountable to the public and, as a result, to young people' (National Youth Council of Ireland, 2006*b*). Efforts to enhance the professional status and the sectorisation of youth work are mutually reinforcing. Speaking on the Youth Work Bill 2000, Dr Mary Upton, the Labour TD, outlined how youth work legislation would help to professionalise youth work because it would give a legal definition for the activity (Dáil Éireann, 2000). The need for structures such as a professional association for youth work has also been expressed, with suggestions that it would 'be welcomed as adding significantly to the sector' (Kearney, 2006*b*: 2). The aim to build a well-defined and developed youth work sector has, as a necessity, required increased State involvement. The State has supported the sectorisation of youth work and, in justifying legislation for youth work, O'Dea, the then Minister of State in the Department of Education, said, 'Youth work is rightly deserving of its own identity' (Dáil Éireann, 2000).

The State Agenda for Intervention in Youth Work

The corporatist approach to understanding State–society relationships has been described as one where '... society is ruled by the State acting in conjunction with a small number of specific interest groups that it has taken into a privileged form of "partnership" while, in return, these interest groups secure support for State policies, thereby reducing conflict against the State' (Share *et al.*, 2007: 96). Corporatist approaches have a long history in Ireland, but in recent times are closely associated with social partnership. The youth work sector, as represented by NYCI, was made a social partner in 1996. Despite ongoing frustrations with the State's perceived lack of commitment to youth and youth work, and despite threats of pulling out of social partnership, NYCI has maintained ongoing involvement with the social partnership process (National Youth Council of Ireland, 2006*d*). In a study, Istituto de Ricera in Milan (IARD) (2001: 71) focused on trends of 'neocorporatism' in European youth work. It referred to a blurred distinction between statutory and voluntary provision, the principle of subsidiarity and the delegation of action from State to civil society as aspects of this. Ireland is noted for the dominance of the voluntary sector in youth work and the IARD report connected this to a modernised form of subsidiarity (Istituto de Ricera, 2001: 133). It suggested that the corporatist structure of youth work is found in countries with a conservative welfare state, where 'On the one hand there is a strong interest of the State in providing socialisation towards the standard biography .... On the other side this objective is delegated to voluntary actors which to a high extent are incorporated into local, regional and national administration' (Istituto de Ricera, 2001: 138).

But what objectives might be behind the State's increasing intervention in Irish youth work in the particular form that it takes? In exploring this question, two main considerations will be analysed here: firstly, the issue of achieving cost effectiveness, value for money and management control in youth work provision; secondly, the desire to shape youth work by utilising its social control potential to fit with other State policy objectives.

The State is not the sole provider of welfare in Ireland; instead, a 'mixed economy of welfare' exists, comprised of public, private, voluntary and informal providers. Despite a history of subsidiarity, which advocated 'State intervention only as a last resort', the Irish State has developed a significant role as a provider and regulator of welfare (Fanning, 1999). However, the voluntary sector is regarded as being very cost effective in providing services and this quality makes it particularly desirable for the State to delegate service delivery here (Boyle and Butler, 2003: 22). The cost effectiveness of utilising voluntary sector provision in youth work is often used by both sector and State in justifying State funding for youth work, for example, the NYCI (National Youth Council of Ireland, 2003*b*) argued, 'If the State had to replace all the volunteer youth workers with paid employees on the minimum wage, it would cost about €100 million.' But, as Jenkinson (1996) points out, voluntarism has also been used as a justification for *not* funding youth work adequately. The State attempts a careful balance between providing just enough funding, but not so much that it depletes voluntarism. For example, Fianna Fáil TD Michael Mulcahy challenged demands for youth sector funding in an Oireachtas Committee debate, saying:

> ... until the 1970s youth work existed very well without any form of State funding whatsoever....there are hundreds if not thousands of people who want to be involved in the youth sector on a voluntary basis and do not need, and in some cases do not want, the involvement of the State in what they are doing .... we need to be careful we do not add to the depletion of volunteerism by allowing organisations to be hijacked by people. (Joint Committee on Education and Science, 2003)

But, as Fanning (1999: 58) points out, even where there was hostility to State encroachment in areas of strong voluntary service provision, over time interrelationships between the State and voluntary sector have developed and the role of the State has increased. Doorley (2003: 5) points out that the trend of growing co-operation and partnership between the voluntary sector and State has in general been mirrored in the youth sector. Barlow and Rober (1996) describe the developing role of the State in western countries as 'steering not rowing', meaning the State is now embracing co-ordination and control functions in the management of public services, rather than necessarily service provision. The rise of 'new public management' (NPM) emerged from a desire to address 'deficits' in public sector management in order to improve efficiencies and cost effectiveness by bringing private sector thinking into public agencies. But the discourse of new managerialism now pervades voluntary sector–State relationships and includes concepts such as, 'value for money', 'targets', 'outcomes', 'strategic planning', 'development plans', 'performance assessment', 'quality assurance', 'coordination', etc. More formal arrangements are desired between the voluntary sector and the State and NPM approaches are strongly proposed in the funding relationship between the two in order to enhance accountability and performance (Boyle and Butler, 2003; National Economic and Social Council, 2005: 23). The discourse and practices of 'managerialism' are strongly evident in the relationship between the youth work sector and the State, as envisaged in the Youth Work Act 2001, and the National Youth Work Development Plan itself is essentially a strategic plan for youth work. Also, under the Act, a key role of the Assessor of Youth Work is to enable State influence in encouraging value for money in youth work funding.

One might ask if the State's interest in managing and controlling youth work extends beyond simply achieving efficient service delivery or value for money. Youth work can reach into the lives of young people and, if controlled by the State, youth work can be aligned to broader Government objectives and can thus provide a useful socialisation and social integration function for the State. A recent evaluation of the impact of youth work in England found that, though its core purpose remains unchanged (i.e. personal and social development), youth work 'is formally recognised as contributing to a widening social policy and social inclusion agenda' (Merton, 2004). In Ireland, attempts to justify the societal value of youth work and appeals for better youth work funding often point to the ways in which youth work can be used in addressing the Government's social inclusion objectives. For example, during its funding campaign, the NYCI argued that 'The Minister continues to ignore the valuable contribution being made by youth workers throughout the country to tackling those issues we prioritise today – educational disadvantage and social exclusion' (National Youth Council of Ireland, 2004). These appeals are strategic since the State's dominant interest in youth work is clearly related to working with 'disadvantaged' youth. The vast amount of State funding available is for projects with a prevention, diversion or re-integration emphasis, and efficient spending is targeted at youth most 'at risk'. Cost effectiveness is invoked to justify youth work funding. If the problem of disadvantaged youth is not addressed now 'it will cost society a lot more in the long run.'[xi] Youth work is sold by the sector itself on the basis of its social control potential in the lives of such troublesome youth.

Alongside this, youth work is attributed with the potential to contribute to other social policy areas, such as promoting active citizenship, participation and the building of social capital (Hall *et al.*, 2000; National Youth Council of Ireland 2004, 2006*a*). These areas feature strongly as policy objectives for both Ireland and the EU, and youth work is increasingly recognised in both arenas with these objectives in mind. While much of the discourse around these areas presents the idea of youth participation as a progressive youth rights issue, the underlying philosophy is conservative. An examination of EU youth policy objectives designed to enhance and promote youth citizenship and participation illustrates this point.[xii] A European comparative study acknowledged that limited youth participation is understood as a 'major youth problem' in most Western European countries as 'declining political engagement and traditional societal participation among youth is perceived as a threat to the future of representative democracy' (Istituto de Ricera, 2001: 17). Fears of declining youth participation are fuelled by the reality that the future of older European citizens will lie in the hands of these young people in a scenario of high age-dependency ratios. As Europe gets older, these young people will be an important source of tax revenue and their adherence to the traditional structures of society becomes even more important, so that they have a strong belief in citizenship and in the concept of the EU and its values. The EU White Paper, *A New Impetus for European Youth*, identifies one of its key messages as enhancing the active citizenship and increasing the participation of young Europeans. The EU is also concerned about aligning youth policy with broader economic objectives, for example, the European Pact for Youth is designed to contribute to achievement of the Lisbon Agenda for economic growth and jobs, requiring that young people 'be fully integrated into society' (European Commission, 2005).

In Ireland, youth work is well understood as being predominantly conservative in character, and funding applications today still refer to youth work's merits as 'keeping kids off the street'.[xiii] The very definition of youth work used in the Act is quite conservative, highlighting the social and personal development of young people, which is *complementary* to formal education. For an increasingly interventionist State with a desire to 'modernise both an economy and other institutions with the potential to influence economic performance' (Share *et al.*, 2007: 98), youth work is ripe for the picking, offering the potential of social control and integration of Irish youth into the status quo. Jeffs and Smith (1988) outlined how the capitalist State can utilise youth work to help it address both accumulation and legitimation functions. As a legitimating activity, the State can use its involvement in youth work to demonstrate society's concern for young people, but at the same time obscure the structural causes of disadvantage. To society, the State's involvement in youth work is evidence that it is dealing with 'the problem of youth'. In terms of accumulation, youth work can 'enhance the productivity of labour' by teaching young people valuable social skills and personal development or by helping to keep them in formal education (Jeffs and Smith, 1988: 37–39). More recently, Skott-Myhre (2005), applying a Marxist analysis to youth work in the American context, suggested that it had lost its radical potential, having been appropriated by capitalist interests. He argued that youth work is being used to 'seduce youth into contact with the "helping professions" and they are then defined, diagnosed and rehabilitated as bourgeois citizens of late stage global capitalism' (2005: 143). Youth workers, he argued, are complicit in the exploitation of youth. Jeffs and Smith (1988: 39) also suggested that the youth work sector can exploit young people by using 'victim' images of young people; these images are mutually advantageous for both the sector and the State, serving to 'justify the existence of youth services, secure their funding and sanction their activities'. Smith (2002) argued that the State agenda in youth work in the UK is to increase control over the power and governance of youth work. He outlined the ways in which Government has aligned youth work with other State objectives through the Connexions Service. He concluded that what remains cannot be called youth work, rather 'a modified form of schooling that also entails a significant amount of case management and some youth work'.

The Position of Young People

Whose interests are served by growing State intervention in youth work? The sections above outline some of the possible interests being met for both sector and State alike. What about the interests of young people? Much of the logic of sector claims for State intervention rests on the argument that, with State backing, a quality youth service can be achieved and that this in turn will enable it to meet the needs of young people. According to this logic, sector and youth needs are neatly packaged into one and the same thing. But this may be too naïve and simplistic a claim given the limited constituency of youth work; the possible decline in the relevance of youth work in meeting youth needs; the prevailing static nature of youth policy; the dominant images of youth and youth work; and the absence of a youth rights agenda in a rapidly changing society.

It is no easy task to determine what the needs of young people are, especially as there is growing recognition that there is no standard biography for youth today and young people do not constitute a homogenous group. But youth work makes claims to its societal relevance on the basis that it is constantly determining and responding to the changing needs of young people (see Sweeney and Dunne, 2003; Lalor and Baird 2006). However, some European and local research indicates low levels of involvement in youth organisations (Eurobarometer, 2007: 20; Lalor and Baird, 2006: 47). The IARD study found that, with the exception of Mediterranean countries in the rest of Western Europe, the percentage of youth who were members of youth organisations and associations was either stable or declining but certainly not increasing. For Ireland, it found 12 per cent of 15–24 year olds were involved in youth associations compared with 44 per cent involvement in sports organisations and 61 per cent involvement in any association. Thus it suggested, 'The importance of voluntary youth work, that used to play an important role in young people's leisure time, has diminished during the last decades' (Istituto de Ricera, 2001: 16). Indicators of low involvement prompt questions around the relevance of youth work to the needs of youth today. Will growing State involvement improve this situation? Some may argue that it will yield better funding and therefore improved services that are more attractive to young people. But in the language of managerialism, young people become 'targets' and responding to needs becomes 'delivering services'. Growing State control over youth work may produce a top-down approach to working with young people, aimed at aligning youth needs with broader social and economic objectives. Will youth work become a formulated service mediated through set packages of funding and project types, simply a collection of 'services for young people'?[xiv] Ultimately, who will have the power to define how the needs of young people will be determined or met?

Despite continuous references to the changes in the lives of young people and the need for youth work to stay relevant (see Department of Education, 2003*a*; Sweeney and Dunne 2006), it is remarkable how static youth work and youth policy remains; this suggests an underlying conservatism in youth work. Much of what is contained in the Youth Work Act can be traced back through 30 years of prior policy proposals. The static nature of youth policy is illustrated by an analysis of policy content, which time and again features points on protecting the voluntary character of youth work, improving funding for youth work, developing structures for youth work and youth service delivery, and developing partnership between voluntary and statutory agencies. The IARD analysis of European youth policy noted static tendencies in the interpretation of youth policy in many national reports; youth policy was interpreted as being identical with the state of youth work. They also noted an absence of any conflict-oriented perspective on youth policy and a lack of analysis about the distribution of power amongst generations, classes or geographical regions. The IARD (Istituto de Ricera, 2001: 111) suggests that one reason for this absence 'may be explained by the lack of conflicts within youth policy where the interests of the State and of youth organisations are so inextricable that there is no room for undisguised conflicts of interests'.

Hurley has critiqued the conservative nature of youth policy, particularly up to the mid 1980s, as being individualistic in focus and for assuming 'the important outcome would be within the young person' (Hurley, 1992*a*: 11). But during the 1980s there was a brief hiatus in this type of 'static' youth policy and a more 'dynamic' socio-political perspective of young people and youth work took hold. O'Ferrall (1983), writing at a time of economic instability and high unemployment in Ireland, suggested youth policy must address the socio-political context of young people's lives and empower young people for social change. But he was sceptical that opportunities for young people to participate in decisions affecting them would be provided, given the paternalism pervading Government youth policy that resulted in keeping young people '... amongst the last important section of society to be essentially disenfranchised' (O' Ferrall, 1983: 108). The State-commissioned Costello Report (Department of Education, 1984) is probably the most notable exception to the 'static' conception of youth policy employed in the Irish context. It argued for a national youth service based firmly within the context of youth needs, and it regarded the social and political education function of youth work as integral to creating a society where young people 'claim it as their right to exert their influence in how society at its various levels is organised and to be themselves part of the action' (Department of Education, 1984: 220).

But the return to static youth policy-making was quick and sharp, continuing right up to the Youth Work Act 2001. One might suggest that earlier provisions to call the Act the 'Youth Service Act' may have been a more apt description, as it makes virtually no reference to young people, their social context or their changing needs. Despite the fact that the 'rights' of both the State and sector are outlined, there is no room given in the Act to assert that all young people have a right to be provided with adequate and equal access to youth services. Youth policy continually prioritises the establishment of a quality youth service without reference to youth needs and rights as a context for such a service, but it also fails to make reference to a rights-based approach to service provision. Hayes (2002) argues, in relation to child policy in Ireland, that it remains welfare based rather than rights based. She suggests that children are treated as the passive recipients of protection by the State. A similar analysis could be applied to youth in Ireland, as their treatment in both sector and State policy suggests they are regarded as mere consumers of services rather than as agents in pursuit of rights. This image of young people mirrors that of broader social and cultural views, and stems from the discourse of youth as a transition stage (as discussed earlier in Chapter 2). Wyn and White (1997: 115) argue that transition views of youth as 'the future', 'citizens in waiting' or as 'adults of tomorrow' '... tend(s) to trivialise the issue of young people's rights and their full participation in society. Young people are also citizens, not just in the future, but in the present.' Even seemingly progressive attempts to increase youth participation in decision-making can sometimes harbour notions of 'participation as a principle' alongside 'participation as an end objective' (Walther *et al.*, 2002: 36). As Kiely has written in Chapter 1, projects such as Dáil na nÓg can be criticised for the lack of any real say they offer young people in influencing public policy in relation to youth rights. Rather they offer opportunities for young people to practise participation for their future roles as adults.

There are a few exceptions to static trends, for example, the National Youth Work Development Plan does provide an analysis of youth in a changing society, as well as consideration of some of the challenges youth work faces into the future. The NYCI, as social partner, has previously stated that, 'The needs, rights and expectations of young people must be recognised in the new Social Partnership agreement' (National Youth Council of Ireland, 2006*c*). However, in later press releases it was clear that the NYCI saw its 'win' in social partnership negotiations as securing 'additional resources for the sector, which was guaranteed in the agreement by a commitment to implementing the National Youth Work Development Plan and the Youth Work Act 2001' (National Youth Council of Ireland, 2006*d*). It is questionable as to whether it is appropriate or desirable for one organisation to maintain a dual mandate to represent both the needs of the institution of youth work as well as represent the needs and rights of youth as a social group. The sector and State are both complicit in positioning young people as passive consumers of youth services but, as an interest group for youth rights, the sector presents very little challenge to the State.

Growing State Intervention in Youth Work: Can it Work?

Hurley (1992*b*), anticipating growing State involvement in youth work, forewarned the sector with the question 'Can it work?' More recently, referring to the introduction of youth work legislation in Ireland, Smith (2007) warned the Irish youth work sector to proceed with caution, outlining a salutary tale of youth work and State intervention in the UK. But such warnings seem to be disregarded by the youth work sector, as the position taken by key youth organisations is to proceed with engaging in social partnership arrangements and in State–sector structures at both national and local level. But youth work is dependent on the State for status, recognition and security of funding, and if we are to believe the warnings from the sector, its future lies in the hands of the State (National Youth Council of Ireland, 2003*b*). This puts the State in a very powerful position in the relationship and challenges the idea of the 'partnership' relationship being an equal one. In exchange for giving a legal and statutory commitment to youth work, the State has clearly taken control of the management of Irish youth work, as evidenced by the tenor of the Youth Work Act 2001. Because of a commitment to 'management by partnership', the sector possibly believes it will be able to stem the worst excesses of State involvement. Yet the power of the State is felt each December as youth work organisations wait with bated breath to see what the Budget will mean for youth work in the year ahead.

Given its dependency on the State, it is difficult to believe that increasing State control will not present some difficult challenges for youth work and the youth work sector. Is the youth work sector prepared to meet the challenges of such a close relationship with the State? In the proposed new local structures for youth work, the formulation of three-year development plans for youth work in each VEC area suggests that youth services are to be co-ordinated with the work of other agencies; this could pose serious challenges for the sector's autonomy and self-determination. Smith (2002) argues that State control and attempts to formalise youth work can damage the very essence of youth work. This is evidenced by the adoption of more coercive forms of participation as well as shifts from association to individualised activity, from education to case management and from informal to bureaucratic relationships. State intervention presents a challenge to universal provision by underfunding mainline work and emphasising targeted provision. What kind of youth work will emerge from formalised arrangements between sector and State or from State-managed contracts for service delivery? For those involved in youth work because of its social change potential, Hurley (1992*b*) questioned how realistic it would be to expect that increasing State intervention would not have a prohibitive effect on such youth work practice. Jeffs and Banks (1999: 100) have argued that the greatest danger of indoctrination in youth work now emanates from the State in its determination to narrow the youth work agenda and to 'restrict the educational experience to what it deems useful, worthwhile and safe'.

Fianna Fáil TD Pat Carey questioned whether developments in youth work have really improved young people's lives:

> With all the developments in youth work that have occurred since 1984, has youth work had an impact on the problems facing young people? It has had an impact on the problems facing many individuals, but as a system it has had little impact in addressing the inequalities in society that create the problems faced by young people in marginalised communities, in cities and rural areas. Despite the individual models of good practice and the commitment of many innovative and creative youth workers throughout the youth organisations, the influence on national policy and on the institutions of the State that impact on the lives of young people has been very limited. (Dáil Éireann, 2000)

There is very little evidence to suggest that the position of young people as a social group has been improved or is likely to be improved by growing State intervention or by evolving partnership relationships between key youth organisations and the State. The relationship seems to be built more on serving the needs of each other, with the result that the needs and issues of young people are not centre stage. So, for those with a concern for the position of young people in Irish society, the answer may be that it cannot work. Hurley (1992: 10, 12) pointed to the conflict of interest that exists for State-controlled youth work '...to the extent that the youth service is viewed as part of the "State machinery", the youth service can be interpreted as representing the interests of society as a whole.' In such circumstances how realistic is youth policy as a liberating tool for youth?

The relationship between the youth work sector and the State has changed considerably over the years. Prior to the 1960s, only a tenuous link existed between the voluntary-based provision of youth work and the State. What exists now is a relationship between the two, which could be characterised in a number of ways as a statutory–voluntary relationship; a purchaser–provider relationship; a dependent or interdependent relationship; or a partnership. Whichever description serves best, it is clear that the relationship is much more formalised and structured now than ever before. The Youth Work Act 2001 is the most important vehicle for defining and understanding what the formal structures underpinning the relationship will look like into the future, but the implications for youth work practice are as yet unknown. Various provisions of the Act will cement State involvement into the very heart of youth work. The Act then represents an inescapable acceptance of growing State involvement in Irish youth work into the future. An assessment of whether this is a good or a bad thing will depend on the answer to the question of whose interests might be best served by this - the State, the youth work sector or young people?

Notes

i There are over 50 youth organisations, 40,000 volunteers, and approximately 800 paid staff, serving 750,000 young people (National Youth Council of Ireland, 2006*c*). See Hurley (2003) for a short description of the youth work sector.

ii It is accepted that they may also differ in terms of their relationships with the State, but for the purposes of this chapter the sector is discussed as a whole, based on the view that it is represented as a whole by the NYCI in social partnership and by the National Youth Work Advisory Committee.

iii The role of the Minister of State for Children has been expanded with the portfolio now to include Youth Affairs.

iv DES funding for youth work rose from €26.066 million in 2002 to €45.037 million in 2006 (NYCI, 2006*a*).

v These initiatives include the Department of Justice, Equality and Law Reform (DJELR) for Garda Youth Diversion Projects; the Department Health and Children for Dáil na nÓg; the Department of Community, Rural and Gaeltacht Affairs for the Young People's Services and Facilities Fund; the Department of Foreign Affairs and Irish Aid for Development Education Initiatives; the Health Service Executive for Neighbourhood Youth Projects and Community Based Drugs Initiatives; the Local Development Social Inclusion Programme (LDSIP) for local youth programmes.

vi Compare the €1.6 million available in the Local Youth Club Grant Scheme to the €9.8 million available for Garda Youth Diversion projects in 2007.

vii This refers to the predetermined budget lines that exist for certain types of service or project.

viii The NYCI mounted a high-profile funding campaign (For Now, For the Future – Invest in Youth Work Campaign) shortly after the launch of the NYWDP. The campaign has involved pre-budget submissions and launches, press releases giving dire warnings of the 'end of the youth sector' and showcase events to highlight the value of youth work (see National Youth Council of Ireland press releases for 2004, 2005, 2006). The campaign is ongoing.

ix For example, in the area of combating educational disadvantage, initiatives set up by youth projects in the early 1990s have been adapted by the mainstream education sector today. Many breakfast and homework clubs are now running under the DEIS scheme (Delivering Equality of Opportunity in Schools includes a range of actions aimed at combating disadvantage) of the Department of Education and integrated into mainstream schooling. This idea was introduced via Special Youth Projects in the early 1990s and some teaching staff members are involved in early school leaving initiatives using a youth work approach. Some youth work staff have been attracted into work as Education Welfare Officers with the Department of Education and Science or Access Officers with third-level institutes.

x This study contracted by the European Commission and carried out by Istituto de Ricera in Milan (IARD) compared national reports on youth work and youth policy from 18 European countries including Ireland.

xi Such references are made by both youth work organisations and politicians when arguing for improved youth work funding (see, for example, NYCI, 2003*b* and contributions made during the Dáil Debate on the proposed Youth Work Act).

xii See Council of Europe 1999; European Commission 2001, 2005, 2006; Barrington-Leach *et al.*, 2007.

xiii In my capacity as a volunteer member with a charitable trust, I read many such references in funding applications.

xiv The recent relocation of Youth Affairs from the Department of Education and Science to the Department of Health and Children certainly provokes concern that the State may increasingly regard youth work as simply service provision to youth alongside child services.

6

The Politics of Community Development: Relationship with the State

Catherine Forde

Introduction

This chapter analyses the relationship between community development and the Irish State and critically interrogates the reasons for and implications of growing State intervention in community development activity. It begins by exploring the manner in which, after independence, the State sought to build and maintain a unitary and nationalist culture and society based on conservative values, strong central government, extensive clientelism and the ascendancy of elites. It is maintained that these characteristics caused the diminishment of civil society and the concomitant discouragement of an autonomous public sphere. The chapter proceeds to argue that the adoption and entrenchment of a neocorporatist or 'social partnership' approach to national and local decision-making since the 1980s has both ensured the ongoing subordination of civil society and allowed the increasingly globalised and neoliberal State to exert unprecedented control over an array of civil society groups, including those involved in community development activities. It explores the impact of neocorporatist arrangements on Irish democracy and the rhetoric that the current Government uses to justify the maintenance of these arrangements. The concluding section of the chapter draws on empirical research by the author to assess the prospects for the vitalisation of Irish civil society.

State–Civil Society Relations in Ireland 1922–1970

In his analysis of twentieth-century Irish culture, Joe Cleary (2007) argues that the Irish struggle for independence differed significantly from revolutions in other European states. While countries such as France and Russia had undergone violent upheavals between aristocracy and peasantry, Ireland's long-standing history of colonisation ensured that it had bypassed such cataclysmic events. Thus, despite the progressive ideas that inspired the 1916 Rising, those who succeeded to power faced a more tranquil future:

> There could be no extended clash between modernism and the aristocratic … since there was so little of the latter to begin with. The attainment of nationalist independence in what is now the Republic brought to power a lower middle class without any such heritage to defend or attack. (Cleary, 2007: 93)

Given these peculiarities, it is perhaps unsurprising that some of the key distinguishing characteristics of Irish society after independence were conservatism, authoritarianism and the predominance of elites. Early governments opted for policies that preserved the privilege enjoyed by the middle class and failed in large part to address the needs of vulnerable groups (Ferriter, 2005; Keogh, 2005). Poverty was endemic in both urban and rural areas and people emigrated in huge numbers to Britain or the United States. Despite the significant role that women played in the War of Independence, the early Irish Republic was a chauvinistic one and successive governments introduced a plethora of legislation that discriminated against women in a range of areas. The 'gendered State' (Ferriter, 2005: 327), which was heavily influenced by Catholic Church teaching, persisted until the early 1970s when a confluence of events forced its dismantlement. Meanwhile economic protectionism, which sought to preserve the interests of indigenous business people and shield native industry from foreign competition (Crotty, 1986), was similarly enduring and remained in place until the 1950s.

The sociologist J.P. O'Carroll (2002) argues that the primary concern of the nascent Irish State was to ensure cohesion and solidarity, which it did by emphasising 'the nation' and the existence of a single common, nationalist, Gaelic[i] and Catholic culture that encompassed and defined every member of society. In order to build and maintain a culture based on these characteristics, the State recognised and drew on the primacy of 'community' as a unifying principle and 'obvious rhetorical device' (O'Carroll, 2002: 14). Using this device, commonalities rather than differences were posited, making the establishment and maintenance of legitimacy a relatively straightforward task for the State. The political model was a simple one, based on clientelistic or face-to-face relations between representatives and their constituents. Fianna Fáil, which was the ruling party for most of the period between 1932 and 1973, espoused a 'catch-all' form of politics that favoured State control, curtailed deliberation and debate in the legislature, discouraged agitation on the basis of class, and resisted the devolution of power to the regional and local levels (Daly, 1999; Ferriter, 2005). Post-independence local government resembled a system of local administration rather than local democracy and became increasingly centralised and bureaucratised throughout the twentieth century (Forde, 2005).

There was a significant degree of civil society activity in the years after independence, although civil society groups experienced a number of challenges and constraints, some of which were internal while others emanated from relations with the State and still others from wider societal problems. To illustrate, three elements of civil society activity are briefly discussed here. First, despite a drastic drop in trade union membership in the 1920s, there was an active labour movement in post-independence Ireland. A number of small but radical groups formed to push for the rights of specific groups of workers. These groups included the Irish Unemployed Workers Movement (IUWM), which in the 1930s organised protests against unemployment and the living conditions of urban slum dwellers (Powell and Geoghegan, 2004), the Federation of Rural Workers and the Irish Women's Workers Union, both of which were active in the 1950s. Notwithstanding oppositional activities such as these, after 1922 the larger trade unions tended to eschew the militancy of the 1913 'Lock Out'[ii] and embraced accommodation with first the pro-Treaty and then the Fianna Fáil Governments (Allen, 2000; Garvin, 2005). An example of this was the support given by the large Irish Transport and General Workers' Union (ITGWU) to the Trade Union Act 1941, which sought to regulate trade union activity. Ferriter (2005: 413) argues that, in supporting the Act, the ITGWU 'sought refuge and excuses in the political consensus which surrounded neutrality'. It could be argued that this willingness to submit to consensus and compromise presaged trade union entry into social partnership from the late 1980s.

The second strand of civil society is the prominent ruralist and Catholic movement Muintir na Tíre, which was established in 1931. Muintir na Tíre sought to revitalise rural communities after the Civil

War (Curtin and Varley, 1995; Varley and Curtin, 2002) through promoting self-help and the modernisation of farming methods (Ferriter, 2005). These were worthy aims given the poverty of rural Ireland, but it is nonetheless true that Muintir's vision was a conservative and integrationist one (Curtin and Varley, 1995), concerned with avoiding class conflict through the establishment of voluntary groups based on vocationalist principles. The idealism of Muintir's vision is evident in its failure to achieve a network of parish councils throughout rural Ireland. Factors that militated against this initiative included the over-riding poverty of these areas between the 1920s and the 1950s (Ferriter, 2005) and opposition from rival groups. In the 1970s Muintir's attempt to replace parish councils with community councils met with limited success (Forde, 1996; Powell and Geoghegan, 2004) due to urbanisation, a growing focus on interest-based community work and unwillingness on the part of the State to provide significant funding for community development activities that it did not initiate or control. The movement retained its conservatism throughout the latter half of the twentieth century and today advocates 'voluntary-State partnership-type relationships as the *sine qua non* of effective community development' (Varley and Curtin, 2002: 26–27).

Women's collective action is the third feature of civil society after independence. From the mid-twentieth century the 'confinement of women to a limited sphere' (Ferriter, 2005: 361) was challenged by the emergence of a number of women's organisations, including the Irish Countrywomen's Association (ICA) and the Irish Housewives' Association. These organisations disputed traditional and gendered perceptions of women and in doing so were the precursors of the Irish Women's Movement (IWM) of the 1960s and 1970s (Connolly, 2002). Despite its role in ensuring that oppressive legislation such as the marriage bar was overturned, the broad-based IWM had a relatively short existence and eventually splintered into a number of single-issue groups (Mahon, 1995). Connolly (2006) points out that, from the 1980s, the women's movement in Ireland began to professionalise and focus on working within the State rather than against it. This strategy has provoked mixed views amongst feminists, some of whom favour this development while others are concerned about 'the coopting of activists by political parties and established institutions, and the demobilising effect of professionalizing movement organisations' (Connolly, 2006: 74).

What has been the legacy of the first half century of Irish independence? This legacy includes a 'monolithic system of government' (O'Carroll, 2002: 15), emasculated local government and an emphasis on consensus. Most significantly, this period ensured the diminishment of the significance and independence of community organisations, which were 'thin on the ground, weakly organised and overshadowed by a political culture dominated by parties, clientelist practices and national sectionally organised interest groups' (Curtin and Varley, 1995: 382). A public sphere (or spheres) autonomous from the workings of State and economy (Habermas, 1992) did not emerge because the deliberation and contestation that are integral to the realisation of such a sphere were discouraged in the pursuit of consensus and unanimity. Thus, long before the economic imperatives of the Celtic Tiger curtailed the development of the public sphere, the demands of nation-building ensured its suppression.

The next section provides an overview of the genesis and development of the corporatist approach that currently dominates socio-economic policy-making in Ireland, and explores the rationale for this approach.

Socio-Economic Development since the 1970s: the Rise of Corporatism

From the late 1950s seismic changes occurred in Irish society. Garvin (2005: 67) points out that 'it took the economic and social crisis of the mid-1950s to force through a fundamental rethinking of Irish economic policies.' Protectionism was dismantled and trade with other countries encouraged. A welfare State gradually developed, albeit at a much slower pace and in a more piecemeal fashion than its British counterpart. Entry to the European Economic Community (EEC) in 1972 and the advent of social movements such as the IWM accelerated the generation of essential social legislation.

By the mid 1980s, the Irish economy fell into recession, and problems of unemployment and poverty stretched the ability of the State to cope with welfare demands. This contributed to the development of what Conroy (1999: 45) calls the 'welfare society', in which responsibility for social provision is shared by the State and a number of other groups, including the family and voluntary and community organisations:

> A welfare society is one where people recognise responsibilities towards each other in the first instance. The role of the State is to provide an enabling environment for groups and individuals to provide services for and between themselves, to facilitate local employment, local services and local participation.

The Irish welfare society is essentially a mixed economy of welfare. This model may be described as a mix of neoliberalism and collectivism or, as Ó Riain and O'Connell (2000) describe it, an amalgam of both developmental and distributive roles, where the developmental role refers to the State's encouragement and facilitation of economic activity, and the distributive role concerns the development of a welfare system that relies to a significant degree on voluntary and community groups to deliver a range of social services. A central facet of the Irish State's developmental role has been the fostering since the 1960s of a heavily globalised economy based on foreign direct investment (FDI) (Ó Riain and O'Connell, 2000). The distributive arm of the State has been described as an example of 'Third Way' economics, or a merging of State or public responsibility with individual responsibility (see also Chapter 4).

The publication in 2000 of the White Paper *Supporting Voluntary Activity* is an example of the Irish State's use of the Third Way philosophy. The White Paper applauds the considerable contribution that voluntary, charitable and community groups have made to Irish society and to the economy of this country since the foundation of the State, and pledges ongoing State support, both financial and otherwise, to those groups that engage in work aimed at countering poverty and social exclusion. At the same time, the White Paper seeks greater accountability from these groups for the funding that they receive, introduces service agreements between the State and voluntary service providers, and posits an unprecedented role for the State in coordinating and integrating the work of statutory and voluntary service providers:

> The solution involves the State acting as an agent in facilitating the various approaches taken at local level and ensuring that the overall effort of all players is integrated and that experience and lessons learned inform the policy development process. (Department of Social, Community and Family Affairs, 2000*a*: 7)

Critics of the 'Third Way' philosophy point out that it includes a movement away from a universalist social policy that directs benefits to all members of society towards more targeted policies that are aimed at particular groups (Conroy, 1999; Esping-Andersen, 2002). Furthermore, under this approach, voluntary and community organisations are used to provide services that would otherwise be the preserve of the State. This saves the State both financial and other resources, while providing it with the opportunity to extol the benefits of voluntarism for individuals and society. Perhaps the most significant disadvantage concerns the level of influence that the State has gained over civil society groups through regulatory mechanisms such as those included in *Supporting Voluntary Activity*. These disadvantages are discussed in more detail later in this chapter (see also the discussion of the White Paper in Chapter 9).

The welfare society represents just one facet of the Irish State's growing interest in and engagement with voluntary and community activity over the last twenty years (Forde, 2006). Another reason for this interest has been the influence of European Union initiatives such as the first, second and third Anti-Poverty Programmes and the rural LEADER Programme, all of which had a presence in Ireland. Harvey (1994) points out that these initiatives took the concept of co-operation between the State and local groups far beyond anything that either party had previously experienced. Perhaps the most important catalyst for growing State involvement in community development is the corporatist or 'social partnership' approach that has characterised Irish economic policy since 1987, when the first national agreement, the *Programme for National Recovery* (PNR), was instituted between the Government, trade unions and employers. In the eleven years since 1997 the Irish institutional landscape has been dominated by neocorporatist arrangements, whereby a broad range of civil society groups and organisations, known collectively as the Community and Voluntary Pillar (CVP),[iii] has been included in negotiations leading to national agreements, of which there have been seven to date.[iv] Like the traditional social partners (trade unions and employers' organisations) before them, these groups have become incorporated into the apparatus of what has become the 'dispersed' (Shaw, 2008) or 'interactive' (O'Donovan, 2000) State (see also Michel Foucault on governmentality, 1979; 1991).

Neocorporatism has been extended to the local level where there are a range of State-led targeted initiatives aimed at generating socio-economic development in urban and rural areas which have experienced high levels of unemployment, poverty and social exclusion. Of the local neocorporatist initiatives, one of the most significant and extensive has been the development of area-based partnership companies and community groups. In 1991, under the prevailing national agreement the *Programme for Economic and Social Progress* (PESP), twelve local partnership companies were established on a pilot basis in areas of high unemployment throughout Ireland. The initiative aimed to develop an 'integrated approach designed to implement a community response in particular local areas to long-term unemployment and the danger of long-term unemployment' (Department of the Taoiseach, 1991: 75). Under the Local Development Programme 1995–1999, the number of partnership companies was increased to 38 and a further 33 local development organisations (commonly known as community groups) were established in areas that are not designated as disadvantaged. These formal structures consist of representatives of the statutory, social partner and voluntary and community sectors. Most partnerships and community groups draw on a community development approach in implementing their activities and employ community workers whose job it is to engage in animation activities with a diversity of groups. The employment opportunities that these organisations provide have contributed to the professionalisation of community work (see discussion of professionalisation in Chapter 7) and growing numbers of community workers undertake training courses in third-level colleges and universities (Ó hAodain and Forde, 2007).

The White Paper *Better Local Government* (Department of the Environment and Local Government, 1996) announced that the local government system would be integrated with the local development system[v] and introduced a number of neocorporatist structures to Irish local government. Strategic policy committees (SPCs) are supposed to offer an enhanced policy-making role for city and county councillors and provide for the inclusion of civil society groups in decision-making. County and city development boards (CDBs) are charged with drawing up and overseeing integrated strategies for economic, social and cultural development within each city or county and overseeing the implementation of these strategies over a ten-year period. They draw their membership from local authorities, the local development sector (including partnership companies), the statutory sector and the social partners.

The Local Development Social Inclusion Programme (LDSIP) under the National Development Plans (NDP) 2000–2006 and 2007–2013 has provided for the maintenance and consolidation of a range of local urban and rural neocorporatist arrangements. Merging of partnership companies with LEADER companies will halve the number of these organisations from 106 to 55 (Pobal, 2007) but these structures will retain their nationwide coverage.

In the last twenty years Irish public policy has been transformed as the complex and multifaceted corporatist infrastructure has taken hold and become embedded at national and local level. The following section argues that, contrary to official rhetoric, the introduction of corporatism with its emphasis on harmony and consensus has served to maintain and entrench the pattern of State–civil society relations that was established in the early years of the Irish Republic.

Corporatism: the Formalisation of State–Civil Society Relations

According to O'Carroll (2002: 15), the adoption of corporatism over the last twenty years represents the continuity of the old 'nationalist and communal motifs' rather than a movement away from their influence. Like these old values, the leitmotifs of corporatism are inclusivity, unity and consensus and, as before, corporatism renders community groups secondary to the needs of the monolithic State.

> Co-option incorporates and controls in ways that are not always apparent ... Negotiations take place in an arena and around an agenda arranged by the State ... Furthermore, through its emphasis on consensus, it deprives society of the benefits to be derived from the airing of communal differences in the public sphere. (O'Carroll, 2002: 16)

Like O'Carroll, Fraser (1992: 88) decries the 'hiving off' of certain topics for discussion 'in specialized discursive arenas' because this tends to benefit dominant groups and weaken less powerful ones. The arenas to which Fraser refers are redolent of 'invited spaces' (Gaventa, 2004; see also Chapter 3) for participation, which may be generated by elites for the inclusion of citizens or service users in decision-making on matters affecting them, but which privilege the needs and concerns of the powerful rather than those of subordinate groups.

Following O'Carroll, Peadar Kirby (2002: 179) identifies continuity in the State's adoption of corporatist arrangements and argues that social partnership represents continuity with the past because it embodies a 'long-standing populist reflex in Irish political culture'. Kirby suggests that this reflex has three main dimensions. First, the resources of the State are used for the 'short-term satisfaction of different constituencies' (Kirby, 2002: 179). Thus, successive budgets offer sops to different segments of the population, without necessarily addressing the core problems that these groups face.[vi] Furthermore, policies such as the National Anti-Poverty Strategy provide a targeted rather than a universal response to the problems of poverty and social exclusion (Coakley, 2004). Such targeted responses may alleviate poverty but are unlikely to eliminate it.

Second, State policies are oriented towards short-term, practical responses rather than longer-term, considered ones. Carmel Duggan

(1999) argues that, while 'spatially focused' policies such as area-based partnerships and community groups can contribute to improving people's quality of life and employment prospects, they cannot make a significant impact on the risk or incidence of societal poverty. This can only be achieved through relevant and effective national policies that tackle the distribution of wealth. Duggan is concerned that initiatives such as local social partnerships may find themselves assuming 'an ideological role in relation to the political management of social exclusion rather than a practical role in its eradication' (Duggan, 1999: 74). Duggan's point is echoed by Meade (2005) who argues that a significant aspect of the State's agenda in establishing local social partnership structures is its desire to quell unease at the inadequacy of State interest in and provision for disadvantaged localities. In essence, partnerships and community groups provide the State and its ancillary bodies with 'good publicity' which they scarcely deserve.

The third dimension of the State's populist reflex concerns the manner in which civil society organisations are co-opted in a manner that renders them dependent on the State. Co-optation 'tends to incorporate civil society organisations in a vertical way, weakening their autonomy and reducing their understanding of politics to a struggle to gain benefits from the State' (Kirby, 2002: 176). Neocorporatism or social partnership thus interferes with the scope of civil society, in the form of voluntary and community organisations, to act autonomously and to engage in the type of deliberative or 'discursive contestation' (Fraser, 1992) that is the lifeblood of an autonomous public sphere (see Chapter 9 for a detailed discussion of deliberative democracy). Their absorption into the institutions of social partnership serves to preoccupy them with this hierarchical process, thus reducing their opportunities to form 'horizontal links out of which collective interests could be formulated and promoted' (Kirby, 2002: 176). Their increasing dependence on the State for financial resources, some of which are channelled through the partnership process, further weakens their capacity to challenge it on issues that concern them.

As well as continuity, it is argued here that corporatism represents a new departure because it seeks the *formalisation* and *institutionalisation* of relations between the State and civil society, a formalisation that was never previously in evidence and the outcomes of which could not have been anticipated by participating civil society organisations or by others. Neocorporatist structures such as partnership companies and community groups are essentially forms of 'manufactured civil society', a term used by Lesley Hodgson (2004: 158) to describe groups that are formed as the result of State initiative and that receive initial or ongoing funding from the State:

> The term manufactured is used because these groups have not developed organically, but have been engineered, created or manufactured by the State. Couched in terms of 'developing', 'strengthening', 'nurturing', 'creating', 'recreating' or 'renewing', the State can be said to be constructing a particular type of civil society built upon a government agenda.

Unlike organic forms of civil society, 'manufactured' forms enjoy very little autonomy and are almost completely reliant on the requirements of their funders. Organic forms have a clear focus which is 'driven by need and values' (Hodgson, 2004: 158) and a strong sense of identity from their inception, whereas the focus of manufactured civil society is determined by the State and therefore does not possess a clear sense of identity. Furthermore, manufactured civil society is an 'invited' participatory space in that membership is by invitation and is not open to everyone, in contrast to the 'claimed' spaces that arise from the grassroots of communities and localities in response to expressed needs, deficiencies and issues.

This formalisation of State–civil society relations and the restrictions it imposes is illustrated in the work of Mary Murphy, who gained 'inside' experience of partnership negotiations in her role as National Policy Officer for the St Vincent de Paul Society, one of the community and voluntary organisations that participated in negotiations for successive national agreements. Murphy (2002: 85) criticises the formality of social partnership negotiations and their reliance on consensus as the modus operandi, and argues that an insistence on consensus can mask or deflect ideological differences or conflicts between participants:

> Consensus and problem-solving models work by setting aside ideological differences to allow shared understandings to develop. They avoid visioning about the future in order to be pragmatic about the present.... This not only denies the possibility of ideological discussion but also limits creative approaches to problem solving around inequality issues.

Murphy adds that attempts by voluntary and community sector groups to engage in informal discussions with organisations from other sectors were rebuffed, and some representatives were reprimanded for their attempts. These experiences are evidence of what Iris Marion Young (2000: 55) refers to as 'internal exclusion' whereby the claims of those who participate in 'invited' spaces are given little credence and accorded little respect by more powerful groups. Echoing Murphy's concerns, the National Economic and Social Forum (NESF) (1997), which is a neocorporatist body[vii] in its own right, refers to 'the limits of consensus' and suggests that an emphasis on consensus in negotiations gives rise to a number of problems. These include a tendency to exaggerate the existence of agreement when in fact parties to the negotiations may differ considerably 'on the nature and direction of the whole social and economic system' (National Economic and Social Forum, 1997: 18). Such differences are inevitable in a society that is fundamentally unequal. Other problems concern the possibility that the emphasis on consensus may curtail innovation and difference by emphasising the need for uniformity, and may produce 'bland agreements, which are little more than the lowest common denominator of what various partners will agree' (National Economic and Social Forum, 1997: 19). Such 'systematically distorted compromises' (Dryzek, 1990: 17) are anathema to a Habermasian (1989) conception of consensus as a deliberative process that is not tied to system imperatives (see Chapter 9 for a fuller discussion of Dryzek's ideas).

Proponents of social partnership including O'Donnell and Thomas (1998: 136–137) argue that corporatist institutions confound the unequal distribution of power within society by creating an opportunity for 'less empowered organisations to exert an "unexpected" influence within the political domain'. This perspective is challenged by a number of writers, including Hardiman (1998), who points out that, in negotiations for partnership arrangements at national level, the interests of the traditional social partners – the employers and trade unions – have been accorded precedence over those of the voluntary and community sector that represents marginalised and disadvantaged groups. She highlights that representatives from the voluntary and community sector were excluded from the process of priority-setting for the *Partnership 2000* (Department of the Taoiseach, 1996*a*) national agreement, and that issues such as social inclusion and equity, with which they were particularly concerned, were given residual status in the negotiations and, consequently, residual funding. In contrast, issues such as pay and taxation, with which employers and unions were most concerned, were accorded top priority. In an opinion piece in the *Irish Times* in 2007 former Taoiseach Garret FitzGerald, who is an advocate of social partnership, argues that, despite the inclusion of voluntary and community groups in partnership negotiations, improvements in social services have not followed. He points out that many of 'the problems of inequality and poverty that still afflict our society reflect persistent failures to target social needs that can be eliminated only by major, well-directed reforms in the provision of services for the young, the old and the ill and disabled' (FitzGerald 2007: 14).[viii] The persistence of these problems suggests that the impact of civil society groups on the corporatist process has not been as significant as they may have wished.

Neocorporatist arrangements have not only ensured the ongoing suppression of civil society but have enabled the State to gain an inordinate measure of control over the groups that make up civil society. The next section explores the rhetoric that governments have used to justify this control.

Civil Society as 'Tool' or 'Solution'

Hodgson (2004: 141) observes that contemporary civil society is being constructed as 'a set of institutions that perform the functions of inculcating morals and values that facilitate social cohesion'. A range of authors, including Robert Putnam (2000) and John Keane (1998), have advocated that states use civil society as 'civic virtue' (Hodgson, 2004: 141) in order to encourage the re-engagement of citizens with the political sphere and to foster a civic culture. Hodgson points out that Tony Blair's New Labour Government followed this advice by generating a discourse centred on the concept of 'partnership' between the State and civil society for the voluntary delivery of a range of welfare services. In this way, civil society has become a tool or 'solution' (Fremeaux, 2005) for the provision of welfare and for the improvement of the community's 'performance', utility and efficacy. Essentially, State discourse provokes 'induced self-help' (Shaw, 2003*b*: 362), as civil society is inveigled to take responsibility for issues and problems that were previously the remit of the State. This one-sided discourse fails to acknowledge the impact of such an arrangement on civil society groups or the communities from which they arise.

Hodgson's work has considerable resonance in an Irish context. Like New Labour, the current Irish Government, which is now in its third successive term of office, adopts a rhetoric that glorifies civil society and the opportunities that social partnership offers to civil society organisations. An excerpt from a 2005 speech by the former Taoiseach Bertie Ahern to The Wheel, an umbrella body for voluntary organisations, illustrates the moralistic manner in which these ideas are conveyed:

> I believe that the quality of life in society, and the ultimate health of our communities, depends on the willingness of people to become involved and active. Active on behalf of themselves and their families, their communities and the more vulnerable members of society. Happy the society that has people to act, rather than lament; who organise rather than complain; who accept a personal responsibility rather than walk by on the other side.

In a later speech in Dublin, Bertie Ahern argued that 'Ireland now needs to develop a strong and corresponding sense of duty and community' (cited in *Irish Times*, 2006*a*: 1), and went on to suggest that 'Patriots today are people who are at least as fully aware of the needs of their community as they are of their own individual rights.' These exhortations recall Frances Cleaver's (2001: 48) discussion of how policy makers simplify the concept of 'community' and 'link participation with social responsibility' in order to encourage citizens to participate in institutions which they had no part in conceiving or building (see also Chapter 4).

In his 2005 speech to The Wheel the Taoiseach extolled the virtues of social partnership between the State and the voluntary and community sector:

> The important role of the non-profit sector in our economy and society has been reflected in the development of relations between the Government, the public authorities in general and the community and voluntary sector. Nowhere is that better reflected than in the evolution of social partnership to include the sector as a full partner over recent years. I recognise that this has placed considerable demands on those who represent the sector in the various institutional arrangements which we have created together. I know that, in return, this participation gives your representatives access to dialogue not only with the Government and public officials, but also with the other social partners, who play such a critical role in Irish life.

While the speech made reference in general terms to the demands which participation in social partnership places on civil society organisations, unsurprisingly it failed to acknowledge the specific problems that civil society organisations experience or the limitations of dialogue with State officials and the other social partners. In averring that the State and civil society were jointly responsible for the establishment of social partnership, Ahern masked the fact that social partnership is a top-down, manufactured construction that was imposed on civil society rather than created by it. In short, it failed to acknowledge the fine line between 'nurturing' and 'stifling' (Hodgson, 2004: 144) civil society.

In an opinion piece in the *Irish Times*, Michael D. Higgins, a Labour party TD, contends that Bertie Ahern's call for an increase in voluntarism is simplistic in the market-driven and consumerist context of contemporary Ireland where the gap between rich and poor is growing wider and the alienation of the poorest threatens 'a naked confrontation between the excluded and the powerful, between the technologically sophisticated and the technologically manipulated, and consumers and the consumed' (2006: 15).

An interesting addendum concerns the publication of a report by the NESF on the subject of social capital and its relevance to Ireland. The report (National Economic and Social Forum 2003: 71) warns that an overly prescriptive and top-down approach to development and change can be counterproductive:

> Too much control, social engineering or provision of external incentives could negate the very principle of an active civil society which is based on voluntary effort and support motivated by a collective desire and endeavour for the common good.

Ironically and paradoxically, the report endorses the partnership approach and suggests that partnership bodies have a role to play in strengthening social capital and encouraging active citizenship in Ireland.

The neocorporatist arrangements that populate Irish public policy represent a form of 'manufactured civil society' that has been imposed on existing forms of civil society and justified using a laudatory idiom that masks the problems that it causes. The effect of this imposition on democracy in Ireland is the subject of the following section.

Corporatism and Democracy in Ireland

Proponents of corporatist arrangements argue that they have improved the quality of Irish democracy. Patricia O'Hara (2002) argues that these arrangements have made a positive qualitative impact on policy and practice in the following ways: the range of interests involved in policy-making is greater than ever before; the diversity of interests facilitates a multifaceted approach to policy-making and the inclusion of social and cultural objectives as well as economic ones; combating exclusion has become a policy objective; and policy planning has become a much more strategic process. O'Donnell and Thomas (1998: 137) go even further by arguing that national and local social partnership initiatives 'represent innovative attempts to reconfigure the relationships between representative and participative democracy which are fostering new forums of deliberative democracy'.

In contrast to the views of these writers, Ó Cinnéide (1998) maintains that democracy in Ireland is experiencing serious difficulties and that what he calls 'creeping corporatism' is one of the main causes of these problems. In the first instance, he points out that the executive branches of Government have become increasingly powerful at the expense of the two deliberative branches, the Dáil and the Seanad. In particular, Ó Cinnéide suggests that the rise of corporatist social arrangements have led to the concomitant decline of parliament as a decision-making body. He argues that national agreements represent 'a major shift in power from elected representatives to full-time officials in the civil service and in the organisations of the major interests' (Ó Cinnéide, 1998: 47). Effectively these agreements bypass elected representatives and promote to the forefront of decision-making a diverse group of nonelected individuals, including Government officials and members of the civil service, representatives of the traditional social partners, and representatives of the voluntary and community sector. These agreements, which affect every member of society, are made by this small cabal of individuals in private or invited spaces that are sealed off from the wider society.

Expanding on Ó Cinnéide's remarks, Meade (2005) points out that civil society groups that have been invited to take part in national social partnership negotiations are those that have the approval of the State and that, in their turn, this small number of groups is represented at the partnership table by paid workers and officials rather than by volunteers. 'For these insider organizations privileged enough to be accommodated, partnership promises a form of recognition that is prized in contemporary politics' (Meade, 2005: 357).

Again, Ó Cinnéide and Meade describe Fraser's 'specialized discursive arenas' (1992: 88), Gaventa's 'invited spaces' (2004), and the manner in which bargaining within these arenas or spaces tends to work to the advantage of dominant groups and individuals (Harrison, 1980; Fraser, 1997; Cleaver, 2004).

Since 1995 corporatism has been extended to local government through the establishment of strategic policy committees (SPCs) and county and city development boards (CDBs). Despite being touted as 'an important exercise in participatory democracy' (Department of the Environment and Local Government, 1996: 29), these reforms are wholly top-down in nature (Ó Cinnéide, 1998; Forde, 2005) and SPCs and CDBs have proved an unsatisfactory experience for both councillors and representatives of voluntary and community groups.

> Voluntary and community sector representatives have found SPC meetings to be intimidating, bureaucratic, mechanistic and a destructive experience. Some councillors have responded negatively to the arrival of the community representatives. (Harvey 2002: 20)

At a meeting with a cross-party group of six Cork City councillors which this writer attended in July 2003, councillors expressed mixed views about the introduction of SPCs. Of these councillors, just two expressed general if noneffusive support for the SPCs and their operation in Cork City. The other councillors criticised the imposition of SPCs on a number of grounds, including community representatives' inexperience in policy making, the time-consuming nature of SPCs, their cost to the taxpayer, and the absence of a democratic mandate due to the nonelected status of several of their members.

The reforms of Irish local government reflect the unprecedented commitment of the Irish State to consumerist and managerialist aims. Viewed together, the provisions of the White Papers *Better Local Government* (Department of the Environment and Local Government, 1996) and *Supporting Voluntary Activity* (Department of Social, Community and Family Affairs, 2000*a*) provide a strong indication that the State's purpose has more to do with the extension of its influence and control over civil society organisations and the spheres that they occupy than a concern with developing a truly participatory democracy. Moreover, the language that the State uses to introduce and justify these developments smacks of Habermasian instrumental rationality and the exercise of Lukes' third dimension of power (Lukes, 2005; see also Chapters 3 and 4). This language is not a 'social critique or a discourse of ethics, but governed by a mechanistic pseudo-rationality' (Higgins, 2006: 15). Nonetheless, such 'pseudo-rational' language and the measures it puts forward are used persuasively to encourage the compliance of those at whom the policies are aimed:

> The new managerial State is certainly a problem, not least because it is constituted as much through language and routine as structure so that we can become insidiously embedded in its ways without even noticing. (Shaw, 2003*b*: 365)

While the language of the State may be persuasive, the disillusionment of some civil society organisations with social partnership is evident in two recent developments involving the sector. The Community Platform, which was originally a member of the Community and Voluntary Pillar (CVP) and which comprises 28 voluntary and community groups, participated in talks for the sixth national agreement *Sustaining Progress* (Department of the Taoiseach, 2003) but declined to endorse that agreement on the basis that it 'offered nothing that was additional to existing policy commitments to address the ongoing problems faced by our members and the groups we represent who experience poverty, social exclusion and inequality' (Community Platform, 2006: 1). The Community Platform also objected to what it suggested was a lack of engagement by the Government with its members and their proposals (Community Platform, 2006; Community Workers Co-operative, 2006*a*). Consequently, the Platform was excluded from several of the consultative fora for the seventh national agreement. This development caused considerable concern amongst the constituent members of the Platform, of which the Community Workers Co-operative (CWC) is a member:

> The absence of the Community Platform means that there is no voice of women, Travellers, other ethnic minorities, refugees, asylum seekers, migrant workers, lone parents, gay and lesbian, etc., at the talks. (Community Workers Co-operative, 2006*b*: 1)

More fundamentally, the exclusion of the Community Platform characterises social partnership as a form of 'closed shop' from which participants may be excluded if they express dissenting views.

The second development concerned the discontinuation of State funding to the Community Workers Co-operative. Founded in 1981, the CWC was one of a number of anti-poverty networks that were funded by the State since the early 1990s. Its remit was to support community development groups in combating poverty and inequality, and it employed a small number of full-time staff to pursue this work. Like many other groupings within the voluntary and community sector, the CWC was supportive of the introduction of neocorporatism and produced a series of publications on participation by the voluntary and community sector in social partnership at national and local level (Community Workers Co-operative, 2001*a*, 2001*b*).

By 2003 the CWC had begun to publicly question the benefits of social partnership to the voluntary and community sector, and called for reflection on the sector's future within the social partnership framework. One of the principal reasons for this change was a Government requirement (Department of Community, Rural and Gaeltacht Affairs, 2003) that projects under the nationwide Community Development Programme (CDP) present their yearly plans for endorsement by the CDBs. This requirement provoked fears that the autonomy enjoyed by CDPs in the drawing up of their plans would be compromised.

In late 2004, the Government announced that it would discontinue the CWC's core funding at the end of the following year. This was done and, although the CWC continued to operate using alternative funding, it lost two full-time workers and had to severely restrict its work.[ix] It continued to express strong reservations about social partnership and, in particular, argued that the independent role of the community and voluntary sector has been undermined by State initiatives in recent years (Regan, 2005).

The difficulties faced by the Community Platform and the CWC raise a number of questions which the following section will attempt to answer. Is the formalisation and institutionalisation of the State–civil society relationship of the past twenty years likely to continue? If it continues, could a challenge to this formalisation occur and, if so, could it emerge from within civil society, given its weak position in relation to power and its reliance on Government funding? Finally, what possible forms could this challenge take?

Conclusion: Stasis or Change?

It is difficult to foresee a significant change in the pattern of State–civil society relations in the near future. This chapter has explored the advantages to the Irish State of cultivating and maintaining a close and unequal relationship with civil society groups, principally through the mechanism of social partnership. The impetus for change is therefore unlikely to come from the State. Indeed, it is implausible to suppose that any State would put itself forward as the guarantor and guardian of an autonomous civil society: 'Must its [civil society's] independence rest simply upon the disinterested benevolence of the State – a most insecure basis?' (Kumar, 1993: 386).

Negotiations for the establishment of the seventh national agreement, *Towards 2016* (Department of the Taoiseach, 2006), were more problematic than those for any previous agreement. The negotiations were more protracted than for its predecessors and frequently stalled on a range of different issues, including public sector pay, the protection of workers and social housing (*Irish Times*, 2006*b*). In July 2008 pay negotiations within the context of the agreement came to a prolonged standstill due to disagreement between employers' organisations and trade unions. These difficulties provide a tentative indication that the social partners – trade unions, employers' organisations and civil society groups – may have begun to tire of the compromises that collective bargaining demands. Despite these difficulties there is no evidence that the commitment of the Government to a formalised neocorporatist relationship with a range of interest groups is diminishing (Cowen, 2009), although the current economic conditions are likely to place considerable ongoing pressure on partnership.

Are there any signs that a concerted impulsion for change may come from civil society, and specifically from the community development sector? A tentative answer is principally based on the results of empirical research conducted by this writer between 1998 and 2004. The fieldwork consisted of a survey and four case studies of the operation of eighteen partnership companies and community groups under the Local Development Programme 1995–1999 and LDSIP 2000–2006.[x] Community workers, community directors (representatives of voluntary and community groups who sit on the boards of partnership companies), other participants from communities, and managers of partnerships and community groups were interviewed for the research. Space restrictions prohibit a full discussion of the results so key elements are focused on here.

In the first instance the survey revealed that, despite particular achievements,[xi] there are a range of associated problems with how these local neocorporatist structures function. Problems concerning the partnership process include the existence of unequal and sometimes dysfunctional relationships between directors from different sectors at board level (in particular, between directors from State bodies and those from the voluntary or community sector); a lack of clarity amongst partners as to what the term 'partnership' actually means; the adherence of partnership boards to rigid corporate practices, routines and conventions; a reliance on a consensus approach to decision-making at board level; sometimes unrepresentative and unresponsive participatory processes; and a heavy dependence on professional staff in the conduct of activities that could constitute the remit of community directors or the wider community. These issues underline the reality that partnerships and community groups are 'invited' participatory spaces, the rules of which are determined externally and imposed at local level. Furthermore, several respondents argued that the insistence on consensus potentially masks differences of opinion between board members from different sectors, thus undermining any genuine deliberative possibilities that partnership arrangements may offer. Additional problems highlighted by the research include a focus on service delivery rather than advocacy, the relative failure of the State and its ancillary bodies to learn from the experience of local partnerships and some ambivalence amongst communities towards local partnership. It seems the prediction of the European Social Fund (ESF) Programme Evaluation Unit (1999: 220–221) that 'Partnerships and Community Groups may become marginalised deliverers to the marginalised with limited potential impact on mainstream policy and practice' has a measure of validity.

Despite these problems, community workers and community representatives did not express any willingness to overtly challenge the hegemony of social partnership. Two examples illustrate this contention. First, in 2003 the writer attended a meeting facilitated by the CWC to discuss the requirement that community development projects (CDPs) present their annual plans to the county and city development boards (CDBs) for approval. Participants at the meeting expressed outrage at the requirement and the potential difficulties and constraints that it would pose for their projects. Despite this outrage, however, they evinced powerlessness to strongly challenge or change the State's decision and the meeting ended with a single decision to draw the concerns to the attention of the relevant minister.

Second, in summer 1999 this writer conducted a case study that sought the experiences of long-standing community directors in a large urban partnership company which was established in 1990 (Forde, 2006). In a focus group the directors disclosed their dissatisfaction with the operation of social partnership, their view that partnership has yielded relatively little for the communities they represent and their concern at the ambivalence with which these communities regard local social partnership. They experienced considerable difficulties in attempting to ensure that their views were heard at board and substructure level and argued that the voices of minorities such as women were not being adequately represented on the partnership board. They were also worried that their communities did not have sufficient knowledge or understanding of social partnership and its objectives. These problems provide further evidence of Young's (2000) 'internal exclusion' and raise fundamental questions about the capacity of 'top-down' initiatives such as partnerships and community groups to effectively engage and involve the communities at which their programmes are directed. Notwithstanding these issues, the directors were unwilling to disengage from the partnership, citing a desire to 'wait and see' what would happen in the future and a commitment to working within the system rather than outside it. Perhaps their ongoing commitment could be characterised as a type of 'false consciousness' induced by the rhetoric surrounding social partnership and the recognition it gives to groups which were previously excluded from decision-making processes. Given this history, their reticence is probably unsurprising and understandable. Whatever the reason or reasons may be, the reaction of the CDP workers and the community directors is a reminder of the risk of assuming that community groups are necessarily able or willing to resist the imposition in a 'top-down' manner of new institutions, procedures and practices. Shaw (2008: 11) argues that community development faces an 'unavoidable choice' between assisting in the maintenance of the status quo and seeking a more equitable alternative. In Ireland it appears that community development has chosen the former and it is difficult to envisage a radical shift in this position in the foreseeable future, although the literature offers some interesting possibilities (Daly, 2008; see also the discussions in Chapters 3, 9 and 10).

Perhaps the best hope for a challenge to neocorporatism and the emergence of an autonomous public sphere emanates from the disparate but growing elements of civil society that function outside the structures of the State and economy. In Ireland these groupings, which are growing in strength, visibility and cohesion, are challenging neoliberalism and global capitalism while attempting to construct alternative and critical public spheres (Meade, 2005; Cox, 2006). These fora, which function on a 'voluntary and communicative basis' (Cox, 2006: 223), offer 'a comparatively independent intellectual space' (Meade, 2005: 368) from which new social and political ideas can emerge. The activities of these groups may sometimes be small-scale and unheralded, but they also offer a chink of possibility for future democratic renewal in Ireland.

Notes

i Despite its efforts, the early State's attempts to realise its idealised vision of a Gaelic Ireland through the media of Irish language and tradition found little resonance with the majority of the population, for whom

English had been the primary means of communication since before independence and who identified more eagerly with popular culture than its Gaelic alternative.

ii A strike by members of the Irish Transport and General Workers' Union (ITGWU) culminated in a 'lock out' by Dublin employers opposed to unionisation.

iii Members of the CVP in 2008 are: the Irish National Organisation of the Unemployed (INOU), St Vincent de Paul, the National Youth Council of Ireland (NYCI), the Congress Centres Network, Protestant Aid, the Conference of Religious in Ireland (CORI), The Wheel, the Disability Federation of Ireland, the National Association of Building Cooperatives, the Irish Centre for Social Housing, the Children's Rights Alliance, the Irish Senior Citizens Parliament, the Carers Association, Irish Rural Link, Age Action Ireland, the Community Platform and the National Women's Council.

iv The current national agreement, *Towards 2016* (Department of the Taoiseach, 2006), will be of ten years' duration, from 2006 until 2015. It is the only national agreement to date to have a projected existence of more than three years. The 'current programme ... runs to some 100,000 words – as against 12,000 in 1987. It covers almost every aspect of public policy' (FitzGerald, 2007: 14).

v The local development system consists of a range of area-based partnership companies, EU-funded LEADER groups and city and county enterprise boards. All of these initiatives are neocorporatist in nature.

vi For example, Budget 2005 introduced a payment of €1,000 per annum for families who avail of childcare. While this payment will reduce families' substantial childcare bills, it will not solve the ongoing problem of inadequate State childcare provision in Ireland.

vii The NESF was established by the State in 1993, and consists of representatives of the Government, Dáil and Seanad, the social partners and farming interests, and representatives of women's organisations, youth groups, unemployed people, older people, and disability and environmental organisations. The role of the NESF is to 'develop economic and social policy initiatives, particularly on employment, and to contribute to the formation of a national consensus on social and economic matters' (Langford, 1999: 101).

viii He adds that 'it is difficult to resist an impression that what emerges from the process consists more of policies that the Government would in any event have been introducing, rather than new ideas emanating from civic society' (2007: 14).

ix The CWC's core funding was restored in 2007 and, together with the Community Platform, it remains within the Community and Voluntary Pillar (CVP).

x The survey consisted of 21 interviews, which were carried out between April 1998 and December 1999. The four case studies were conducted between winter 1998 and summer 2004.

xi The survey revealed three principal achievements of partnership companies and community groups. In the first instance, they have established and/or worked with an impressive range of formal and informal structures - boards of directors, subcommittees, working groups, community fora, community networks and interest groups - the purpose of which is to facilitate participation by statutory bodies, the traditional social partners and the voluntary and community sector. Second, partnerships and community groups devote considerable resources, both financial and human, to working with communities and community groups. This work includes training and education for board members and community groups, the use of diverse methods of communicating with communities and groups, and the employment of significant numbers of professional staff whose role is to engage in community animation. Third, they have developed an array of innovative actions at local level, some of which they directly deliver themselves, and some of which are contracted for delivery by local voluntary and community organisations.

7

Professionalisation and Youth and Community Work

Seamus Bane

Introduction

In this chapter I look at a significant issue that has a particular relevance for youth and community work as both sectors prepare to meet the challenges of a rapidly changing Ireland. That issue is the move towards professionalisation. Youth work and community work face many common issues and they are often grouped together in discussions of their role, methods, practices and approaches. Indeed Banks (2004: 2), while acknowledging that there are differences, suggests that youth work, community work and social work are 'related, but still distinct, occupational groups involved in care, social control, informal education and advocacy with a range of vulnerable, troublesome or "disadvantaged" user/client groups'. However, while acknowledging that there are similarities between youth work and community work this chapter treats each as separate entities with their own focus and characteristics. Social work is not part of this discussion and, given the contested nature of the term, I try to avoid describing either occupation as a 'profession'.

The first section explores the term 'profession' and the characteristics and understandings associated with it. It introduces some of the key sociological theorisations of the concept in order to explain how and why the term has come to signify the kinds of authority and prestige that are much sought after by a range of occupational groups in contemporary society. The next section then considers the professionalisation of youth and community work in the Irish context. It identifies some of the forces and trends that are pushing those occupations to seek the label 'profession'. Following this is a critical analysis of the implications of professionalism, in which I explore some of the issues that might be considered by those involved in the practice of Youth and Community Work were those occupations to become the preserve of those who are labelled 'professionals'. Finally, I explore the potential for a 'new professionalism' and ask whether either or both occupations might constitute themselves in new and creative ways. Specifically I ask if there are ways whereby the practice of these occupations can best serve *all* involved in the process while remaining true to their respective core values and principles.[i]

Origins of the 'Profession'

In everyday discussion the term 'profession' can be used as simple shorthand for the job that one does. However we also speak approvingly of work or events being produced in a professional manner, for example, the smooth running of community, music, sports or arts events. In the world of work and in a common or everyday sense, to be identified as a professional carries cachet, indicating a level of competence and a seal of assurance that whatever is being undertaken will be carried out to a high standard. It is an appellation that is valued by those both within and outside the 'professions'. It is also, as the following definition shows, a status that is highly prized and protected by those within given professions. The website of Professions Australia (http://www.professions.com.au) offers the following quite comprehensive definition:

> A profession is a disciplined group of individuals who adhere to ethical standards and who hold themselves out as, and are accepted by the public as possessing special knowledge and skills in a widely recognised body of learning derived from research, education and training at a high level, and who are prepared to apply this knowledge and exercise these skills in the interest of others. It is inherent in the definition of a profession that a code of ethics governs the activities of each profession. Such codes require behaviour and practice beyond the personal moral obligations of an individual.

This definition suggests that professionals do indeed see themselves and present themselves as somewhat above and distinct from the everyday. They are defined as experts with a set of knowledge and skills that are not widely available or indeed understood. They are bound by codes of behaviour 'beyond the personal moral obligations of an individual' and they have an obligation to apply their knowledge and skills 'in the interests of others'. The professional then would appear to be a person of some importance in society in terms of both their role and status.

The status of 'professional' as traditionally understood is probably best exemplified in popular constructions of the oldest of such occupations: law and medicine. Practitioners could expect, once they had completed their studies and training and gained their qualifications, to carry on their work in a particular way. Underlying assumptions regarding the integrity and legitimacy of their professional status were not questioned or challenged by the vast majority of people. The reference point of the 'professional code of ethics' guaranteed practitioners considerable freedom, autonomy and discretion in how they carried out their work, whether as an individual 'business', which many were, or as employees. Even as an employee within an organisation the professional was accorded an independence not shared by others, for example, the doctor employed in the hospital who has freedom to make clinical decisions independent of hospital managers.

In sociology, however, much of the recent literature challenges the concept of the 'professional' and highlights the absence of a universally accepted definition of what constitutes a profession. Hugman (1991), Macdonald (1995) and Banks (2004) locate their explorations of professions generally in the English-speaking, Anglo-American world and suggest that different definitions of what precisely constitutes a profession raise questions as to the validity of the appellation in strictly social scientific terms. While acknowledging that study has been undertaken on the role and status of professions in many international settings, this chapter primarily draws on literature that analyses the development of professions in the UK and Ireland. Hugman's (2005: 31) observation – drawing on the work of Macdonald– sets the boundaries for this discussion when he states that 'there is considerable agreement that the idea of "profession", the attributes of "professionalism" and the process of "professionalisation" refer to occupations that have developed claims to particular types of status, power and authority and a basis for asserting these claims within the wider society.'

While acknowledging that the title 'profession' may itself be somewhat contested, in the British and Irish context it nonetheless represents a status and position that has been achieved by some occupations and is sought by others. In considering why this designation is much-sought we begin by first looking at the origins of the 'profession' and at how some occupations evolved over time and became professions as they exist today with the status and power they enjoy.

Macdonald (1995) points out that the attainment and protection of knowledge and its transmission is a key starting point in the sociological studies of professions. He argues (1995: 158) that:

> Professions became possible only when knowledge emerged as a socio-cultural entity in its own right, independent of established social institutions, and when society came to be based on knowledge in a way quite different from earlier periods; and when the market had reached sufficient salience as a feature of society for the private provision of knowledge-based services to become viable.

Drawing on a number of sources, notably Gellner, Macdonald (1995: 157–160) argues that the development of modern, 'rational', scientific analysis and study laid the foundations upon which professions were built. In premodern times knowledge and facts had to fit into a moral, religious or cultural framework that helped people to make sense of and understand their world. Thus, while people in premodern societies could observe events and their consequences, the way in which they made sense of them was controlled by a range of factors, including religion, tradition and the culture of the society. In this situation, a crop failure, a defeat in battle or ill-health could be interpreted as punishment by the deity. This overarching framework held society together and maintained group cohesion. In the premodern era, such cohesion was seen as the only way in which the group could survive and prosper (Macdonald, 1995).

By the fifteenth century, beginning with the Renaissance, perspectives shifted with regard to understanding the world and how it worked. This continued and grew in sophistication and depth with the Reformation and the Enlightenment and was firmly in place by the start of the nineteenth century. New rational, empirical and scientific ways of understanding natural and social phenomena developed that were not dependent on religious or social constraints. Events and objects were studied as discrete entities and deductions were made that established 'scientific facts' about those events and objects of study (Macdonald, 1995).

The process by which knowledge became separated from the authority of religion and other 'non-rational' belief systems and became the product of 'rational', scientific study was peculiar to Western Europe. This historical process that facilitated the emergence of knowledge 'as a socio-cultural entity in its own right' (MacDonald, 1995: 158) facilitated the emergence of huge social and technological changes manifest in the Industrial Revolution and subsequent developments.

Increasingly, science and reason would define nature, the human being (and humanity in general) and newly emerging industrial societies as objects of examination, study and controlled intervention. Science and reason would also propose ways by which society and humanity might reach ever higher levels of knowledge and civilisation. In addition, Macdonald (1995: 159) argues: 'it became possible for individuals to develop an area of learning and expertise and to become repositories of knowledge in their own right.' Having become repositories of knowledge, whether it was law, medicine, engineering or another, it then became possible for such individuals to sell their learning and expertise to others in the free market that accompanied the 'European miracle'.[ii] In the free market in which they operated, the emerging professionals attempted to maximise their market position and squeeze out their rivals – be they individuals or groups.

Theorising the Idea of the Professional

1. Functionalist Perspectives

In considering the emergence and role of professions, sociologists have tried to explain the phenomenon in a variety of ways. Emile Durkheim (1858–1917), the founder of functionalism, was one of the earliest to write about the role of professionals in society (Macdonald, 1995; Porter, 1998). Durkheim was influenced by the positivism and rationalism of the era in which he lived and believed that human society, like the natural world, could be examined and studied. Society as it evolved was seen as a given – almost as an act of nature – and the role of the social scientist was to study it so that it could be understood and made to function better, but not necessarily changed in its basic structures. As mentioned, the change from premodern and preindustrial to modern and industrial society that saw the emergence of professions also saw huge changes in the way in which people lived their lives. With the growth of industrialisation and the concurrent specialisation in the production of goods and services, traditional bonds weakened and individual identity emerged as a stronger and more significant factor than group consensus. Individuals now had to depend on others, most of whom they would never meet or know, to produce the necessities to enable them to live.

According to Talcott Parsons, another sociologist who was influenced by Durkheim, 'for social order to succeed, members of society needed to share a moral commitment to the rules of society'

(Porter, 1998: 22). Tensions, which Durkheim labelled *anomie*, were inevitable in times of major social and technical change as represented by the Industrial Revolution. The maintenance of the structures of society and the management of these social tensions required, for Durkheim, 'the development of strong State regulation and the emergence of powerful occupational associations that would provide a buffer between the State and the individual' (Porter, 1998: 17). Thus, in complex modern societies with a sophisticated division of labour, which Durkheim labelled organic, the emergence of professions would be an important element in helping the structure of society to function and maintain itself. As repositories of specialised knowledge the professions could provide leadership in both their particular areas of expertise and in the wider society by their adherence to professional codes of ethics. This adherence to a code of ethics became one of the key elements in the identification of an occupation as a profession. As exemplars of high moral probity professionals would serve an important function in setting standards of behaviour and civility, and also in defining the place of individual people within society.

2. *Trait Theory*

According to Macdonald (1995: 2), Durkheim believed that the existence of professions and in particular their observance of a code of ethics would 'save modern society from the breakdown in moral authority, which in his view threatened it'. Taking as given Durkheim's assumptions regarding the role and importance of the professions in society, later studies attempted to establish empirically the characteristics or traits that an occupation must possess if it is to be classified as a profession. Once these traits were identified, a given occupation 'could be compared to the list of traits, and the degree to which it matched was then taken as an indication of the extent to which that occupation was professionalised' (Hugman, 1991: 2). Indeed, as Macdonald (1995: 3) observes, some writers were able to develop schemata that allowed the classification of 'occupations into "professions", "semi-professions" and (presumably) "non-professions"'. One such template is provided by Daryl Koehn (1994: 56) who identifies five traits that distinguish those who qualify as 'professionals':

> Professionals: (1) are licensed by the State to perform a certain act; (2) belong to an organisation of similarly enfranchised agents who promulgate standards and/or ideals of behaviour and who

> discipline one another for breaching these standards; (3) possess so-called 'esoteric' knowledge or skills not shared by other members of the community; (4) exercise autonomy over their work, which is work that is not well understood by the wider community; and (5) publicly pledge themselves to render assistance to those in need and as a consequence have special responsibilities or duties not incumbent upon others who have not made this pledge.

While many of these traits are claimed in the definition of professions cited earlier, questions have been raised in relation to the usefulness of trait theory. Both Macdonald (1995) and Banks (2004) argue that the 'trait' theoretical framework does not have a uniformly accepted base position. Referencing Koehn's schemata, Banks observes (2004: 19) that many alternative lists have been produced. She further notes that for Koehn (1994) the public pledge or code of ethics was 'the only defensible trait of professionalism'.

Furthermore, Hugman (1991: 3–4) points out that those traits that were typically presented as the template against which other occupations could be assessed were traditionally those associated with law and medicine. He argues (1991: 3) that these occupations 'should themselves have been part of a critical analysis' of what constitutes a profession. An uncritical acceptance of the characteristics of these occupations as the exemplars of a profession creates a circular argument in that the model presented has not been properly tested. In addition, he suggests that the traits themselves are accepted as 'unproblematic social facts' rather than claims that must be tested and proven. Hugman (1991: 3) also argues that trait theory accepts the claim of an occupation to exclusive authority in its own domain of expertise as uncontested rather than 'a subject for enquiry and debate'. In all of this, Hugman (1991: 3) challenges trait theory as ignoring 'the problem of power in the success of an occupation in achieving professional status within a society'. This point is further reinforced by Rixon (2007: 35) who recognises that those fields of work undertaken by middle-class white men have been most readily classified as professional.

3. Critical Perspectives

Adopting a critical perspective, Macdonald (1995) suggests that the development of the professions from early modern times to their present position of status and power can be understood in terms of the

'Professional Project'. Borrowing from Weber's idea of 'social closure', he argues that having established themselves as players in the free market of the nineteenth century, the professions set about consolidating and developing their power and status in society by closing off access to their disciplines so that entry could only come from a small and controlled source. The acquiring of specialised knowledge required significant periods of study for young would-be professionals. As access to education was limited to those who could afford it, entry was dominated by the landed gentry or wealthy merchant class. Porter (1998: 63) points out that educational credentials – or what Weber called the 'patent of education' – 'can be used to enhance both the status and class situation of those who gain them'. By limiting the number and type of person who could become a professional, these groups were able to implement a type of social closure that consolidated their economic power and social status. As Porter puts it (1998: 64), 'having attained a monopoly, they have also succeeded in restricting the supply of their services, which has had the effect of pushing up the prices they can charge. In terms of status, social closure, combined with a claim to such attributes as altruism and ethicality, has had the effect of giving them a position of honour within society.'

Macdonald (1995) draws attention to the 'fundamental' but often hidden symbiotic relationship that exists between (would be) professions and the State. Because 'professions aim for a monopoly of the provision of services of a particular kind; monopolies can only be granted by the State, and therefore professions have a distinctive relationship with the State' (Macdonald, 1995: 66). These factors facilitated older professions, notably law and medicine, to establish themselves as significant status groups and wielders of power in society. Later on, the ability and willingness of new professional groupings – such as social workers or nurses – to develop organisational structures that would preserve and expand their respective spheres of influence helped to consolidate their power and status. The process of social closure that defines who is or is not a professional leads Hugman (1991: 82) to characterise professions as 'not types of occupations but historical forms of controlling occupations'. In the fields of youth work and community development, where so much emphasis is placed on inclusivity, participation and equality, such exclusive practices may be seen as inimical to stated purposes and methods.

In developing a critical analysis of the claims and status of the professions, it is worthwhile to consider also the contribution of post-structuralist theories and concepts. As noted earlier, professional groupings require State sanction and support to legitimate their claims to monopoly status. Within the fields of youth work and community development, considerable attention is therefore paid to the quality of relationships between the State and youth and community organisations, particularly to the power of the State to sanction, curtail or support the actions of those organisations (see Chapters 5 and 6). From such analyses it can appear that the State holds power 'over' community and youth organisations in relationships that tend to be overtly hierarchical. The French intellectual and post-structuralist Michel Foucault (1994) developed a more heterogeneous conception of power that helps us to appreciate how professional groupings may influence the actions and behaviours of the State and the broader population. As Finlayson and Martin (2006: 167) explain, Foucault recognised that power is also a positive force that is dispersed throughout society, a force that has the ability to create new kinds of knowledge and behaviour.

In contemporary Irish society regulations and procedures relating to 'child protection' are being adopted by youth and community organisations (see also Chapter 8). The content and form of those regulations has been greatly influenced by the advocacy and intervention of a range of social actors, including NGOs, professional social work bodies and child welfare experts. Foucault's concept of 'governmentality' explains interactions such as these, where government is not only delivered from 'above' by the State, but emanates from multiple sources. Professional or aspirant professional groups develop new forms of knowledge, which legitimate their intervention in the lives of citizens (Finlayson and Martin, 2006). Meanwhile intervention creates new forms of knowledge about those citizens. For example, professional youth workers may claim a privileged right to 'manage' young people based on their distinctive knowledge and competencies. The forms of behaviour that are created and encouraged, as Finlayson and Martin (2006: 168) point out, facilitate the State in the 'management of a population and its doings, legitimating and making possible widespread intervention'. The power relationship that emerges sees the profession being enlisted as a player in this management task. However, youth workers' practice, which is derived from their exposure to and understanding of young people's needs and concerns, further legitimates their claims to a distinctive knowledge base and bolsters their claims of professional status. Young people and community members learn to monitor their own conduct or to define their identities in line with professional knowledge – accepting or responding to labels such as 'at risk', 'socially excluded' or 'disadvantaged'. For example, as noted by Kiely, the knowledge base of official health promotion in Ireland has found its way into those youth work programmes with a health education focus. Citizens can, however, also contest and challenge forms of professional knowledge, just as mental health activists often contest psychiatry. Therefore, professional groupings may have privileged status within society, but this status is not fixed and is open to being resisted and redrawn (see Finlayson and Martin, 2004 for further discussion).

It is obvious that from a critical perspective there are limits to the usefulness of the term 'professional' as a sociological concept. The concept has developed and been used to exclude others and to exercise control over those who are not part of (nor allowed to be part of) given professions. For Ivan Illich (1977: 22), the power and status that has been acquired by the professions means that 'democratic power is subverted by an unquestioned assumption of an all-embracing professionalism.' He argues (1977: 14) for 'the endorsement of a patronising and sceptical attitude towards the experts – especially when they presume to diagnose and prescribe'. For Illich, the destruction of professional dominance in all areas of life is crucial to the growth of participatory politics and the (re)claiming of power by the people.

In spite of such criticisms many occupational groups continue to seek the designation or status of 'profession'. Not least among the occupational groups that may consider such a status to be a desirable goal are those of youth work and community work. Before looking at the potential implications for the work of these groups were the status to be achieved, we will look briefly at some of the drivers pushing youth work and community work towards this goal.

The Drive for Professionalisation in Community Work

A brief review of the origins and development of community work shows that the move to professionalism has been a feature of its evolution in Ireland. In a literature review entitled *The Role of Community Development in Tackling Poverty in Ireland,* Motherway (2006: 15) traces the emergence of community development from the co-operative movement of the nineteenth century, through the self-help movement of Muintir na Tíre in the 1930s and on to the anti-poverty focus that emerged in the period from the 1970s to the 1990s. For most of the early years in the history of community development it was a voluntary activity that was run independently of and sometimes in opposition to the State by people who did not receive financial reward. With the rediscovery of widespread poverty in the 1970s and the influence of the EU through the 1980s, the Irish Government became increasingly interested in the community development approach as a way of addressing deep-seated social problems. Motherway (2006: 16) notes that it is only in relatively recent times that community development has become 'official'. He points out (2006: 15) that this recognition has come about due to 'the growing acceptance of the importance of participation and inclusion, including formal partnership processes' (see also Chapter 6). The implementation of participation and inclusion has become activated in the concept of 'Social Partnership' which has become and remains 'at the heart of Government policy, both nationally and locally' (Motherway; 2006: 17). As this partnership model has developed with financial support from the State, the role of the paid community worker has become more prominent and that of the volunteer less so. In describing the various structures through which partnership is operated, Motherway (2006: 17) concludes 'most areas now have well-established and experienced community development sectors, with a range of bodies and individuals involved, and more *professional community development workers* than ever before' (my emphasis).

The evolution of community work as an occupation with increasing numbers involved in a paid capacity can be seen as creating a critical mass in which the idea of the professionalisation of community work could take root. However, the employment context within which community development workers operate is far from a secure one. Government funding for organisations delivering programmes such as the Local Development Social Inclusion Programme, the Community Development Programme and the Family Resource Centres is allocated on a three-year basis. Consequently, employing organisations are unable to offer contracts for more than three years. This creates difficulties for work that is 'not a process that takes place in a short timeframe as it seeks to address deeply rooted inequalities and forms of disadvantage' (Community Workers Co-operative, 2007: 10). Paid staff have no real job security and frequent staff turnover means disruption and discontinuity for the communities affected. With a fixed pool of money available to them, employing organisations can be anxious to divert as much money as possible into actions and outcomes. Staff members may often feel that their employment conditions suffer in this balancing act. In such a volatile situation it is understandable that community development workers would seek the security and status associated with the label of 'professional' as a way of recognising and valuing the work they do.

In light of these issues a recent draft document, *Standards for Community Work Practice*, produced by the Community Workers

Co-operative (CWC) and representatives of community, academic and statutory sector organisations, highlights 'the need to establish a set of standards to govern (and protect) the practice of Community Work and community work as a profession overall and to inform the training and education of community workers'(Community Workers Co-operative, 2007: 4). The document also speaks of community work as 'unique in being both vocational and also professional'. It identifies 'a distinct discipline and ethos' and community development 'as a set of core values/social principles covering human rights, social inclusion, equality and respect for diversity; and a specific skills and knowledge base'(2007: 12–13). While not disputing the foregoing it could be argued that some of the characteristics listed are those that have been utilised in the past by occupations that have designated themselves as 'professions' and sought to exclude and protect their market position. In seeking to advance the case for establishing community work as a profession the document recognises a key dilemma such a designation might bring. It records a gradual realisation by those involved in the process 'that it was possible to develop standards, training and education endorsement processes, which would not contradict the community work tradition of ensuring access to the profession for those involved as participants in community work initiatives'(2007: 5). However it might be argued that distinguishing between 'those involved as participants' and the 'practitioners' could be seen as identifying the 'client' and the 'experts' that characterises the classic professional relationship. Another characteristic of the traditional profession is highlighted when it suggests that 'community workers have obligations to themselves, the community, their employers, funders, one another and *society*' (2007: 7; my emphasis).

Shaw (2008: 24) suggests that 'in a context in which "community empowerment" is virtually Government policy, it is hardly surprising that there is almost no area of social policy that is immune from the community treatment.' We have already seen how community development has become the vehicle by which the Irish Government seeks to address poverty and social exclusion through the medium of social partnership (see Chapter 6). In this scenario community workers become the enablers of community development and the key 'deliverers' of Government policy. In such a context it may not be surprising that community work and community workers would come to be seen as requiring certain skills and training so that they can be effective deliverers and recorders of official policy. There may be a shift in emphasis away from the more person-centred skills – group work, engagement skills, etc. – towards developing 'competencies' that support the more bureaucratic aspects of State community sector relationships. It would appear that the expansion of the role of community development in Government policy has seen a corresponding growth in the number of courses on offer at third-level institutions.[iii] It is not suggested that this is a negative development but rather that the interests of those institutions in terms of defining new areas of knowledge and in attracting new groups of students are other significant factors in the professionalisation of community work.

The Drive for Professionalisation in Youth Work

The *National Youth Work Development Plan* (Department of Education and Science, 2003*a*: 11–15) highlights the context and the challenges facing youth work at a time when Ireland has seen rapid and major change in the social, cultural, economic, technological and legislative areas in a relatively brief time frame. All of these challenges have strengthened the demand from both paid and volunteer youth workers and youth work employers for training and, more significantly, for certified training in order to meet what are seen to be the increasing challenges of youth work. The plan also presents youth work as 'a *profession*, in the sense that all those who do it, both volunteer and paid, are required and obliged, in the interests of young people and of society as a whole, to carry out their work to the highest possible standards and to be accountable for their actions' (2003*a*: 14; emphasis in original). This could be seen as a carefully worded discourse, designed to ensure that different groupings within the youth sector are kept on board. Nonetheless, the presentation of youth work in the plan as a *profession* and not as a *vocation* no doubt stems in part from the long-held belief within the youth work sector, both paid and volunteer, that their work with and commitment to young people was seen in a patronising and condescending manner. In the words of a National Youth Council of Ireland (NYCI) presentation to the Joint Committee on Education and Science (2003: 2), there was a 'suspicion that youth work was the Cinderella of the Irish Education System'. Such suspicion may be justified given the history of State support in the past 30 years (see Chapter 5). While the passing of the Youth Work Act in 2001 generated considerable optimism within the sector, the delay in implementing its provisions led to the pessimism evident in the above assessment. It also highlighted the sector's concern regarding the perceived value of youth work to the State as an intervention with young people. In such a context it would not be surprising that those involved in youth work would feel the need to seek legitimacy and recognition from the State, and thus argue for it as a highly professional activity.

As outlined by McMahon (Chapter 5) the nature of State funding for youth work also poses difficulties for the sector. Since 1969 mainstream youth work has been supported through a grant-in-aid from the Department of Education and Science. Each year a figure is made available to the youth sector and distributed to youth work organisations. These organisations in turn employ staff to support the hundreds of volunteers all over the country that work with young people in local communities, both urban and rural, through youth clubs and groups. Support is in the form of grant-in-aid that is not mainstreamed within the departmental budget and, while the grant continues to be made available on an annual basis, there is no commitment that the funding is guaranteed. The need to address this situation is identified under Goal 3 of the *National Youth Work Development Plan* (Department of Education and Science, 2003*a*: 23) but its recommendation that a funding review be undertaken has not been actualised. Such a situation can create difficulties for staff retention and continuity of work, and youth organisations must frequently fundraise to meet staff costs. In terms of employment conditions, workers may also desire the introduction of clearer pay-scales and progression routes: conditions that are more in line with those granted to professionals who perform 'like work'. In such circumstances the label of professional might be seen as offering protection and security for a worker.

As with community work, ongoing developments in the youth work sector have emphasised the need for training and certification. The *National Youth Work Development Plan* (NYWDP) records that 'the need for a coherent national framework of validation and accreditation for youth work training is now widely accepted. It was one of the most common themes arising in submissions to the NYWDP' (Department of Education and Science, 2003*a*: 33). With an increasing demand for certification there has been an increase in the access routes for workers to achieve this and more third-level institutions now offer courses in youth work. Responding to the demand for certified training and accreditation, the NYWDP established the goal of setting up the North–South Education and Training Standards Committee (NSETS) to validate youth work courses on the island of Ireland. This process includes many bodies, among them youth work organisations, third-level institutions and practitioners. The demand for certification within the sector mirrors the general growth in credentialism in education (including life-long learning) that has emerged in recent years. A factor that has contributed to this growth was the coming into effect of the National Qualification Framework as part of an EU-wide effort to make certified training and education comparable and transferable across all member states. Under the ambit of the Further Education and Training Awards Council (FETAC) a range of further education and training courses are now available for what might be called non-traditional learners. Among others there has been the development of pilot programmes certified at FETAC Level 5 in both youth and community work. The increasing demand for qualified practitioners and the concurrent increase in third-level certified courses may be seen as a move towards a service that is delivered by practitioners who have undertaken a long period of study at higher level. As mentioned, this has traditionally been presented as one of the fundamental criteria in the definition of a profession and is undoubtedly a force in the drive to professionalisation for youth work and indeed community work.

In relation to youth work there is one other major issue that can be seen as a significant driver of professionalisation. That issue is child protection and its importance is emphasised in the *National Youth Work Development Plan* (Department of Education and Science, 2003*a*: 26) when it states that 'the safety and well-being of children and young people has to be the paramount concern.' Also recognised is the 'question of the protection of youth workers themselves, paid and voluntary, both from unfair allegation and from any threat to their safety, physical or otherwise'. As with community work the context in which youth work takes place is seen to be increasingly complex, demanding increasingly specific skills and training. There may also be particular issues for volunteers and their retention. They may develop a greater sense of being overburdened by fears of litigation, the demands of child protection and the complexity associated with the ever-increasing specialisation of youth work itself (see also Chapter 1).

With the coming into effect of the Youth Work Act 2001, the youth work sector now finds itself within the compass of the statutory structure and in a network of partnerships and relationships that it has to make work. There is no doubt that in a wide variety of areas and activities youth work has been engaging with statutory bodies, for many years in some instances and to the significant benefit of many young people. While issues may arise for all involved in these new relationships, some of which will be referred to later, one inevitable consequence is that youth workers will more and more find themselves in situations where they will be dealing with other occupations and professions. For many of these other occupations their work in the context of young people will be focused on individuals who are identified as 'at risk' and in need of specific and targeted case-work interventions to minimise those risks. For the youth work role to be recognised and the input of youth workers to be respected by other professions, youth workers may be required to possess case work skills not traditionally seen as part of their repertoire. A study by Corney (2004) of youth work training courses in a number of Australian universities, gives some credence to this view. He found that 'all cases touched on or specifically taught the practices of counselling, case management and therapeutic group work within their curriculum' (2004: 521). The pragmatic reasoning behind this was 'to enable them to gain employment as a youth worker'. In a very practical sense it can be argued that youth workers need to have these types of skills in order to function and be seen as equals when engaging with other organisations that also have a statutory remit around young people. However, it can also be seen as a driver of professionalisation as these individual, case-work skills are seen as esoteric and not available to the untrained. Finally, because partnership and interagency work increasingly places youth and community workers around the same tables as other, relatively long-established professions, it may also fuel demands for the same status as those other professions. In such a context, a desire for official recognition of their occupations as 'professions' will continue to be an issue of concern for many youth and community work practitioners.

The above developments are real issues for those involved in both youth work and community work. However, there are fundamental questions for both occupations in pursuing the path of professionalisation for their occupations and we will consider some of these in the next section.

Implications of Professionalisation

The question of whether their particular occupations are or should be constructed as professions has been the subject of debate within youth and community work for years. Banks (2004: 32) points out that there has long been 'a strong voice within these occupations arguing for the importance of a coherent occupational identity and status, in order to maintain credibility with the public and other more powerful professions'. On the other hand, she points out, many within youth and community work have opposed this trend and see 'the development of exclusive professional bodies and requirements for training and expertise as creating a distance between the workers and those with whom they work'. Interestingly, in the 1980s the CWC described professionalisation as an 'anathema' (Whelan, 1989).[iv] In considering the desirability or otherwise for either youth work or community work to seek professional status for their occupations, there are some key issues that might be explored.

Bearing in mind Macdonald's (1995: 66) observations that professions aim to be the monopolies of their particular services and that only the State can grant monopolies, then youth work and community work would be explicitly tying themselves into a particular and significant regulatory relationship with the State. There is some evidence that such a relationship may not be to the best benefit for those occupations or the constituencies they serve and support (see Chapters 5 and 6). The incorporation of the community and voluntary sector in the partnership process has allowed the community 'to be constituted as a significant actor in its own right in policy discourse if not in the development process itself' (Curtin and Varley, 1995: 382). However, becoming a significant actor in policy discourse may have come at a price for the community and voluntary sector. Anna Lee, who has been involved in community and local development for a number of years, observes that: 'activists are conscious of a double-edged sword: the sector has achieved status; it has been brought in from the cold to participate in State partnership. Yet, they contend, this achievement has tended to work against the very foundation of community development – pushing through radical social change, against the wishes of the status quo' (2006: 14).

This, however, is not just an Irish phenomenon, as noted by Shaw (2008: 27) who argues that community development is itself a contested term and it can, like education, 'act in ways which, in Freire's terms, domesticate or liberate'. She goes on to suggest (2008: 31) that 'community as it is deployed in policy discourse and practice to pursue the objectives of Government can create a spurious unity, which makes managing communities more straightforward.' In such a capacity the role of the community worker is to control and manage 'problems' on behalf of the State while using the veneer of 'participation'. Such practices also reinforce notions of professional distance and hierarchy between workers and communities. That values such as participation and empowerment can be used in ways that may be diametrically opposed to the intentions of the worker highlight the contradictions that beset the very notion of community development in the current policy context.

While the experience of youth work is somewhat different than that of community work, there are still serious questions to consider. A major and fundamental one was highlighted by Mark Smith at a conference on Youth Work in University College Cork in April 2007 when he reflected on the experience of statutory youth work in England. Smith spoke of the introduction of the Connexions Service in England, the thrust of which was to focus youth work intervention on 'those facing substantial, multiple problems preventing them from engaging with learning' or 'those at risk of not participating effectively in education and training (Jeffs and Smith, 2002)'(April 2007, conference notes). The impact of this was that youth workers would focus more and more on the individual, and in particular the 'at-risk' individual, in an effort to ensure that they would remain in and complete their education or training course. In addition, Smith (April 2007, conference notes) referred to the manner in which youth workers in the employment of local authorities are more and more required to befriend young people who have been identified by the police as '"threatening" young people'. The role of the youth worker then becomes one that 'will discourage their anti-social behaviour and offer alternatives to "hanging about in public areas"' (Smith, 2007: no page no. available). Not only are youth work resources being directed away from the vast majority of young people towards a minority defined as 'threatening', but the integrity of youth work practice is potentially endangered.

For Smith (2003*b*: http://www.infed.org) the net effect of this has been a fundamental reshaping of the values of youth work:

> There has been a shift from voluntary participation to more coercive forms; from association to individualised activity; from education to case management (and not even casework); and from informal to formal and bureaucratic relationships (Jeffs and Smith, 2002). Significantly, the new targets surrounding accreditation will inevitably accelerate the movement away from informal education towards formal education, formation and training. The overall effect is a radical alteration of the shape of work within youth services. Jobs may involve some youth work – but they are increasingly becoming something else.

Interestingly, the result of this enforced new role for youth workers has been, according to Smith (2007), a rejection of local authority youth worker services by significant numbers of young people and a consequent growth in provision and participation in faith-based, charity and community or estate organised youth work. He claims that, in the UK, church-based organisations now employ more youth workers than the State and they are backed by up to 100,000 volunteers. In light of the coming into effect of the Youth Work Act 2001, this experience provides grounds for serious consideration before Irish youth work seeks to become a profession regulated by the State. However, there is also a potential downside to the growth of youth work services that are seen as manifesting a vocation or a particular religious faith. Workers might be expected to function under terms and conditions which would be unacceptable elsewhere because their work is seen as a 'calling'. While accepting that many youth workers 'do have a particularly strong sense of personal commitment to the work' (Department of Education and Science, 2003*a*: 14), the author would argue that all workers, paid or unpaid, deserve the best possible working conditions and supports in the work they do.

A recent trend that is relevant to debates about the future of youth and community work is that of 'deprofessionalisation'. Healy and Meagher (2004: 244) have analysed this trend in social work in the UK and Australia, describing it as 'the fragmentation of and routinization (sic) of social work and the concomitant loss of opportunities for the exercise of creativity, reflexivity and discretion in direct practice'. They associate it with the increasing privatisation of welfare services and new cultures of managerialism, a point that is also made by Rixon (2007: 35). Banks (2004: 42) observes that 'more and more tasks and procedures are prescribed, targets set and general standards applied' and in addition 'the division of labour between occupational groups is blurring, as interprofessional working is increasingly required.' Writing about community development in the Irish context, Lee (2006: 17–18) sees skilled workers being diverted from the 'labour intensive', 'time consuming and resource-consuming process' of 'doing' community work towards management roles, due to the conditions attached to the programmes they deliver. In youth work this process is noted by Corney (2004) in his review of training courses in a number of Australian universities. In relation to the training of youth workers in areas such as counselling, case management and therapeutic group work he found that 'the policies of economic rationalism, when applied to youth work, see youth workers as case managers and counsellors working a managerialist and blame-the-victim values framework that is antithetical to the primary political and ideological values of professional youth work'(2004: 521).

Banks (2004: 43) also identifies the growth of 'competency-based training' as another element of the deprofessionalisation process. Such training equips workers with a range of technical skills to carry out tasks, but may not include (critical) discussion or analysis of the values and philosophy that underpins work practice. The authority and autonomy to analyse and prescribe has traditionally been an important aspect of the role of the professional. When this authority and autonomy is downgraded in favour of the more technical aspects of the role then the task and role of the manager becomes more important and powerful. Associated with that is the blurring of the boundaries between different forms of professional intervention. Interestingly, David Treacy (see Chapter 8) comments on the apparent absence of tension or conflict associated with school-based youth work. This is surprising given that 'youth work' and 'formal education' are generally presumed to operate from divergent value bases.

In addition to the above, recent years have seen the status of the professions come under greater public scrutiny than ever before. The perception and standing of practitioners in the fields of law, medicine and others have been affected by the actions of some of their members. Recent high profile examples include the former Drogheda obstetrician Michael Neary, who had, over a number of years, unnecessarily removed the wombs of some 172 women. He was found guilty of professional misconduct and struck off in 2003. More recently the Dublin-based solicitor Michael Lynn's business collapsed, with Lynn owing financial institutions some €80 million. Following legal action by the Law Society he left the country and faces the prospect of arrest upon his return. Some professionals have, it would appear, not adhered to ethical standards and codes of behaviour. It might be argued that we are in an environment where, as Banks (2004: 191) observes, 'professions in general, and the social professions in particular, are in a state of change, with some commentators predicting their demise and others their transformation.'

A New Professionalism?

We have already seen how the concept of the profession has been critiqued as a means by which certain groups can control access to and membership of a particular occupation. The relationship between the traditional professions and the public is one of remoteness where the expert professional, possessing exclusive skills and knowledge, dispenses expertise as a solution to the client's difficulties. These characteristics are not commonly associated with the values and practices of either youth or community work and would appear to be at odds with the ways in which both occupations typically espouse the conduct of their work. Community work cannot deny that it is a political activity and for many it is about social change in favour of those less advantaged (Shaw, 2008). According to the Community Workers

Co-operative (2007: 13–17), community development operates from a set of core values, which are:

- Collectivity – working with and supporting groups to collectively analyse, identify and address their issues.
- Empowerment – empowering individuals and communities, and addressing unequal distribution of power.
- Social justice – working to promote human rights for all.
- Equality and anti-discrimination – all people are of equal worth and importance.
- Participation – the meaningful involvement of excluded groups in decision-making, planning and action.

While Shaw (2005*a*: 3) also identifies 'making relationships' as being at the heart of community work, she adopts a sceptical attitude towards community development's 'values' (see also Chapter 3). She asserts (Shaw, 2005*b*: 3–5) that community development is:

- Contextual – it is always related to the specific time, place, economic and social context.
- Constructed – community development as we know it has a history that shows it to have been 'invented' for specific historic purposes.
- Contested – different ways of understanding the world, socially and politically, will give rise to different versions of community work.
- Ambivalent – it has both positive and negative potential.

Given the political and contested nature of community development, it might be argued that the role of 'professional' workers, be they paid or unpaid, is to question and animate the assumed values of the occupation in a truly reflexive dialogue that broadens the democratic opportunities for all. To do this community development needs to engage all its stakeholders in a conversation about its central purpose. Bearing in mind that it is always contextual, there may be no one answer to the questions that will arise and potential answers must be arrived at through a conversation of equals (in Chapters 1 and 8, Kiely and Treacy argue that a similar conversation needs to happen in Irish youth work). Such a process may offer a way of 'professional working' that distinguishes community development from other interventions and allows it to remain true to its democratic values, in ways that other traditional professions may not.

The vast majority of youth work as it is practised in Ireland cannot be seen to be political in the way that community development may lay claim to. It can, however, define an empowering model of practice based on the values that underpin practice. According to the National Youth Council of Ireland (http://www.youth.ie/youth_work/) the values that underpin youth work are:

- Empowerment of young people
- Equality and inclusion
- Respect for all young people
- Involvement of young people in decision-making
- Partnership
- Voluntary participation

Echoing Shaw (2005*a*), Smith (2003*b*: http://www.infed.org) also emphasises that 'our relationships are a fundamental source of learning.' I would suggest that youth work in Ireland often 'starts where the young person is at' rather than operating out of an explicit social change model. These starting points are not necessarily antithetical and beginning 'where the young person is at' can demand a critical assessment of the social forces impacting on them and consideration of the structural changes required to ensure the equality and inclusion of all. However, developments recorded by Smith in England (and by Kiely and Treacy in Chapters 1 and 8) suggest that practice can become more focused on 'domestication' than 'liberation' or that youth work values might not be invested with enough clarity or meaning to inspire practice that is liberating.

Conclusion

The importance of the beliefs and values espoused by both youth and community work is emphasised by Rixon (2007: 32), who holds that 'what practitioners do is mediated through their own beliefs and values.' In both the *National Youth Work Development Plan* and the *Draft Standards for Quality Community Work*, the commitment of those involved in their respective activities, both paid and unpaid, is acknowledged. Their personal beliefs and values lead people to give time and energy beyond what is required of them by the demands of the job. Perhaps the new professionalism in youth work and community work is to connect with those beliefs and values in a critically reflective way so that they are engaged in 'a professional practice and a political practice' (Shaw, 2008: 26). Perhaps the professional responsibility of youth and community workers is to give meaning to what are often vague or poorly defined values by actively and consciously resisting the more elitist aspects of professional power.

In the regular 'doing' of their work, youth and community workers will find themselves subject to a range of forces, including the requirements of funding organisations, policy change, reporting deadlines and the various other demands placed on their time and energy. Such demands are particularly acute where staff levels or funding is insufficient to maintain services, or where there is poor support from the worker's parent organisation. All of this can contribute to losing sight of the values that the workers (and the organisation) might claim underpin their practice. In such situations the practice may become more about doing things 'for' rather than 'with' people. Alternatively, workers might seek to redefine systems of accountability in partnership with young people and communities, so that their practice is invested with a real commitment to democracy and participation.

Fortunately, the traditional understandings of professional groups are under increasing scrutiny and have been critiqued on the basis of power, class and gender (Rixon, 2007). The goal of becoming a profession in the traditional sense, in the opinion of this writer, is not one that is in the best interests of either youth or community work. However, this by no means implies that such workers should ever be less than professional in observing good practice and being true to the values they claim as integral to their work.

Notes

i Those values and principles are contested and the chapters by Kiely (Chapter 1) and Meade (Chapter 3) in this volume critically interrogate them in a more detailed way.

ii During the three centuries between the medieval period and the early modern age (approx. 1501–1800) Europe came to a position of dominance in global trade and politics. The term 'European miracle' refers to the combination of factors and processes that led to this dominance, including the decline of feudalism, the emergence of the nation-state and colonialism, the growth of science and rationalism, the rise of capitalism and the development of industrial production that accompanied this phenomenon. The term comes from the 1981 book by Eric Jones, *The European Miracle: Environments, Economies and Geopolitics in the History of Europe and Asia.*

iii Some of the courses available include:

- BA Community Youth Work – Dundalk IT
- B.Soc.Sc. in Youth and Community Work – UCC
- Diploma in Community and Youth Work – NUI Maynooth

- B.Sc. (Hons) in Community Youth Work – UUJ
- Diploma in Youth and Community Work – Brunel University

iv This reference is 'Community Work in Ireland' from 1989 and is available on PDF on the Combat Poverty Agency (CPA) website (http://www.cpa.ie). It was co-edited by the CWC and CPA and Mary Whelan's chapter looks at training and professionalisation.

III

Futures

8

Irish Youth Work: Exploring the Potential for Social Change[i]

David Treacy

Introduction

This chapter will seek to examine the concepts of 'social control' and 'social change' and briefly refer to theoretical models (Hurley and Treacy, 1993) that provide a framework for examining and debating youth work practice in terms of its outcomes in society. The models are referred to here simply to contextualise the debate about the role of youth work as an agent of 'social control' or 'social change'. In this chapter it will be argued that in most cases youth work in Ireland is practised in ways that are conservative in orientation. This will be illustrated by examining the ever-evolving role of youth work and the relationships generated by State funding of youth organisations. As youth work is an informal education process complementary to formal education as defined in the Youth Work Act 2001, it is important to also examine the role of formal education in maintaining significant inequalities in Irish society that affect the life opportunities of young people from working-class areas.

I will examine how the underfunding of the youth work sector by the Department of Education and Science over 30 years has resulted in youth organisations pursuing funding from other statutory funders such as the Department of Justice, Equality and Law Reform and the Department of Health and Children. The focus of many of the funding schemes administered by these departments requires youth organisations to address society's concerns about 'problem young people' or young people with 'problems'. It will be argued that this strategy has resulted in confusing the role of youth work with an educational process and has contributed to a growing concern that youth work practice may be losing its direction. This confusion may be compounded by the reassignment of the youth work remit from the Department of Education and Science to the Office of the Minister for Children and Youth Affairs.

I suggest that youth work in the Irish context is still a relatively new discipline and it is therefore imperative for the sector to develop a clear vision of purpose that recognises young people's right to participate in public spheres; emphasising a practice that enables their voices to be heard above those of the vested interests in society. Youth workers need to develop their capacity as 'reflective practitioners' and there is a responsibility on youth organisations to facilitate this process. In addition, pressures to produce 'learning outcomes' and / or moves towards a defined curriculum for youth work practice should be resisted. Instead the youth work sector needs to restate its commitment to the importance of relationships as the focus of its work. Finally, I outline a number of challenges that will confront the sector in the coming years and propose how these might be addressed.

Defining Social Control and Social Change

'Social control' is the term used by sociologists to describe the role that social institutions such as education and social welfare play in maintaining social order and ensuring that the status quo remains in place in respect of who controls wealth and power. Defining 'social change' can be a little more complicated. Theorists of all perspectives agree that every social system or society is continuously changing. The Functionalist sociologist Talcott Parsons (1951: 480), in his analysis of social change, distinguished between change *within* and change *of* the society. Social change *within* society is the orderly process of ongoing change *within* the established boundaries of society, and the social change of society refers to the processes that result in changes of the structures of that society. From a functionalist perspective changes *within* society are acceptable if such changes do not result in a radical redistribution of power or control over the wealth in society. Conflict theorists (Gramsci, 1971; Willis 1977; Apple 1982) argue that society will not change from *within* to a sufficient degree to destabilise the kinds of inequalities in society that maintain the social class structures. They argue that meaningful social change will only come from a radical upheaval in society and the substantial redistribution of power and wealth. However, the distinction between 'social control' and 'social change' is blurred by the recognition of the fact that the cumulative effect of changes *within* the system may result in changes *of* the system.

Returning to the question 'Is youth work contributing to "social control" or "social change"?' the first step is to explore our understanding of the role and the purpose of youth work in Irish society.

The Role and Purpose of Youth Work

The Youth Work Act 2001 defines youth work as 'a planned programme of education designed for the purpose of aiding and enhancing the personal and social development of young persons through their voluntary participation and which is: a) complementary to their formal, academic or vocational education and training; and b) provided primarily by voluntary youth work organisations.'

Young (1999*a*: 3) argues that the emphasis in youth work on the personal development of the young person must be seen 'in terms of the development of the person, their sense of themselves, identity and the values that underpin their actions in the world.' In addition, she states that the emphasis on social development should be considered 'not in terms of "life skills" or learning about issues but rather as the development of young people as social beings in a social world' (Young, 1999*a*: 3). I agree with this broad interpretation, and suggest that youth work must support young people to learn from their experiences, develop the motivation and capacity to examine their values, reflect on the principles that guide their own judgements, and develop the skills to make informed decisions. But how does this happen in the youth work context?

Understanding How Youth Work Works

Coombs *et al.* (1973) offer a classification of education, which is helpful in exploring learning in a youth work setting. The three categories are:

1. *Formal Education*: that which is provided by the State and the education and training systems set up or sponsored by the State.
2. *Informal Education*: the vast area of social interactions in which people acquire attitudes, values, skills and knowledge from daily experience of telling, advising, informing and influencing each other.

3. *Nonformal Education*: the many deliberate educational enterprises set up by agencies outside the formal education system.

These categories are useful when making the distinction between learning in informal social settings and in formal educational settings. While the emphasis of the Youth Work Act 2001 is on a 'planned programme', it is important to recognise that learning occurs in both the nonformal and the informal educational opportunities that arise in youth work processes. Nonformal educational opportunities may be regarded as the programmes provided that have a specific content and are orientated towards particular outcomes. Informal opportunities refer to the variety of unplanned scenarios that arise in youth work contexts, for example, the conversation over a cup of coffee, the argument between two young people over the pool table, etc. Relationships between the young person and the youth worker and between the young people themselves become the catalyst for this learning. As social learning occurs in all youth work situations, the learning outcomes can be both positive and negative for the young people and the broader society. Unintended social learning can reinforce gender stereotyping, racism or bullying if the youth worker does not intervene in the social learning process. It is important therefore that youth workers are conscious of influencing the social learning that is occurring in informal settings as well as that occurring in the content of programmes. The key is to ensure consistency between the nonformal and programme content, all of which should be underwritten by respect for difference. The mismatch between formal and nonformal learning, if not managed or acknowledged, may reinforce negative messages to young people about themselves and their place in their communities.

Youth work relationships must be based on mutual respect, appreciation, trust and concern. Indeed it is 'through such reciprocal relationships, engagement and dialogue that young people can best be supported to become aware of their values; gain critical abilities needed to mediate those values; grow in their ability to make decisions which can be sustained through committed action' (Young 1999*b*: 84). Thus, youth work, like other social processes, is undertaken with an implicit or explicit purpose. As documented by Kiely in Chapter 1, the purpose, methods, programmes and outcomes of any youth work intervention are influenced by the prevailing values of the youth workers and the organisations in which they work. Youth workers, by their own characteristics and behaviour 'can inspire honesty, co-operation, altruism, optimism, care and concern for others; or dishonesty, hypocrisy, pessimism, putdowns and competitiveness' (Rosseter 1987: 54). Therefore, youth workers should strive for a good level of personal awareness regarding their own beliefs, values and attitudes, and 'must bring integrity to their relationships with young people' and demonstrate 'behaviour consistent with their exposed values' (Jeffs and Smith 1996: 52). Thus it becomes important to have a frame of reference that can enable youth workers to examine their own practice and its outcomes, an issue that will be explored later in the chapter.

Theoretical Models of Youth Work

Describing youth work in the Irish context in the 1980s, I wrote that 'as a result of the lack of research or written reflective practice, there was not an adequate body of knowledge to help workers to name, predict and act. There is a need, therefore, for a typology of youth work … based on different perspectives on the social purposes of youth work, derived from general social theory and specifically the sociology of education'(1989: 32). As a consequence, Louise Hurley and I (1993) set out a framework for understanding youth work interventions based on sociological theories and concepts; a framework that also attempted to explain the role of social institutions in society. We presented four models of youth work, which were ideal types rather than descriptions of really existing projects, so that youth workers could compare, contrast and trace the possible influence of different political values and assumptions in the practice context. While recognising that it is somewhat dated, I believe that this framework (briefly summarised in the following paragraphs) remains a helpful tool for critically reflecting on the contrasting social purposes that youth work may serve (refer to Hurley and Treacy (1993) for more detailed discussion). At the very least, it reminds us that education is never neutral and that youth work practice is implicitly and, occasionally, explicitly political.

The four theoretical models of youth work in Hurley and Treacy's (1993) framework are the Character Building Model;[ii] the Personal Development Model;[iii] the Critical Social Education Model[iv] and the Radical Social Change Model.[v] In the Character Building Model the needs of society are prioritised over those of the young people, as it is assumed that young people should learn to abide by the cultural consensus, accept the dominant moral values of society and contribute to the maintenance of social order through their allegiance to existing social institutions and structures. By contrast, the Personal Development Model focuses more on the individual, emphasising the personal needs of the young person, with little reference to the social situation or environment in which the young person lives. The youth worker's role is to enable young people to acquire the skills to take on the responsibilities of adult life and to develop the necessary social skills to participate within society (Hurley and Treacy, 1993: 28–30). Despite their apparently different purposes, I argue that both models seek to enable young people to slot smoothly into society and to negotiate and regulate their lives in ways that do not disrupt the status quo.

Alternatively, the Critical Social Education Model is concerned with raising young people's awareness of how dominant value systems promote inequality and justify the oppression of a range of social groups. Young people are encouraged to analyse, critique and re-imagine social relations and to seek changes within existing social and political structures (Hurley and Treacy, 1993: 41-43). A more overtly critical and even revolutionary purpose is articulated in the Radical Social Change Model. Here the purpose of youth work is to promote a socialist consciousness in agreement with and actively alongside working-class young people (Davies, 1977; Taylor, 1987). Programmes are developed to indoctrinate young people with pre-set socialist perspectives and to recruit them as political activists to revolutionary political organisations (Hurley and Treacy, 1993: 45–57). For both of these models there is a strong focus on young people's creative energies with the hope that they might be unleashed in the name of social and political transformation.

While acknowledging that the models are academic constructs rather than rigid categorisations of practice, I would argue that Irish youth work practice, in the main, reflects the philosophy of either the Character Building or the Personal Development Models. The reasons for this are explored in the following sections.

The Role of Youth Work in Irish Society – Social Control or Social Change?

Historically youth organisations have tended to be conservative in their outlook and view of society. In both the UK and Ireland the pioneers of youth work were motivated by an often moralistic perception of pressing social issues. In the UK this motivation was largely linked to a concern for the decline in moral standards related to industrialisation (Leighton 1972), while in Ireland a commitment to nationalism and Catholicism was the primary motivation for pioneers in the early years of the State (Hurley, 1992*a*). Historically, youth work was carried out by predominantly middle-class youth workers and targeted at working-class young people. As documented by Davies and Gibson (1967: 34), youth work as a distinct form of practice emerged as a response to middle-class anxiety about a perceived moral decline among the working class and was informed by 'a powerful social conscience and a deeply held religious conviction' (Davies and Gibson, 1967: 34). Though motivations and values have changed over time, the primacy of voluntarism and delivery by voluntary organisations still provide the backbone of current youth work provision. The development of youth work responses is still guided by specific values and philosophies derived from a set of diverse voluntary traditions.

The State became involved in direct provision of youth work in both Ireland and Britain because of growing concern about social issues, particularly the perception of increasing juvenile crime and the problems generated by unemployment, etc. State intervention occurred in England in the 1930s and expanded rapidly in the 1950s and 1960s. In Ireland, we witnessed limited State intervention in the 1930s, which had intensified by the late 1980s and became more pronounced from 2000 onwards. The thrust of statutory involvement has been to fund and support the voluntary sector to work with young people and to take on direct provision only in very limited circumstances.[vi]

Throughout the 1970s and 1980s, and particularly with the increasing employment of paid youth workers in Ireland, the focus of practice began to move from the Character Building Model to the Personal Development Models of youth work (Treacy 1989; Hurley, 1990; Galvin, 1995). The emphasis on personal development as a model of practice was also evident in Government reports published at this time (Department of Education, 1977, 1980). Interestingly, in 1985, the Irish Government established a National Youth Policy Committee and its report, known as the Costello Report (Department of Education, 1984), promoted an alternative view of the purpose of youth work, a point already noted by Kiely and McMahon (see Chapters 1 and 5). It emphasised the empowerment of young people and encouraged youth workers to engage in processes that enabled young people to become critical participants in society: a view of youth work more in line with the Critical Social Education Model. The report explicitly acknowledged the inequalities in society and claimed that greater equality could be achieved through enhanced participation by young people in political, economic and social institutions (Jenkinson, 1996: 41). It is important to emphasise that the shift in thinking reflected in this document did encourage individual projects to develop practices that were informed by principles such as participation, liberation and empowerment.

However, it did not translate into a change of approach in the majority of youth work projects and organisations. The continued dominance of the Character Building and Personal Development Models is clearly illustrated when we consider how the youth work sector presented itself to government and state funding bodies and defined its own role in addressing the issues facing young people in society.

As explained in Chapter 5, the National Youth Council of Ireland (NYCI) is the representative body of all voluntary youth work organisations. In 1994 the Council produced a significant policy document entitled *Towards the Development of a Comprehensive Youth Service* (National Youth Council of Ireland, 1994). This document offers an insight into the dominant perspective of the youth work sector at that time, illustrating how it sold its potential as a vehicle for addressing the issues facing young people. The following example is highlighted, not as a criticism of NYCI, but merely as a reflection of a view that was pervasive during the period. The document recognised that inequalities are reinforced and perpetuated from one generation to the next by the education system. It stated that 'substantial differences exist among social groups in their access to educational resources, their treatment by the education system but particularly in the outcomes of the educational programmes which they receive' (National Youth Council of Ireland, 1994: 43). Nonetheless it proceeded to assert that 'education cannot achieve its objectives unless accompanied by significant changes in the young person's life experience as a whole and this is where the Youth Service can have an effect as an essential element of the education system' (National Youth Council of Ireland, 1994: 43). The NYCI clearly saw the role of youth work, in partnership with the statutory sector, as promoting the integration of young people into the existing social and economic structures in society. It also stated that 'acute forms of disadvantage such as substance abuse, homelessness, and the disadvantage experienced by young offenders, young Travellers and young people with disability can be dealt with by the youth service working in tandem with statutory agencies' (National Youth Council of Ireland, 1994: 44). It seemed that the emphasis of such a youth service would be on supporting young people to adapt to their circumstances, to cope with rather than challenge the existing order of things. This document proceeded to call for the 'formulation and adoption of a policy framework for the development of services to disadvantaged young people which recognises the present and potential future role of the voluntary youth service in catering for the needs of disadvantaged young people' (National Youth Council of Ireland, 1994: 44). Therefore, the sector's response to poverty and social inequality was to call for long-term funding for youth work in order to cater for specific groups of young people. The 'youth service' sought to become part of the institutional response and to passively involve young people defined as 'disadvantaged' as consumers of their services.

When the causes of social exclusion are located in those who are under-represented, then those individuals and groupings become the main focus of intervention. As observed by Tett (2006), the reasons for their exclusion are attributed to their failure to engage appropriately with existing social systems. This failure is put down to factors such as a lack of motivation to participate on their part, little encouragement from peer group and family, and financial constraints. The youth work response that emanates from this perspective fails to harness the practice's emancipatory potential in the interests of engaging young people in the pursuit of social change.

Youth Work and the Formal Education System

The second reason for my assertion that youth work is practised predominantly in socially controlling ways relates to its status as an educational process 'complementary to the formal education system', as stated in the Youth Work Act 2001. Despite the fact that Ireland has been transformed economically, inequalities remain deeply rooted in society and are particularly evident in the field of education. Statistics relating to education have highlighted consistently the ongoing failures of the formal education system to meet the needs of particular learners. According to Kelleghan *et al.* (1995), one in ten children leaving primary schools has a literacy problem. A report prepared for the Department of Education found that more than 30 per cent of children in primary schools experience severe literacy problems (Eivers *et al.*, 2005). A similar report by the same authors published in late 2005 reaffirmed these findings and also noted that in some poorer areas up to 50 per cent of pupils have literacy difficulties (Eivers *et al.*, 2005). A national survey of new entrants to higher education highlighted the importance of socio-economic status in determining the success or failure of individuals within the education system. The survey noted 'persistent social inequalities ... reflected in the over-representation of children of certain groups among new entrants to higher education, relative to their share of the population' (O'Connell *et al.*, 2006: 136).

There is continued evidence of a direct relationship between the social background of a child and his or her educational outcomes. 'The worrying tendency for educational disadvantage to cluster in specific schools/areas and to be reproduced across generations raises serious equity issues and highlights the need for effective educational interventions'(Department of Education and Science 2003*a*: 7). The findings also imply an education system that compounds rather than compensates for existing disadvantages. This is evident in the emphasis placed on achievement in education. Students are encouraged to strive for a high level of results and when those who succeed are rewarded, the education system fosters and promotes the concept of 'achievement'. Despite the inequality described above 'the meritocratic system is perceived as the fairest way to distribute educational advantage' (Connolly, 2007: 124). So if youth work complements the formal education system and at the same time pursues a social change agenda, one might expect tensions to arise.

More and more local youth services in Ireland are engaging with schools by supporting young people to stay in school. To the best of my knowledge, there is no evidence to suggest that this engagement has been very problematic in the Irish context. Nonetheless, the overriding tendency in the youth work literature is to portray youth work as being at odds with traditional or mainstream notions of education and teaching. For example, Rosseter (1987) describes youth workers as educators who practise an 'open' rather than a 'closed' form of education practice. He suggests that the differences between the two areas are rooted in the fact that youth work is based on voluntary association whereas schooling is compulsory. Others such as Walther *et al.* (2004), writing about youth work in German schools, suggest that there is a discrepancy between voluntary youth work and the involuntary nature of educationally based youth work. Tett (2000) and Bowie (2002) have also identified the potential for conflict between teachers and youth workers because of their different styles of engagement with young people and because the aims, culture and procedures are very different in youth work and schooling practices. It would be worth exploring if such tensions are manifest in the Irish context. The implication for the youth sector is that it needs to develop a clear analysis of the place of marginalised young people in society and begin to address the causes of inequalities in partnership with young people. Just because youth organisations are funded to address the symptoms of social inequalities, this does not necessarily mean that they do so in ways that are consistent with a social change agenda.

Challenges for the Future

In this chapter I have argued that the primary focus of current youth work practice is on the personal development of individual young people. Significant recent developments in youth work policy were discussed in Chapters 5 and 7. I would suggest that the creation of the North–South Education and Training Standards Committee (NSETS), the post of the Assessor of Youth Work, the publication of the Journal *Youth Studies Ireland* and the possible establishment of the Youth Work Development Unit provide a unique opportunity for a debate on the purpose of youth work in this State. There are a number of challenges that the sector faces at policy and practice levels and these must be addressed if youth work is to have a greater impact on the causes of inequality and not just its consequences. This shift in emphasis requires workers and organisations 'to see the connections between their experiences, young people's experiences and the impact of global capitalism at micro and macro levels' (Husein, 1997: 65). In the following sections the key challenges are discussed in greater detail.

Being Clear about the Boundaries of Youth Work

Smith suggests that '[youth] workers may know they are not teachers or social workers but are unable to find enough in the concept of youth worker to explain their role' (Smith, 1988: 53). Research in Northern Ireland found that no universally agreed definition of youth work prevailed and concluded that '... there seemed to be more consensus on what youth work was *not*' (Harland and Morgan 2006: 9). There are a number of reasons why the purpose of youth work is particularly unclear in Ireland. Firstly, the voluntary nature of provision together with the lack of a professional association means in reality that the title 'youth worker' is not legally protected; anybody can call themselves a youth worker regardless of qualifications and experience. Secondly, the need to find new sources of funding has been a major spur towards the greater involvement of youth organisations in a series of initiatives often well outside their normal spheres of activity.

For example, the Health Service Executive's sponsorship of health promotion programmes, neighbourhood youth projects and, recently, youth cafés, has emerged as an important source of additional funding. The development of a hundred Garda Youth Diversion Projects, funded by the Department of Justice, Equality and Law Reform in the last ten years and delivered by no more than five youth organisations, is also a considerable development. Both of these important new funding streams have had an impact on the role of individual youth organisations. Youth work has been remodelled to deliver employment training programmes, general and specific life skills coaching, health promotion, sex and drugs education, crime diversion schemes, school attendance initiatives and social inclusion measures. However, funding does not come without strings attached and funding pressures threaten to submerge many of the distinctive and diverse traditions that youth workers have long championed. While this funding has enabled the maintenance and development of certain aspects of provision for young people, the overall effect has been to obscure the fundamental purpose of youth work and cause confusion regarding that purpose among young people and sometimes among youth workers themselves.

The confusion about the role may well be further compounded by the integration of youth work into the Office for the Minister for Children and Youth Affairs and the transfer of funding for youth work from the Department of Education and Science to the Department of Health and Children. The Minister for Children and Youth Affairs has stated that this move will facilitate the co-ordination and integration of services for children and young people. There are some concerns that, while this will provide opportunities for cross-agency planning and 'joined up' responses to young people's needs, it may further undermine youth work's claim to be a distinct practice governed by a particular set of values, as youth work is seen as just another service to be delivered to young people.

The future of the Youth Work Act 2001 within this new arrangement will rest on the extent to which the Vocational Education Committees (VECs), through the Irish Vocational Education Association (IVEA), and the youth work sector, through NYCI, can convince the Office of the Minister for Children and Youth Affairs that the Youth Work Act already provides for the co-ordination and integration of youth work with other services to young people. Both the IVEA and NYCI have made submissions to that effect. The future of youth work will depend on the capacity of the youth work sector to retain a clear sense of purpose whilst contributing to the policies and provision of other organisations that work with young people.

Young (1999*a*) has identified ways for the sector to increase youth work's credibility. These involve being clear about youth work's purpose and articulating it unambiguously, highlighting youth work's particular strengths in meeting the personal and social development needs of young people, and constantly improving youth work practice, provision and management so as to make everyday youth work a truly meaningful practice. Unfortunately, recent developments in the UK,[vii] which have shifted the focus of youth work to 'measurable outcomes' related to 'education for work', run contrary to the emphasis that youth work has traditionally placed on the 'person-centred' approach. In Ireland, the youth work sector has now reached this point and as a consequence there are serious ethical issues for youth workers, policy-makers and funding bodies. The concern is that the continued concentration on targeted funding requires youth organisations and youth workers to set aside their professional judgement regarding with whom they ought to work. Where the focus is upon the control of young people, then inevitably those who pose the least threat will receive the least attention. However, this will mean the neglect of work with those who tend to be less visible, less troublesome and less demanding. Young (1999*a*) believes it is important for youth workers to keep focused on the fact that they do not work with young people solely because they are 'in trouble' or the 'cause of trouble'. Indeed, youth work programmes that focus on particular issues, such as harm minimisation or alternatives to school, may be criticised for addressing the symptoms rather than the root cause of the problem (Morgan *et al.*, 2000). For national youth organisations, the challenge is to focus on the causes of inequality in Irish society and not just on the symptoms. They must remain resolute in their view that 'young people are not a "problem" to be solved, and youth work is not about solving problems' (Department of Education and Science, 2003*b*: 14) and must challenge the negative stereotyping of young people by the State, the media and others.

The Challenges of Accountability – Avoiding the Pressure to Define Youth Work 'Outcomes'

The youth work sector is now entering a phase where organisations are being asked to make explicit what was previously hinted at and accepted as implicit. Developments in the UK show that 'funders are seeking to impose conditions which require youth workers to show that they have reduced offending, anti-social behaviour or risk activities in a given area' (Banks and Jeffs, 1999: 100). It may be only a matter of time before funders such as the Irish Youth Justice Service demand definable outcomes for their investment in Youth Diversion Projects. As has happened in the UK, youth workers will feel the pressure to concentrate on the 'product' aspect of their programmes rather than on the 'process', which traditionally gave youth work definition. Educational interventions relate in some way to either the sort of individual or world that those undertaking the work wish to achieve and 'interventions that do not pay attention to ends, but merely process, cease to be educational in intent' (Jeffs and Smith, 1998/1999: 7). Nonetheless, it could be argued that growing pressure to formalise youth work and to produce identifiable outcomes will erode the capacity of workers to construct 'communities of enquiry' (Haynes, 1988: 133). According to Haynes (1988), these refer to the spaces created to work with young people constructing programmes and creating experiences of shared mutual learning, which respond directly to the expressed needs of the participants. The youth work sector in Ireland must learn from the UK where the setting of targets and funding by results has redefined the objectives of the programmes provided by the youth service 'in line with a series of hard or quantifiable outcomes, such as a qualification, a place on another scheme or programme or entry into further education' (Mizen, 1999: 30).

Mizen (1999) describes how these targets have resulted in youth work providers selecting those young people who are most likely to achieve the prescribed outcomes and have therefore undermined provision for those for whom such objectives are neither feasible nor desirable. In some cases, where contracts are now linked to 'payment by results', the impact of punitive financial penalties impose either 'conformity or a requirement that workers lie about the outcomes and the work undertaken to secure continuation funding' (Banks and Jeffs, 1999: 100).

The need to think about accountability in broad and more creative terms is vital. Youth workers are and should be accountable to their peers, to the young people involved and the communities in which they work. Because youth work proposes that young people are active participants or partners in the youth work process, good practice should be accompanied by systems in which young people evaluate not just the programmes but also the total experience of their involvement. In Dublin, Sphere 17 Youth Service has created a process that enables young people to become active members of the board and to be partners in the recruitment and selection of staff. This is an important statement about the place of young people in this project.

Stacey (2001) describes a model of 'youth partnership accountability' where the young people have significant control over their project or service, with the youth workers taking up positions as supporters. The workers still take action or make decisions, but with the explicit permission of the young people. This type of partnership changes the power dynamic between young people and youth workers and requires an exploration of trust, respect and reciprocity. To actively engage with this model would require the development of a process of critical reflection by both the young people and the youth workers. In addition, systems should be in place to support young people to have their concerns and complaints appropriately dealt with in an open and honest manner. In addition, the structures and processes of a youth organisation should be publicly visible, for example, all decisions should be published and scrutiny from the young people, their families and the community should be actively sought. Systems should be created to collect feedback from all stakeholders and should support organisations to address the issues raised in the feedback.

Negotiating the Scope for Youth Worker Discretion?

Despite my assertion that youth work practice is in the main a vehicle for 'social control' it can be argued that 'the front line nature of youth work organisations and the contradictions of policy makers' expectations of this area of work allows a degree of freedom for practitioners' (Jeffs and Smith, 1990: xi). Most youth workers would probably not describe the purpose of such work as social control and would tend to stress the development of critical thinking, questioning and extending young people's choices (Banks and Jeffs 1999: 99). There are projects which clearly articulate such a vision and apply it through their practice. I illustrate this with two examples based on my experience in Dublin City. BelonGTo (the Lesbian, Gay, Bisexual and Transgender Project) and Pavee Point (the Travellers' youth project) clearly identify critical social education as the model underpinning their practice. Both projects work with the young people to enable them to articulate the issues affecting their lives and then work with them to raise awareness and campaign on these issues at national level. Other projects, such as Rialto Youth Project and St Michael's Youth Project in Inchicore, use the arts as a vehicle to enable young people to explore the issues in their lives. By working in partnership with the Irish Museum of Modern Art, the projects have drawn on artistic expertise to work with the young people to produce fine art and drama. Young people gain expertise and confidence, but are also exploring the issues that most affect their lives. These all demonstrate that it is still possible to address questions of inequality and exploitation in day-to-day practice and perhaps to do so by using more creative and participatory means.

The Youth Work Relationship

The relationship between the youth worker and the young person, while a constant in youth work, is described 'as the most elusive of all aspects (of youth work).... Indeed, most accounts of practice focus upon activity, assessing the work with young people in terms of "doing" rather than "being"' (Richardson, 1997: 91). In my view, this is also true of youth work in Ireland, where the relationship as the key to the learning process has been 'downplayed' because of anxieties generated by child protection concerns: 'While youth workers recognise that "relationships" are at the core of the work, they also know that personal and relational language is a deeply problematic area of public communication' (Spence 2007: 14). The lack of clarity about youth work's purpose coupled with an anxiety about child abuse have meant that youth workers in Ireland have in the main reverted to interpreting the Department of Education's Child Protection Guidelines as if they were the conclusive statement on the 'rules for engagement' with young people. Because of its informal setting the youth work relationship can feel like a friendship: open, equal, with lots of the elements of friendship such as good natured 'slagging' and play. The language used by youth workers is often the language used by young people. In such a context, youth workers need to know what the youth work relationship is about and need to be clear about its boundaries. Under these circumstances, awareness, debate, guidance and the pursuit of clarity about good practice is essential for the safety and integrity of both youth workers and young people (Sercombe, 2007). Such a debate in the UK and Australia has resulted in an agreed statement of values and principles of ethical conduct for youth workers in each jurisdiction. In Ireland it is appropriate at this time to move towards a similar ethical framework for the engagement of youth workers with young people.

A further validation of the importance of relationships in youth work is described by Smith (2003: 48) who argues that 'there is a danger of losing "relationship" as a defining feature of youth work practice when the emphasis is on organising youth work around concepts such as outcomes and curriculum.' He argues that there is significant evidence of friendships and how they influence how people feel about their lives and the world. He cites Putman (2000) who shows, for example, that joining in with the life of a club can significantly extend an individual's life expectancy and sense of well-being. According to Smith (2003*a*), Putnam's discussion of these issues, which is informed by the concept of social capital (as noted by Meade in Chapter 3), provides youth workers with a powerful rationale for their activities. Their working environment in the group, club or organisation is potentially central to the fostering of social capital within communities and provides a means of cultivating social networks and the norms of reciprocity and trustworthiness. Furthermore, Putman argues that crime can be reduced, educational achievement enhanced and better health fostered through the strengthening of social capital across and within communities. Putman's (2000) work also problematises the targeting of interventions at those who present the most significant social problems, arguing that it ties youth workers to the achievement of specific and individualised outcomes that further social cohesion and order. Smith (2003*a*) argues that the youth work sector must have the confidence in its own ability to stand with and for young people.

The Challenge of Becoming 'Reflective Practitioners'

Youth work practice is produced and experienced in specific social and historical conditions and involves particular moral and political considerations. As noted earlier, what youth workers engage in is 'intrinsically political, affecting the life chances of those involved in the process by affecting their access to an interesting life and material well-being' (Carr and Kemmis 1986: 39). Youth workers therefore need to be open and committed to the concept of personal change and to develop their capacity as 'reflective practitioners'. To develop as 'reflective practitioners' youth workers must build communities of peers who engage in critical conversations about practice (Smith, 1994). The cultivation of judgement is dependent upon forms of communal life that facilitate engagement and conversation about what is good (Bernstein, 1983: 225). Here is a powerful case for the collective exploration of practice. It provides a rationale for youth workers, looking not just at what they may be feeling or thinking but at their interactions, and how these should be located within a dialogue about what may be appropriate for a particular community of practice. In Young's view (1999*a*: 110), 'This is crucial, not only for their personal development but also in order to enable them to become well versed in the reflective and deliberative processes through which they seek to support young people.' This should begin as part of their pre-service professional training and continue throughout their in-service training and development. Creating an open and transparent culture in an organisation is a major challenge for all management staff. However, if the sector wants young people to reflect on the way they live their lives and youth workers are asked to develop the capacity to 'critically reflect' on their practice, then management has an obligation to put in place systems that support such reflection. Such systems may include the provision of practice supervision as well as task supervision. The management must role model or mirror such practices in the manner in which they engage staff in the planning and evaluation processes of the organisation.

Conclusion

Writing this chapter has been an interesting experience as it has provided me with an opportunity to reflect on developments in youth work in the past ten years. Having been a senior manager in the sector over that period I have found it challenging to be wholly objective. That youth work practice primarily centres on the personal development of young people should come as no surprise as this can be said about most youth work practice in the UK and Northern Ireland too. Furthermore, it is difficult to escape the conclusion that, despite the expansion in youth work provision over that last decade, much of that provision can be described as substandard recreation at its worst, with young people as consumers of services. At best it can be seen as limited to narrow personal development outcomes that are targeted at *some* young people. This is not to deny the existence of exceptional projects and exceptional youth workers who work with young people in a manner that has significant impact on young peoples' lives. But the number of projects that hold the engagement of young people in processes of social change as a central and explicit objective is very limited.

However, a concern with or commitment to social change is not just a theoretical issue and should not be dismissed by practitioners as such. In reality, youth work that describes itself as 'person centred' and starting where the 'young person is at' must work in the best interests of young people and as such needs to be concerned about their place in society and how they are treated by that society. Despite significant evidence of the persistence of inequality there is a perception that social class has declined as a significant factor in the routine structuring of social and economic relations in contemporary society. Even where the extent of poverty and deepening inequality is recognised, 'class may be reduced to only one among equally significant variables in a complex system of stratification, and thereby minimised as an explanatory concept' (Law and Mooney, 2006: 525). Yet, social class continues to exercise a profound influence upon the life chances and experiences of young people in the spheres of education, health, employment and housing, and even has an influence on social experiences such as leisure and friendship. Despite this, working-class young people have become the object of overlapping pathologisation processes. This is reflected in the debates about educational attainment, patterns of ill-health and, most publicly, in the mass media in relation to questions of criminal justice (see Devlin, 2006*a*). Terms such as 'deprived', 'marginalised' and 'disadvantaged' are used to describe categories of people thought to be outside the conventional arrangements of 'social stratification and transform the impoverished working class into illegible ciphers of amoral cultures of despondency' (Law and Mooney, 2006: 525).

The persistent inequalities in Irish society that affect the lives of working-class young people are acute social issues and should be of concern to all youth work practitioners. When practice fails to address or acknowledge how inequalities in society impact on young people, it actually attempts to convince young people that if they work hard they can achieve anything. Alternatively, when youth work practice begins to question inequalities and dominant social values it begins to becomes consciously political. Therefore, there is a need for youth work to place young people at the heart of its practice and for youth workers to act as advocates for young people, not just the individuals they are working with, and to take up the cause of young people as a social group that is disadvantaged by society. One positive recent example is where a number of key youth organisations led by the NYCI campaigned against the introduction of Anti-Social Behaviour Orders (ASBOs). This campaign did not prevent the introduction of ASBOs but it did succeed in modifying the approach to their implementation, thus reducing the criminalisation of young people. But these examples are too few and no youth organisation has taken a committed stand on the class-based inequalities in society.

Finally, the youth work sector has been successful in using opportunities to obtain additional funding and recognition by promoting itself as an intervention that can be successful in dealing with the problems of young people or 'problem' young people. Youth work organisations have sold 'the learning experience' and the particular qualities of their institution in order to get the funding they need to survive. Complex processes have been reduced to easily identified packages; philosophies to sound bites; and young people and their parents become consumers (Jeffs and Smith, 2002; Smith 2003*a*). It could be argued that the youth work sector has been successful in integrating itself into mainstream society, and with the participation of NYCI in the social partnership process, the sector is well positioned to contribute to the process of social change and combat the social inequalities that are so prevalent in Irish society. However, the converse could also be argued: that the sector has become too mainstreamed or co-opted to be a strong independent critical voice on behalf of young people (a point also made by McMahon in Chapter 5).

I suggest, therefore, that the youth work sector needs to develop a clear vision of purpose that provides a practice that recognises young people's right to participate in the public sphere and enables young people's voices to be heard. The future of youth work is dependent on the sector taking this opportunity to review its approach and hopefully put the position of working-class young people, their lack of opportunities in society and the need for social change at the heart of the debate. In doing so, the sector may finally answer the fundamental question of 'What is youth work for?' and do so before youth work's purpose is conclusively defined by others.

Notes

i I would like to thank Celene Dunne for reading this chapter on more than one occasion and providing very helpful feedback.

ii This model of youth work mirrors the functionalist perspective in sociology. Functionalists such as Durkheim (1956) viewed the person as a 'bundle of desires' who needs to be regulated and controlled for the sake of social order and individual happiness. Hence, there is concern regarding the effective regulation and control of the individual through key socialising agents including the family, education, religion and the media. Youth work from this perspective recognises that young people are in a stage of transition from childhood to adulthood and must be prepared for specific roles in society. It recognises that young people have the capacity and proclivity to rebel – therefore their energy and drive should be directed in a constructive fashion towards socially acceptable ends. The purpose of youth work is to successfully transmit the existing moral and social values of society to young people. Consequently, decision-making structures are hierarchical in nature – adults dominate and all major decisions are decided by them.

iii The Functionalist perspective is challenged by a broad sociological tradition called Phenomenology, which is more concerned with interpreting the social world than explaining it. Within this sociological school are two broad strands, namely the interpretive paradigm (Weber, 1947) and 'interactionism' (Mead 1934). Interpretative approaches attempt to understand social reality from the perspective of the participant in the situation. Interpretivists argue that humans are thinking, feeling beings capable of action and creativity. Interactionism as a micro-sociological approach focuses on the interaction of individuals and small groups or the processes that occur when people come together in social situations. Interpretivism and interactionism both present a perspective in which individuals negotiate, regulate and live their lives within the status quo. Change in society occurs through the everyday interactions of people and is very gradual.

iv The radical humanist paradigm (Willis 1977; Apple, 1982) is a resistance theory based on conflict theories arising from Marxism. Radical humanism recognises that the individual is dominated by the social institutions of the State and that certain classes are oppressed marginalised. For example, they believe that education promotes ideas and beliefs that benefit the ruling class in society. This perspective recognises that conflict and contradiction are inevitable in society as different groups compete for power and resources. Change in society can only occur through the empowerment of the oppressed and their liberation from oppressive social structures.

v This model is based on the radical structuralist paradigm, which concentrates upon structural relationships within society. Advocates, drawing on Marxist theory, differ between those who concentrate on exploring the structural links between the education system and social order and those who seek to explore the ways in which cultural beliefs and practices support capitalist society (Bowles and Gintis 1976). Youth workers with a commitment to radical social change argue that the individual can do little to effect change in society. They see societal conflict and contradiction as inevitable as different groups compete for power and resources. Eventually, however, these contradictions will reach a crisis point that engenders revolutionary change and the displacement of existing social structures. It is through such major conflict and change that emancipation of the person from the social structures in which they live takes place.

vi The establishment of Comhairle le Leas Óige (currently City of Dublin Youth Service Board) in Dublin City under the auspices of the City of Dublin Vocational Education Committee in 1942 is the exception.

vii The changes proposed for the role of youth work were contained in *Transforming Youth Work: Developing Youth Work for Young People*

(Department for Education and Employment, 2001) and the integration of the local authority youth services into the Connexions Service. Both these initiatives shifted the focus of youth work to targeting individuals who were at risk of drug, alcohol or substance abuse, or at risk of offending or anti-social behaviour.

9

Community Development and Participatory Theory: Problems and Possibilities

Chris McInerney

Introduction

In 1990 the Irish Government established the Community Development Programme (CDP) 'in recognition of the role of community development in tackling poverty and disadvantage' (Department of Social Welfare and Combat Poverty Agency, 1995). In its early years, the official description of the programme saw it playing a role in 'encouraging greater participation in public decision making', 'influencing change in structures, policies and processes which contribute to poverty and exclusion' and 'seeking an equitable distribution of power and resources in order to ensure a fairer society' (Department of Social Welfare and Combat Poverty Agency, 1995). Since its establishment the programme has grown considerably, from 15 projects in its first year to 181 by 2007, making the programme one of the principal mechanisms of support to community development in Ireland.[i] However, it is not just in terms of size that the CDP has changed. Its mission and structures too have been adapted to fit new political and economic realities. For example, in its early stages, support for 'setting standards and promoting good practice' was provided by the specialist staff of the CPA but by 2009 this role has disappeared, and fears for the continued existence of this independent agency have proved to be well founded (*Irish Times*, 2008*a*; *Irish Times*, 2008*b*). Instead, most operational responsibilities are now assumed by civil servants located in the Department of Community, Rural and Gaeltacht Affairs, few of whom have any specialised knowledge of community development or social exclusion.

More importantly though, significant changes in the functions of the programme have been introduced. Nowadays, the CDP is largely described in terms of service delivery, such as: 'provision of information, advice and support to particular target groups...'; providing 'practical assistance to community groups, for example, photocopying'; 'provision of adult education courses and training opportunities'; 'support for local enterprise and job creation initiatives'; and 'support for participation in local development initiatives' (Department of Community, Rural and Gaeltacht Affairs, 2008).[ii] More significantly, CDPs are expected to 'deliver policies and provide services in the public interest and it is essential that this is done in an equitable, transparent and non-partisan way' (Combat Poverty Agency, 2007: 19). This potentially leads to the conclusion that the State is using 'local community groups as a low cost public expenditure mechanism for the delivery of its responsibilities for welfare provision' (Combat Poverty Agency, 2007: 20). Gone are any references to structural change, greater participation in public decision-making or the distribution of power in Irish society. Gone too is the role of external scrutiny with the virtual elimination of the CDP advisory committee, which had comprised representatives of funded projects, relevant statutory agencies and key community sector organisations.

While the experience of the CDP is only one small vignette of the community development landscape in Ireland, it is highly significant and illustrative of the change in the nature of community development within the last two decades. From a position where there was some degree of open engagement in the early 1990s, by 2009 it might be argued that the State has little interest in community development as a process of empowerment and inclusion, seeing it more as a means of service delivery and, ultimately, social control.

The objective of this chapter is to reflect on the capacity of community development to function in such an era of economic, political and ideological contraction and associated patterns of State control. It more especially explores whether community development retains a capacity to realise its progressive potential to address social exclusion, given that the concept has become so widely used and many of its original meanings vacated. These issues are explored largely though the lens of participatory democracy which is frequently linked with community development (Taylor and Mayo, 2008). The chapter, therefore, looks at the promise of participatory democracy in Ireland, at the reality of some participation experiences and, more broadly, at the potential and pitfalls in approaches to participatory democracy. The chapter concludes by introducing a number of possible future scenarios for community development in Ireland and suggests that the community sector's potential for progressive action is contingent on the quality of social, political and economic analysis undertaken and its willingness to test the boundaries of its engagement with the State.

Some Understandings and Assumptions

In exploring the future shape and role of community development it must of course be realised that analyses and understandings of some fundamental concepts may differ. In particular, the community development landscape in Ireland is populated by a host of approaches, beliefs, values and ideologies. Many of its original, more progressive foundations have been harnessed by the State and a myriad of local development networks and, in some cases at least, have become distanced from notions of democratic participation, equality, social inclusion and more progressive approaches to the expression of citizen voice (Craig, 1998; Taylor and Mayo, 2008). At this point, then, it cannot be assumed that all community development practitioners will assume these terms to mean the same thing, nor that all have the potential or even wish to operate from within more progressive, inclusive spaces (see Chapter 3). It is useful at this stage, therefore, to set some definitional boundaries.

Competing Community Development Frameworks

Different analytical starting points and ideologies generate related community development practices, which, in turn, generate distinct equality, participation and power outcomes. These outcomes, and the factors that produce them, are well illustrated in Kenny's (2002) presentation of four community development frameworks that give rise to different community development practices. The first of these is the charity framework, which is informed by 'thematic discourses' about empathy, virtue and compassion; moral discipline and service; and dependency and patronage (Kenny, 2002: 286). Within this framework the potential exists for distinctions to be drawn between the deserving and the undeserving poor and between those willing or unwilling to help themselves. Power clearly rests with the community development practitioner who may view their target group as a passive rather than an active actor.

The second framework, described as the 'welfare industry framework', is based on two principles, namely that it is the role of the State to intervene to ensure 'stability in peoples lives' and that such intervention should be based on principles of 'social justice, social equality and redistribution' (Kenny, 2002: 289). Here, while there may be an emphasis on redistribution, it is suggested that there is a strong charity influence and a tendency to establish a professional–client relationship, rather than a citizen empowerment orientation. Welfare frameworks are likely to focus more heavily on income aspects of social exclusion and on achieving minimum living standards and, as a consequence, may ignore many significant, non-income realities.

The third framework is termed the activist framework and is organised around principles of solidarity and mutuality. This approach is frequently member oriented, heavily emphasises community participation and envisages change taking place at the structural level, the ideational level and at a skills level (Kenny, 2002: 290). In particular this framework envisages that 'the realm of politics is extended beyond governments, political parties and experts' (Kenny, 2002: 292), much like what was envisaged by Barber in his efforts to describe a model of strong democracy (Barber, 1984). The activist framework is reflected in the definitions of community work approaches advocated by the Community Workers Co-operative (CWC) in Ireland and Community Development Exchange (CDX) in the UK. So, for example, the CWC understands community work as being about a 'collective focus rather than a response to individual crisis', as being concerned with 'challenging inequitable power relationships' and 'promoting redistribution of wealth and resources in a more just and equitable fashion', as well as promoting 'solidarity with the interests of those experiencing social exclusion'.[iii]

The last of the four frameworks is the 'market' framework and it emphasises discourses of 'individual self-interest and self-help'. This framework, which can be easily aligned with neoliberal analyses, sees the role of community development organisations as being to assume a greater responsibility for service delivery while the State retains control for policy and funding, not unlike versions of associative democratic theory and new public management concepts discussed later.

In practice, elements of all of these frameworks may inform an individual or organisational approach to community development. However, it is likely that one will dominate to form the core of a belief and value system which will subsequently determine the degree to which more progressive or more radical perspectives will be adopted. In contemporary Ireland, as argued by Forde in Chapter 6, the market framework would appear to increasingly inform much of what is described as community development practice, while activist outlooks find themselves marginalised by the narrow orthodoxy of consensus governance.

Approaches to Social Exclusion

Given that community development is often associated with efforts to address social exclusion, it is also important to acknowledge that there are many different approaches to defining and understanding what exclusion means. While there is limited space in this chapter to explore these understandings in any great detail, discourses have been identified which see exclusion as the result of the absence of paid employment (social integration discourses), as a function of income distribution (redistribution discourses), or as a product of the particular characteristics and inactivity of those who are excluded (the moral underclass discourse or MUD) (Levitas, 2004). What these discourses have in common is the emphasis they place on the individual who experiences social exclusion. Other approaches reject this individualised focus and insist that the emphasis be placed instead on failures in the operation of key societal systems which produce exclusion: the democratic and legal system; family and community systems; welfare systems; and labour market systems (Berghman, 1995).

Other efforts still try to take a more holistic view of social exclusion. For example, the UN Capital Development Fund (UNCDF[iv]) highlights that social exclusion has both income and non-income or human poverty components, as shown in Table 9.1 below. Within this, income poverty is seen as largely relating to unemployment, underemployment and low productivity, and to the status of or access to welfare provision, all of which can be directly related to the distributive and

Table 9.1: A Holistic Understanding of Social Exclusion

Income poverty	Non-income/human poverty
Unemployment/underemployment	Poor access to basic services
Low productivity	Presence of conflict and insecurity
Status of/access to welfare	Disempowerment
	Exclusion from decision-making

Source: Adapted from United Nations Capital Development Fund (UNCDF) (2003), *Local Government Option Study – Draft Report*, East Timor (unpublished).

the social integration discourses on social exclusion. Non-income or human poverty, on the other hand, is seen as having its origins in poor access to basic services, the presence of conflict and insecurity and, crucially, to disempowerment and exclusion from decision-making.

The particular value of the UNCDF approach is its explicit identification of disempowerment and exclusion from decision-making as a significant element of the experience of poverty or social exclusion. It thus places the operation of the democratic system centre stage and challenges community development practice to take cognizance of income and non-income or human poverty.

Even from an admittedly limited exploration of these two concepts, community development and social exclusion, it quickly becomes clear that frameworks of understanding are key determinants of the potential for more progressive community development approaches. Charity, welfare industry or market approaches to community development, just like social integration, redistribution and MUD discourses on exclusion, are likely to produce analysis and action that prioritise change in the behaviour of the individuals who experience exclusion. Here, liberal and neoliberal emphases on the roles, rights and responsibilities of individuals are reflected. By contrast, an activist community development framework, allied with a systems failure analysis of social exclusion, suggests that structural and systemic failings be addressed. It is of course problematic that the very 'systems' that are failing are those that are exerting an increasing influence over the functioning of civil society and dictating the shape of community development practice.

In the next section, attention turns towards the role of community development in deepening the democratic experience, particularly as it relates to the participation of civil society organisations in the democratic process. This will illustrate how different community development frameworks extend or restrict the scope of democratic participation by such organisations.

The Promise, Reality and Potential of Participatory Democracy

The Promise

The links between community development, participation and participatory democracy have been referred to earlier. In Ireland, Government has, on occasion, flirted with the notion of cultivating a more participatory democratic culture, as evidenced in the *White Paper on a Framework for Supporting Voluntary Activity and for Developing the Relationship between the State and the Community and Voluntary Sector* (Department of Social, Community and Family Affairs, 2000*a*). While democratic understanding in Ireland, like most countries in the world at this point, is dominated by the liberal orthodoxy of electoral representation, this White Paper made a number of significant statements emphasising the need for an increased emphasis on a participatory approach. In speaking of the need to promote more active citizenship, the White Paper envisaged citizenship as 'a political activity which gives citizens the opportunity to shape the society in which they live. Groups are given the opportunity to become involved in identifying local needs and developing strategies to meet these needs' (Department of Social, Community and Family Affairs, 2000*a*: 64). On the surface, this suggests an expanded role for citizens as political actors but in reality it limits the involvement of groups to identifying and meeting local level needs only, largely within the confines of voluntary associations, and subject to the primacy of electoral politics. This approach has been reaffirmed more recently in the *Green Paper on Local Government Reform*, which introduces the potential for experimentation with various forms of local participation such as participatory budgeting, but which again reaffirms the 'role and primacy of the elected member' (Department of the Environment, Heritage and Local Government, 2008: 82).

While these initiatives hint at a more progressive vision of deeper citizen involvement, they illustrate the ongoing struggle that exists in the minds of political and administrative elites, between involving citizens and their organisations in decision-making on one hand, but being unwilling to disturb the dominance of representative and administrative decision making on the other. Limited as it was, implementation of the recommendations of this much anticipated White Paper, which was developed with substantial community sector involvement, lost considerable momentum when responsibility for it was transferred to the Department of Community, Rural and Gaeltacht Affairs. Follow-up on many of its proposals has been limited and concerns have been expressed that the ambitious rhetoric has shrunk considerably on contact with the real world of politics and public administration (Harvey, 2004).

The Realities

The increased control exerted over the CDP and the failure to fully embrace the potential of the *White Paper on a Framework for Supporting Voluntary Activity* illustrate the degree to which progress on participatory democracy has stalled or been redefined. The nature of the redefinition illustrated by the CDP example and, it could be argued, by a range of other State–community sector relationships can be explained as a shift from one form of associative democracy to another, that is, from one form of more open-ended, participatory democracy to another narrower, more restricted version.

The form of associative democracy, more visible during the earlier period of the CDP, advances the notion that democracy needs to be underpinned by a 'social base' provided by associations, without which aspirations towards political equality or economic equity cannot hope to be achieved (Cohen, 1996). In the absence of this social base, it is suggested that the needs of poorer interests will not be represented. Moreover, associations can make contributions to problem solving in relation to issues faced by poorer groups. However, as evidenced by the struggles to promote community organisation and participation amongst Travellers in Ireland, it cannot be assumed that such associations will automatically arise (Cohen, 1996), particularly those required to generate political equality. Public support is needed to induce them into existence (Cohen and Rogers, 1997). Associative democracy therefore 'proposes to use State resources to address representational asymmetries', thereby encouraging organisation amongst previously under-represented groups (Baccaro, 2002: 3). This however leads to the question as to whether it is sufficient to simply support such organisation without, at the same time, ensuring that marginalised groups are included in deliberative fora, thereby contributing their local knowledge on specific or generalised problems. As well as contributing to enhanced policy efficiency, therefore, inclusion in deliberative processes may generate a capacity for mutual acceptance of opposing viewpoints, through which attachment to entrenched positions may be lessened (Cohen, 1996: 113). This approach to associative democracy reasserts that the State should play a role in supporting or stimulating the development of associations or organisations, such as community development projects, to engage with and promote the voices of marginalised communities.

Other approaches, however, have taken the role of associations in a different direction and view them as a channel through which functions can be devolved from the State to a variety of citizens associations and organisations (Hirst, 2000). The aim of this vision of associative democracy is to distinguish between the functions of service delivery and the supervision of such services (Hirst, 2000: 29). In such a scenario the task of the State becomes more focused on revenue generation, which can then be used to contract self-governing associations to undertake service provision, for which the State assumes oversight and quality assurance responsibilities, leading to a reduction of State involvement in the minutiae of day-to-day service provision and leaving it more able to deal with the increasing complexity of modern societies. It may also serve to insulate the State from blame when problems arise within different service providing arenas, as has been suggested in the case of the Health Service Executive (HSE) (Kenny, 2005). It has been suggested that this conception of associative democracy is not unlike many of the prescriptions of New Public Management (NPM) (Savoie, 1995), which can be seen as the public administration component of neoliberal ideologies. In Ireland, the Strategic Management Initiative, launched in 1994, and the subsequent public sector modernisation process can be seen to reflect much of the language of NPM.[v] Thus, the current trajectory of the CDP is increasingly towards the provision of services to local communities, and to address persistent problems such as long-term unemployment. At the same time, the presence of such projects within deliberative fora is far from certain and, indeed, in some cases, they have been deliberately excluded. For example, Local Traveller Accommodation Consultative Committees (LTACCs) were set up specifically to advise on the provision of accommodation for Travellers under the Housing (Traveller Accommodation) Act 1998. However, in a number of instances, local authorities choose to bypass organisational structures, often CDPs established with State funding to enhance Traveller participation, despite legislative provision for their inclusion. Moreover, instead of organising or facilitating processes to enable Travellers to (s)elect representatives to sit on the LTACC, in some cases these were simply hand-picked by the local authority (National Traveller Accommodation Consultative Committee, 2004).

The Potential

The demonstrated capacity for this one form of participatory democracy, associative democracy, to be interpreted in quite different ways and leading to quite different results, underlines the importance of delving a little more deeply into participatory democratic theory so as to understand its potential to contribute to the achievement of equality and social inclusion.

Within the boundaries of what is generally called participatory democracy, various approaches exist, the fundamental aim of which is to realise the ambition of greater participation by citizens and/or citizens' organisations in decision-making. At a general level, Pateman

(1970) has argued for participatory democracy as a means of challenging liberal democracy's almost inexorable trajectory towards inequality. She argues that in order for a society to be fully democratic, members of that society need to be trained and educated for democracy, a process that happens through the very act of participation. Moreover, as such participation contributes to the building of the integrative elements of democracy, that is, citizens become more actively and deeply engaged with the democratic system (Sorensen, 1997), it is assumed that the capacities of citizens are developed (Pateman, 1970). However, in order to create a democratic polity, participation opportunities must exist. By contrast, it can be equally suggested that in the absence of participation opportunities, democratic polities cannot be said to exist. The justification for participatory democracy therefore 'rests primarily on the human results that accrue from the participatory process' where 'maximum input (participation) is required and where output includes not just policies (decisions) but also the development of the social and political capacities of each individual, so that there is feedback from output to input' (Pateman, 1970: 43).

Macpherson (1977) also bases much of his advocacy of participatory democracy on criticisms of the dominance of elitist models of democracy which he sees as inherently linked to the production and maintenance of social and economic inequality. Consequently, achieving a more participatory democratic system is premised on achieving certain prerequisites to greater participation (Macpherson, 1977: 99). The first prerequisite is a change in people's consciousness and the second is a reduction in social and economic inequality. However, between these two desired scenarios lies a significant dilemma or a 'vicious circle', within which 'we cannot achieve more democratic participation without a prior change in social inequality and in consciousness and we cannot achieve the changes in social inequality and consciousness without a prior increase in democratic participation' (Macpherson, 1977: 100). Of the four frameworks presented earlier, it is clear that only the activist approach is openly concerned with equality, consciousness raising and democratic participation and, in Macpherson's terms at any rate, is a necessary tool with which to build participatory democracy.

Deliberative Democracy

Alongside these general treatments of participation, a number of more specific participation formulas can be identified, deliberative democracy being one of the most widely referenced. In general terms, this can be seen as 'any one of a family of views, according to which the public deliberation of free and equal citizens is the core of legitimate political decision making and self government' (Bohman, 1998: 401). Young (2000: 22) elaborates further, describing it as a 'form of practical reason. Participants in the democratic process offer proposals for how best to solve problems or meet legitimate needs and so the democratic process is primarily a discussion of problems, conflicts and claims of need or interest.' It is often assumed, therefore, that deliberative democracy has the capacity to move away from bargaining and individual interest more towards reason, recognition and accommodation of the valid interests of others (Cohen, 1996; Cohen and Fung, 2004).

To operate in a deliberative mode it is suggested that a number of fundamental elements should be present. First, participation should be informed by distinct norms and values, namely equality and symmetry whereby all participants have a right to initiate discussion, to question and to debate. Second, the topics for deliberation, the agenda, must be open to question by all participants and, third, the rules of the deliberative process should be open to question (Benhabib, 1996). Other recurring ideals cited within deliberative approaches that supplement these aspirations are reciprocity, inclusion, equality, reasonableness, publicity and accountability, where reciprocity refers to the requirement of mutual respect and being willing to treat others as one might like to be treated; inclusion emphasises the involvement of all those affected by an issue in discussion; equality extends this further so that, even where inclusion does occur, all should be able to participate on an equal basis without fear of domination; reasonableness requires a willingness not only to have opinions, but to listen to the opinions of others; and, finally, the principle of publicity emphasises the value of deliberation taking place in public and is linked to a commitment to accountability where participants are answerable for collective decisions as opposed to individualised actions (Bohman, 1998; Young, 2000). Taken together, these deliberative guidelines present a challenging framework, both to build alternative concepts of democracy, but also to analyse the deliberative credentials of existing governance processes.

Within the deliberative school, Barber's account of strong democracy (1984: xi) proceeds from a robust critique of the contemporary liberal democracy, which he claims has 'undone democratic institutions' and has made 'politics an activity of specialists and experts whose only distinctive qualification, however, turns out to be that they engage in politics'. By contrast, 'strong democracy is the politics of amateurs where every man is compelled to encounter every other without the intermediary of expertise' (Barber, 1984: 152). Effectively, Barber sees strong democracy as being based on the participation of citizens; on the transformation of conflict through such participation without there being predetermined limitations, such as a prevailing economic orthodoxy; and on the capacity for citizenship, individualised and atomised by the weight of liberal thinking, to become more concerned with public rather than private interests.

On a more practical level, empowered deliberative democracy (EDD) represents an attempt to more concretely address the institutional and democratic challenges posed by often vague notions of participation and deliberation. While other approaches arise largely from theoretical origins, EDD, by contrast, draws on the empirical experiences of a number of participatory processes in the United States, Brazil and India to extract some of the key ingredients of a progressive participation and decision-making formula. These experiments include new approaches to policing and education management in Chicago, participatory budgeting in Porto Alegre in Brazil and alternative techniques for community planning in Kerala in India (Fung and Wright, 2001). In doing so, it sets out three principles upon which participation should be based. These require, firstly, that an EDD framework should be concerned with the resolution of specific and 'tangible' problems. Secondly, it should seek to achieve the active participation of those directly affected by the problem and of relevant officials. Finally, the use of deliberative approaches to locate solutions should be privileged (Fung and Wright, 2001: 17). In emphasising the role of deliberation, it should be noted that EDD requires participation in *actual*, deliberative *decision-making*, not just in powerless, non-decision-making, deliberative arenas, many of which may represent little more than bogus post-decision legitimisation. It is perhaps EDD's grounding in practice as opposed to theory that also enables it to engage in useful self-criticism and which ultimately makes it a more credible and useful tool for deepening democracy. Amongst the self-criticisms it self-identifies are: the vulnerability to problems of power and domination, particularly domination by elites; the potential for powerful actors or 'institutional contexts' to limit the extent of deliberation; rent-seeking behaviour by powerful groups; the creation of unrealistic expectations of local participation, especially in the context of political apathy and, finally, difficulties in sustaining participatory approaches over the longer term (Fung and Wright, 2001: 33).

Therefore, in order for EDD to operate effectively, particularly in marginalised communities, there is a need to increase the capacity of citizens or residents to engage in decision-making processes from which they have been traditionally excluded. It can be argued that community development, particularly activist-oriented community development, has a real role to play in building such capacity. This was shown in the case of the RAPID programme in Tralee, where some local CDPs played a highly effective role in supporting residents to engage as decision makers in local-level estate management and community safety processes (McInerney, 2006).

The Limitations of Participation and Deliberation

While there are clearly a variety of approaches to participatory democracy, these are not without their own weaknesses. The core failing of deliberative processes, according to Mouffe (1999), is the inability to escape from the realities of power and antagonism. To address this, a model of 'agonistic pluralism' is advocated, in which confrontation is still seen as inevitable, but in which political enemies are transformed into political adversaries and antagonism into agonism. In this approach, an adversary is seen as an opponent with legitimate views. As a result, antagonism, or the struggle between enemies, gives way to agonism, a struggle between adversaries (Mouffe, 2000: 103). The ambition of an agonistic model, therefore, is to recognise the existence of such antagonisms but, while doing so, it seeks to create mechanisms to defuse actual or potential hostilities, in the process reconciling the exercise of power with the ideals of democracy. Consequently, it seeks to generate 'an ensemble of practices' that make possible the creation of democratic citizens by 'multiplying the institutions, the discourses, the forms of life that foster identification with democratic values' (Mouffe, 2000: 95–96). This echoes other approaches that encourage a multiplicity of deliberative arenas 'so as to vary the kinds of power that permeate each one', thereby facilitating 'critiques of power from different directions' (Mansbridge, 1996: 56).

Participation Barriers

Just as it has been shown that not all variants of community development will be equally concerned with equality or inclusions, so too participatory processes must be challenged and subjected to more rigorous scrutiny, much in the same way as Cooke and Kothari (2001) have done with the notion of participation in the international development literature. In introducing the notion of participation as the 'new tyranny', they aim to highlight how much of the radicalism of participatory development has been corrupted into new forms of control and professionalised manipulation. Much the same charge might be levelled at efforts to supplement the elitist base of liberal democracy with participatory infusions, which in themselves may have limited capacity to adjust the imbalance of democratic power. A number of sources of this imbalance can be identified.

Economic Predeterminism

According to Barber (1984: 253–256) there exists within liberal democracy a distinct form of economic predeterminism, which he describes as having three core components. Firstly, modern capitalism has generated a 'doctrine of economic determinism', which effectively eliminates deliberation on the nature of economic development from nominally participatory arenas, thus failing the deliberative standards described earlier. Secondly, the 'privatistic character of economic individualism' significantly retards the potential to identify already elusive common or public goods. Thus, the neoliberal emphasis on individual success renders citizens less open to actions to achieve broader societal goals. Finally, the very size or 'giantism' of the modern multinational corporation itself presents significant challenges to democracy, such that the modern corporation may be seen as 'incompatible with freedom and equality, whether these are construed individually or socially'. In the Irish case, despite the widening of the agenda for discussion in the *Programme for Competitiveness and Work* (Department of the Taoiseach, 1994) and subsequent national agreements, influenced in part by the presence of a Rainbow Coalition Government, it remains the case that the concerns of large and economically powerful actors both dominate and motivate processes of bargaining and negotiation (Hardiman, 2006), in keeping with expectations of pluralist or neopluralist democratic processes (Barber, 1984; Dryzek, 1996; Manley, 1983). The strength of this influence is also visible in the almost permanent refrain from Government and the business sector that anything perceived as disturbing the confidence of multinational industries in Ireland as a destination for foreign direct investment (FDI) can scarcely be tolerated.

Power and Participation

A further and related barrier to progressive participation is the unwillingness to name and address issues of power (see also Chapter 3).

While not always explicitly named, the unequal distribution of power inevitably acts as a further barrier to democratic participation, leading to calls that democracy should be centrally concerned 'with devising ways to manage power relations so as to minimise domination' (Shapiro, 2004: 11). In a similar way Fraser (1990: 77) sets an important and challenging agenda for democratic theory, suggesting that it 'should render visible the ways in which social inequality taints deliberation within publics in late capitalist societies' and also show how 'inequality affects relations among publics in late capitalist societies; how publics are differentially empowered or segmented and how some are involuntarily enclaved and subordinated to others.' These power relationships, however, are not always explicit within the operation of mainstream democratic institutions, or within parallel arenas trading under a deliberative banner. Claims have been made, for example, that social partnership in Ireland operates in a deliberative mode (O'Donnell and O'Reardon, 2000: 250), albeit that the existence of a distinct hierarchy of power within it is openly acknowledged (Adshead and McInerney, 2006; Hardiman, 2006). Evidence of how this power hierarchy functions is offered by a recent analysis that concluded that Irish antipoverty policy over the duration of the various national partnership agreements has been confined to a 'residual policy category, shaped primarily by the needs of macro economic policy' and that 'the engagement of pro-poor actors in the negotiation process had no significant impact' (E. Connolly, 2007: 37; see also Chapter 6). It would appear, therefore, that the moral or communicative authority of this sector proves to be of little value when faced with the economic power of the major partners.

Institutional Inertia

A further barrier to the realisation of positive participatory outcomes is the inability of institutions, particularly State institutions, to embrace the type of change needed to move beyond elitist modes of decision-making. Thus, achieving inclusion and equality within participatory environments is not simply a given and requires social institutions that can provide an environment within which communication is enhanced (Young, 2000: 31). While this may introduce concerns about material well-being, it may also introduce an imperative to focus on the 'institutional organisation of power' and to recognise that 'where there are structural inequalities of wealth and power, formally democratic procedures are likely to reinforce them because privileged people are able to marginalise the voices and issues of those less privileged' (Young, 2000: 32–35). In this regard, what passes as the norms of 'articulateness' confers further privilege on those who have enjoyed the benefits of access to education. An inherent element of such assumed articulateness is a capacity to fit in with pre-established communication norms (Young, 2000). These privileged modes of expression are reinforced by expectations that political communication be free of passion and excess emotion, the presence of either of these indicating a lower level of political maturity or know-how. This can only be changed by adopting a different view on political communication, where emphasis is placed, alongside existing forms, on modes of communication that include public greeting; the use of rhetoric; and a recognition of the value of narrative and storytelling (Young, 2000).

Such manifestations of power imbalances and privileging of certain forms of communication over others may not always be overt and instead may be couched in terms of 'capacity' deficits. And while participation and the more onerous assumption of representation functions need to take account of different levels of capacity, they also need to acknowledge different forms of capacity, without which certain types of education, experience and knowledge may be discounted (Barber, 1984; Cornwall, 2004; Young, 2000). Without this participation, arenas may fail to recognise that 'not only do different people have vastly different capabilities and opportunities to engage in political, social and civil activities, but the formulations of State policy often exclude the needs and experiences of particular groups' (Jones and Gaventa, 2002: 15). Implicit within this also is the imperative to move beyond narrow preoccupations with the capacity deficits of citizens towards an acknowledgement of the capacity deficits of democratic institutions, requiring a renewed focus on inculcating a deliberative ethic and related responsiveness within public administration systems. For example, there is an acknowledgement in the *National Action Plan Against Poverty and Social Exclusion, 2003–2005*[vi] 'that embedding anti-poverty practice across local authorities is a slow task and will take time to achieve given current organisational culture in local authorities' (Department of Social, Community and Family Affairs, 2003: 55). Resistance to change has also been reported in relation to other efforts to reinforce institutional capacity, such as the establishment of social inclusion units in a limited number of local authorities. In some cases at least these:

> experienced resistance to their work at a variety of different levels and for a number of reasons, particularly in the early stages of their establishment. Local authority staff queried the function of the Units

> and the role of the local authorities as social inclusion agents, fearing that this role would add to their burden. (Walsh, 2005: 4)

Elitism within Participatory Models

Finally, imbalances in participation can result from the capacity of participatory processes to facilitate elite domination of participation opportunities. And while participatory models clearly see themselves remedying some of the weaknesses of orthodox liberal democracy, in some cases they may just repeat them. However, taking Barber's vision of strong democracy as an example, it can be seen that responsibility in this area is largely abdicated:

> Though strong democracy may respond practically no better than liberal democracy to the immediate crisis of the desperate and the powerless, its politics of public seeing and common willing is better suited than the politics of private interests to envisioning their status in a common future. (Barber, 1984: 207)

Thus, the challenges presented by discussions on power and equality not only confront the hegemony of orthodox liberal democracy but the participatory democracy agenda as well. Participatory or deliberative processes also contain within them potential for domination, especially when all voices are not equally listened to or valued or where the potential to exit from the deliberative arena is effectively restricted by institutionalised rules of participation, usually set by the State (Cornwall, 2004: 9; see also Chapter 6). Indeed, experiences with processes of decentralised governance throughout the 'developing world' clearly illustrate the process of elite capture of representative roles within participatory processes, a factor that is hardly unique to such contexts. Recorded experiences in developing countries of so-called innovations in decentralised governance simply facilitating decentralised, elitist controls provide salutary warnings for processes of local governance in Ireland (Blair, 2000; Narayan *et al.*, 2000; Crook and Sverrisson, 2001; Smoke, 2003; Cornwall, 2004; Phillips, 2004; S. Hickey and Mohan, 2005).

Participation – Within or Without the State?

For those engaged in or aspiring towards activist community development in Ireland, a constant dilemma is how to manage the expectation of engagement and co-operation with the State. Inclusiveness and the opportunity to be involved in participatory processes continue to be presented as progressive democratic indicators, the assumption being that civil society engagement with the State can only produce positive outcomes. And while this may sometimes be the case, at other times such engagement may be far from productive. In particular, less well-resourced civil society actors, especially those with a focus on social inclusion, may struggle to translate participation opportunities into participation outcomes, as evidenced by experiences within arenas of national social partnership (E. Connolly, 2007). Despite this, the allure of participation continues to present a tempting opportunity, even if a 'faces of power' based analysis might suggest that there is limited chance to impact on decision-making (face one); agendas are largely set (face two) by the State or by powerful economic actors; and there is a need to repress genuine preferences (face three) due to the nature of the governance environment and the preferences it sustains (Shapiro, 2004; see also Chapter 3).

By contrast, Dryzek (1996) does not see civil society engagement with the State as an inevitability. Instead, in realising its democratic potential, he envisages it as having four principal roles, including changing the terms of political discourse; legitimating different forms of collective action; convening policy-oriented fora and generating responses from Government as a result of fear of political instability, a view not unlike the early aspirations of the CDP (Department of Social Welfare and Combat Poverty Agency, 1995). Consequently, Dryzek proposes, civil society should retain a distance from the State thereby ensuring that it flourishes in an oppositional, as opposed to a co-operative or co-opting, climate.

In situations where a civil society organisation chooses to engage with the State, Dryzek (2000: 84) suggests that 'benign inclusion' can only happen when certain conditions are met. Firstly, a group's desired outcomes must be capable of 'being assimilated to an established or emerging State imperative' and, secondly, 'civil society's discursive capacities must not be unduly depleted.' Whether such conditions can be met is far from certain, leading to the suggestion that where inclusion is likely to be symbolic at best, 'inclusion in the polity beyond the State is more appropriate' (Dryzek, 2000: 85) and may actually contribute more to democratisation. Thus, so-called inclusion can have negative consequences and can, as described by Papadapoulos (2003), lead to the deradicalisation of grassroots movements, as a result of being asked to 'behave responsibly in governance bodies' (Fung and Wright, 2001: 34). As a result, such movements, fearful of losing access to what they see as important decision-making arenas, may engage in varying degrees of self-censorship or co-option (Dryzek, 1996). The dangers of co-option have already been identified in the Irish case and 'anecdotal evidence suggests that dependence on State funding can result in voluntary groups effectively practising "self-censorship" so as to avoid any risk to funding' (Hughes *et al.*, 2007: 441).

For others, civil society frequently plays a dual or 'both' role, both engaging with and opposing the State at the same time (Cohen and Arato, 1994), though clearly such diverse strategies can often produce considerable tension. Engagement usually happens within 'invited spaces', frequently seen to suffer from rigid interpretations of participation; the allocation of only limited responsibility to community participants; an absence of clarity on roles and responsibilities and an unwillingness by participants to question the actions of the State. Popular spaces on the other hand are often seen as arenas where opposition and dissent are possible, in which deeper participation can be generated and more attention paid to process issues, though their linkage to decision-making mechanisms remains unclear (Cornwall, 2002; Cornwall, 2004). In a similar way, Mansbridge (1996) identified the need to distinguish between different participation arenas or spaces and suggested that citizens may need to 'oscillate between protected enclaves, in which they can explore their ideas in an environment of mutual encouragement, and more hostile but also broader surroundings in which they can test those ideas against the reigning reality'(Mansbridge, 1996: 57). The 'Share the Wealth Campaign' undertaken by the National Anti-Poverty Networks in the late 1990s is an example of an effort to create such a popular space, though it was limited in scope, received inadequate support from community sector organisations and was short lived. More recent examples are difficult to come by as community development organisations find themselves increasingly distracted by both governance and service delivery responsibilities.

Locating the Potential for Progressive Community Development in Ireland

The earlier outline of the CDP in Ireland illustrates the hazards and potential contradictions involved in the State playing a direct role as a funder and facilitator of community development. However, beyond this, the community and voluntary sector has found itself increasingly enmeshed in multiple relationships with the State, at national and local level, leading to suggestions that it has experienced significant losses of autonomy. Invariably, this has been influenced by the increasing dependence of many organisations on the State for financial support, the suggestion being that 'the close relationship that many organisations consequently have with government and the fact that 60 per cent of the sector's overall income comes from public funds have led to concerns that their independence in advocacy and agenda setting may become compromised' (Hughes *et al.*, 2007: 440).

However, a more recent assessment suggests that the State actually provides 75 per cent of funding to community and voluntary organisations, with the remaining amounts provided by personal giving and fundraising (20 per cent), corporate sources (2 per cent), and trusts and foundations (2–3 per cent) (Harvey, 2008). Having justified earlier that the State should play a role in supporting associational life by funding the emergence of representative organisations, the significant issue becomes, not the provision of State support, but the nature and disposition of the mechanisms though which such funding is disbursed. This has moved from a pattern of more dispersed funding through different departments and statutory bodies to one where central Government takes a more hands on, directive role. The outcomes of this are presented in quite stark terms:

> Occasionally the rollback has taken more sinister overtones, with the prohibition of advocacy within new communities funding programmes, the requirement of external endorsement for the plans of community development projects, discouragement of the role of policy officers, threats to review organisations that speak out (e.g. Trocaire, Pavee Point), the lack of consultation on significant funding changes in 2007 and even the prohibition of advocacy by childcare networks. (Harvey, 2008: 13)

It could therefore be argued that the era of governance and social partnership, despite introducing the community and voluntary sector into national and local governance arenas has, at the same time, neutralised its possible impact through the exercise of an increased level of central Government control. So, while having originally encouraged a form of associative democracy through the creation of secondary associations to represent marginalised groups, it has subsequently redefined the role of associations and, in the process, has undermined the potential for democratic enhancement through the exercise of increased control and domination over these associations. This would appear to justify suggestions that 'it is foolish in the extreme to delude ourselves that financial dependence on government largesse does not bring with it the threat of sudden financial loss, should the social agendas of the two sectors diverge' (McAliskey, 2007).

In such a context, what are the options facing those involved in community development in Ireland today? Subservience to the State; acceptance of externally driven agendas; externally imposed models of community development; or some form of alternative, oppositional role? A number of possible scenarios suggest themselves.

Scenario One: Accept the Status Quo

One option, attractive to many community sector organisations, is to simply accept the existing status quo. This may well suit those operating from within charity, welfare or market frameworks, for whom there is little desire or motivation to go beyond the boundaries established by State funding. Ideologically, these approaches may accept existing structural relationships and may see little need to challenge patterns of control established by the dominance of elected and administrative elites. Within this scenario, existing models of pluralist democracy are accepted and ambitions of a more participatory form of democracy are largely abandoned. As a result, the limitations of aggregative electoral processes persist while the potential to develop a more democratically integrated citizenry is abandoned.

This scenario may also account for others engaged in community development who, despite believing in the need for deeper social and economic change, may simply have become resigned to a belief that significant change in existing relationships of power and decision-making are unlikely to be achieved in the current political climate. Instead, time and energy are devoted to a more limited agenda of local service delivery and development, sometimes producing an unwillingness to engage in any meaningful way in local or national networks. Politics, in this case, is left as the preserve of the elected and administrative expert, and citizenship becomes a potential as opposed to an actually experienced status.

Scenario Two: More Autonomous Service Delivery Role

A second scenario accommodates community development organisations which may accept a largely service delivery role, but do so in a way that demands recognition of their autonomy and independence. In such a scenario, community development organisations are still located within an associative democracy framework, where relationships with the State are negotiated and formalised and set out the rights, roles and responsibilities of both parties. In this case, however, the assumption of a significant, service delivery role does not imply that advocacy about services, institutions, structures and power relations should cease. Indeed, from an activist community development perspective, provision of services to disadvantaged communities inevitably requires a deeper questioning of such relationships. In this way, taking on a largely service delivery function does not require democratic potential to be sacrificed.

The dilemma here of course is whether State agencies providing funding to community development organisations for the delivery of services or to mediate service delivery can countenance any criticism of their own performance. More fundamentally, within this scenario, there is a danger that the State will cease to see such organisations as an essential, autonomous part of the democratic system, instead viewing them in some way as a ground-level extension of its own infrastructure. One way to avoid this is to increase the role of intermediary funding organisations, a role previously played by the CPA and currently by organisations such as the Family Support Agency and Pobal. Where such agencies are allowed to operate with sufficient freedom, not just to administer but to develop programmes, it becomes possible to strike a proper balance between legitimate expectations of financial and contractual accountability on one hand, and the constructive, critical capacity of community development organisations on the other. Crucially, however, there would appear to be a trend away from such quasi-independent, intermediate agencies, as evidenced by the recent integration of the CPA directly into the Office for Social Inclusion in the Department of Social and Family Affairs, following the 2009 Budget and the significant undermining of the institutional and developmental capacity of Pobal.

Scenario Three: Ambitious Pragmatism

The third scenario for community development organisations is to explore more fully the 'dual' role, acting in partnership with the State but, at the same time, consciously developing and pursuing more challenging agendas (Cohen and Arato, 1994). Potential to realise this scenario requires a rejection of an exclusively service delivery role, instead reasserting advocacy based on a more comprehensive, evidence-based and challenging analysis of social, economic, political and cultural relationships. As such, it allows potential to pursue Dryzek's four-point agenda, involving: changing the terms of political discourse; seeking legitimation of different forms of collective action; convening policy-oriented fora and generating responses from Government as a result of fear of political instability.

Within partnership or invited spaces (Cornwall, 2004), ambitious pragmatism, informed by more challenging analysis, can be pursued. However, this scenario implies a need to challenge the nature of political discourse and deliberation within these arenas which most often operate according to rules, norms and conventions of the State and/or the more powerful participants within them. While these arenas may be seen as offering limited potential for progressive change, they may contain some opportunities to pursue social inclusion goals, provided their potential is appropriately harnessed. Moreover, efforts can be made to shunt these spaces more towards co-governance models, where the types of deliberative standards outlined earlier (Benhabib, 1996) can be realised and where practice from other countries might be emulated (Smith, 2005). In certain cases, the experience of the RAPID programme illustrates how this potential can be realised in practice, with effective neighbourhood structures being created and the emergence of practices of shared decision-making supported by community-controlled leverage funding (McInerney, 2006).

However, scenario three also envisages the need to simultaneously operate outside of partnership arenas, to pursue more progressive agendas within popular spaces (Cornwall, 2004) or within 'enclaves' of resistance (Mansbridge, 1996: 57). Here, not only is there a challenge to reconvene and own collective spaces, which have been largely squeezed by the preponderance of invited spaces, but there is also a need to re-establish their legitimacy as part of the democratic system. These spaces can be constructed at a local, regional or national level, but to do so requires community development organisations to recognise the need for broader alliances of solidarity and a commitment to collective analysis and action. Such alliances are particularly important in light of the State's efforts to foster and control the establishment of local and national structures to act as the exclusive voice of the community and voluntary sector. This control has been exercised, for example, through the creation of one-size-fits-all local community and voluntary fora, which may have only limited interest in social inclusion and equality issues but which may, in some cases at least, be seen as a useful way to neutralise more challenging, oppositional voices.

The challenge of operating within this dual role, namely being willing to produce more challenging analysis from within popular spaces while pursuing an approach of ambitious pragmatism within invited spaces, has not been substantially tested in Ireland. However, there are some indications that it is a necessity that is increasingly recognised (Community Platform, 2008) and one that will be required if the management of the recently declared economic recession is to be prevented from hitting the most vulnerable in society most severely.

Scenario Four: Disengagement from Governance and Service Delivery

Finally, scenario four presents the most radical option for those committed to activist community development. As such, it envisages democratic participation being realised by the development of strong and autonomous civil society organisations and by preventing any blurring of the spaces between civil society and the State. It envisages, therefore, a complete disengagement from governance and/or service provision roles, based on the premise that the State's current pursuit of a neoliberal economic and administrative agenda cannot accommodate concerns about equality and exclusion, given that they are, to a large extent, the very origin of that exclusion (Dryzek, 1996). This fourth scenario questions whether a truly progressive vision of community development can only be found in self-exclusion from 'invited' spaces established and controlled by the State, thereby enabling the creation of 'popular' spaces within which the fundamentals of inequality and power can be confronted. However, for many community development organisations, which have by now become established and professionalised in their own right on the basis of funding from the State, the likely financial implications of this are such as to make it a less-than-attractive option. Equally, alternative sources of funding from philanthropic sources are unlikely to be available to pursue more radical approaches or to question prevailing economic or political orthodoxies, as many, though not all, of the main philanthropic bodies begin to align their priorities with those of Government. Finally, to realise this scenario would require a level of mobilisation within civil society that has not been visible for many years and does not look likely to re-emerge in the immediate future.

Conclusion

In this chapter I have presented some of the possible scenarios for community development practitioners. However, the choices they represent go beyond the more limited sphere of community development and actually represent competing choices about the future of democracy in Ireland in the twenty-first century. I would argue that the current democratic trajectory and State-dictated approaches to community development significantly undermine both democratic practice and democratic potential. Increasingly, there is a drive towards the emasculation of oppositional voices, particularly, but not only, those from the community and voluntary sector who seek to articulate an equality and social inclusion agenda. Moreover, State resources are frequently utilised to reinforce a narrower democratic outlook and to control and/or marginalise dissent. In terms of democracy, I would argue that there is a visible reassertion of a more limited, pluralist model where powerful economic factions dominate, particularly business and trade unions, while other inputs are devalued and their roles assimilated into the service delivery apparatus of the State, thereby denying their essential contribution to building accountable and healthy democracy. Clearly then, the trend is towards a narrow and conceptually unstretched vision of democracy.

Achieving a more progressive vision of participation, within which activist community development has a place, requires a more substantial debate on the future of democracy, initiated either by community development organisations or by the State or both. In the current political and economic climate I would have to question whether the State – political or administrative – has the wherewithal to initiate such an open debate. Consequently, responsibility falls to community development actors, particularly those with an activist analysis, to explore the potential for and value of genuine, participatory approaches to democracy. Within this lies the challenge to reassert the validity of and necessity for a strongly autonomous civil society and the legitimacy of community development practices that seek to redress political and economic inequality, rather than simply camouflage it.

Notes

i Other substantial supports to community development have been provided by various local development programmes, e.g. the Local Development Social Inclusion Programme and the RAPID programme (Revitalising Areas through Planning, Investment and Development).

ii <http://www.pobail.ie/en/CommunityLocalDevelopmentProgrammes/CommunityDevelopmentProgramme>.

iii See <http://www.cwc.ie> and <http://www.cdx.org.uk>.

iv UNCDF offers a combination of investment capital, capacity building and technical advisory services to promote microfinance and local development in the Least Developed Countries (LDCs). See <http://www.uncdf.org/english/about_uncdf/index.php>.

v The Strategic Management Initiative (SMI) was launched in 1994 to enhance delivery of public services. As part of the SMI, each Government department produces a strategy outlining how it will contribute to implementation of the initiative. A subsequent report, *Delivering Better Government* (Department of the Taoiseach, 1996*b*), identified a number of areas where public sector changes were needed. These include: delivery of services to 'customers and clients'; reducing 'red tape'; delegation of authority and accountability; improved 'human resources management'; improved financial management and ensuring value for money; use of information technology; and improved co-ordination between departments. The SMI process has now become part of what is described as a 'public services modernisation' programme. For more information see <http://www.bettergov.ie/index.asp>.

vi The National Action Plan on Inclusion is the plan produced by the Government in accordance with an agreed EU-wide approach to planning on social inclusion. It follows on from the Irish Government's own National Anti-Poverty Strategy, originally announced in 1995 and published in 1997.

10

Youth and Community Work in Ireland in the Context of Globalisation: Towards a Politics of Transformation[i]

Eilish Dillon

Nothing is truly local. That can be an illusion. So much of what goes on, the forces affecting our lives, are not necessarily local ... We see the connection between the issues affecting people's lives everywhere ... We find it works, because sometimes people are so isolated, communities are isolated and issues are isolated.... There's a need to put the local into a global and historical context.... Making some of the links more obvious ... between the local and the global ... opens up the possibility for shared struggle.

(Helena McNeill, Lourdes Youth and Community Services)

Introduction

These days 'globalisation' is everywhere and it seems to get the blame or the praise for much of what happens at a local level in Ireland. Indeed, so pervasive are discourses of globalisation that the term has come to characterise virtually all aspects of contemporary society. It is variously associated with the power of the global market - usually in contrast to the reduced power of the State - with the Internet and international media, with migration and travel, with progress, insecurity, risk and freedom. In theoretical terms, the term globalisation has become a short-hand term for contemporary understandings of global interrelatedness, interdependence and integration, with the associated notions of transnationalism, borderlessness or time–space compression. It is often used as a substitute for 'modernisation' or economic liberalisation and regarded as synonymous with global capitalism or Western imperialism (Callinicos, 2007*a*). Thus, the argument goes, as we live in 'a global village', any analysis of contemporary Irish society is incomplete without an analysis of globalisation.

Is globalisation 'real', and if so, is it 'real' everywhere and for everyone? Does it matter? These are just some of the questions that have permeated debates about globalisation in recent years. I include them here to introduce globalisation as a constructed and contested understanding of processes of global interconnectedness. Like all such constructions, and particularly those that have come to mean 'all things to all people', its usefulness depends on its meaning and its application, for example, is globalisation something 'out there' that bears little relevance to the lives of people in Ireland? Is it 'on the radar' for youth and community work at all? If it is, how do different political perspectives in youth and community development – for example, 'pragmatic' or 'alternative' (Powell and Geoghegan, 2004), 'mainstream' or 'critical' – affect our responses to it?

In this chapter, I contest dichotomous understandings of globalisation, which, for example, privilege convergence over diversity, the external over the local or the State, force over agency and inevitability over the creation of alternatives. In view of these contestations, I discuss the questions and challenges for youth and community work in addressing globalisation. These suggest a more critical engagement by youth and community work with a politics of transformation. Such a politics cannot be based on easy prescriptions, but a good starting point for youth and community work in Ireland is to take critical positions in relation to addressing the inequalities associated with neoliberal globalisation. A critical analysis of globalisation presents particular challenges in relation to how youth and community work are positioned vis-à-vis the State and how alternatives are conceptualised and constructed. These involve questioning 'mainstream' positions and constructions of participation, education and collective action, for example (see also Chapters 1 and 3). Of specific concern is the need to move beyond a preoccupation with the local. I introduce the work of some organisations that are involved in facilitating the construction of alternatives within youth and community work, in order to identify some of the challenges associated with constructing a politics of transformation.

Contesting Globalisation

Is the term globalisation useful for an understanding of the challenges and potential of youth and community work in the contemporary Irish context, particularly considering the vast terrain to which it is applied? As discussed below, not only is there disagreement about what globalisation means, but also about whether or not it provides any useful analytical clarity. One of the difficulties with how the term globalisation is often used is the conflation of an unspecified 'category' of 'globalisation' with 'the reality' or 'realities' of contemporary lived experience. Bahnisch (2002: 2) argues that 'globalisation has indeed been the metanarrative of an age supposed to be sceptical of all metanarratives.' Arguably, if globalisation is about everything or nothing, then it cannot present any specific clarity. This suggests the importance of addressing different debates on globalisation and interrogating their specific relevance for youth and community work. All totalising understandings of globalisation have their limitations: when globalisation is understood as 'borderlessness', it can fail to take account of the borders that are erected and defended against people; when understood as 'interdependence', it underemphasises dependencies and inequalities; when constructed as 'imperialism', it can reduce multidimensional power processes to a singular point of origin and limit responses to resistance alone; and when the 'global' or 'external' is overemphasised, it can limit the power of the 'local'.

In the next section, I explore debates about and contest discourses of globalisation with a view to identifying the challenges they present to youth and community work in Ireland. I argue that thinking on globalisation presents specific questions and challenges, particularly related to the discourses of convergence and divergence, the role of State and civil society, and in relation to alternative responses to globalisation.

Globalisation as Convergence and Divergence

Some Debates on Globalisation as Convergence and Divergence

Since the 1980s, a central dichotomy in thinking on globalisation has related to 'sameness' and 'difference'. Some argue that globalisation homogenises cultures, integrates economies and that it is about convergence. Others emphasise the divergences associated with globalisation in terms of diversities and inequalities. Sklair (1991) and Cochrane and Pain (2000: 16) usefully suggest that globalisation involves a myriad of interrelated economic, social, political and cultural processes, practices and institutions. Economic theories of globalisation engage with understandings of globalisation as 'the progressive integration of the modern economy' (Callinicos, 2007*a*: 62), the contemporary manifestation of global capitalism, or the hegemony of neoliberal economics. Todaro and Smith (2006: 120) explain neoliberalism in the following terms: '[T]he neoliberals argue that by permitting competitive free markets to flourish, privatising State-owned enterprises, promoting free trade and export expansion, welcoming investors from developed countries, and eliminating the plethora of government regulations ... both economic efficiency and economic growth will be stimulated.'

Economic debates about convergence and divergence in relation to neoliberalism call for a careful reading of the different effects of globalisation on different people in different contexts (Willis, 2005). It is important therefore not to take 'the critical pot off the boil', so to speak, when it comes to globalising processes of neoliberalism and their unequal and often contradictory effects (Rai, 2002; Rapley, 2004; Schirato and Webb, 2003). Rapley (2004), for example, focuses his analysis of 'Globalisation and Inequality' on 'Neoliberalism's Downward Spiral'. He argues that we should be less concerned about globalisation and more about the form that globalisation processes are taking. He asserts that we live in a 'neoliberal age' in which a neoliberal wave has spread across the world. Focusing in particular on the widening gap between the rich and the poor – what he calls a 'distributive crisis' – he argues that globalising elites play a dominant role. His analysis highlights the importance of interrogating particularly powerful globalisation processes, especially those, like neoliberalism, which result in 'winners' and 'losers', growing global inequality, 'dislocations of power' and 'new forms of poverties' (Harcourt, 2003: 75–76). Schirato and Webb (2003: 204–205) describe the antisocial tendencies of the politics and processes of neoliberal globalisation, arguing that they 'function to "undo" social structures and institutions in states too weak to resist them'. Willis (2005: 174) shows that 'the potential benefits of time–space compression are not available equally to all', for example, use of the Internet, and she goes on to argue that 'for some groups, growing interactions with people and places from the other side of the world are not necessarily desirable.' What are the implications of neoliberal globalisation on movements of people, for example? Harcourt (2003: 76) links increasing numbers and types of migration to globalisation. Though she argues that these can be positive, and that 'globalisation has produced a whole new set of cultural and social relations of migrants and citizens', she points out that they present 'new types of demands for distributive justice'. In this context, understanding globalisation in terms of divergence can highlight both the potential and the challenges related to diversity.

These analyses remind us of the need for critiques of the structures and institutions that create inequalities at a myriad of levels, and of the effects of them on different 'real' people across the globe. Such inequalities are often conceptualised in terms of global 'North–South' divides, but given the divergences associated with globalisation, they are increasingly understood as relating to what Bezanson (2004: 130) calls 'a geographically heterogeneous "included/excluded" axis'. In the Irish context, for example, who are the 'winners' and 'losers'? What kinds of power relations operate to 'include' and 'exclude' certain people or groups from the potential benefits of globalisation? Who are the 'included/excluded' in youth and community work, and on what basis? I return to notions of 'inclusion' and 'exclusion' below.

Analyses of the unequal material effects of neoliberalism are strengthened by critiques of its discursive effects. At a discursive level, market 'forces' are constructed not only as 'the only way', but as 'outside of control', the implication being that they are irresistible. Baker *et al.* (2004: 126) remind us that 'the market is not a naturally occurring phenomenon.... Economic activities take place within a framework that is produced by political choices, is continually shaped by the State and is dependent on its enforcement agencies.' Likewise, Schirato and Webb (2003: 204), who identify neoliberal ideology as central to globalisation, discuss how it saturates the public sphere, 'naturalizes technological developments and their uses as natural and irresistible, and ... narrativizes the freedom of the few as a (necessary) prelude to the freedom of all'. These critiques of globalisation highlight the need to explore the constructed nature of much of what is taken for granted as 'natural', 'true' or 'inevitable' about neoliberalism. This has particular relevance in the Irish context.

Contesting Convergence and Divergence – Challenges for Youth and Community Work in Ireland

As discussed above, an overriding discourse of globalisation is that of convergence, and this is particularly evident in debates related to the global economy. Discourses of convergence appear useful in terms of understanding global/local 'interconnectivities'. While this seems to appropriately describe different global interconnections through international trade or international human rights instruments, for example, the notion of interconnectedness is an apolitical one suggesting some kind of neutral global relations. It does not adequately take account of where connections do not sufficiently occur nor does it interrogate the power relations involved in these relations. In general, discourses of convergence are open to the essentialist promotion of and acceptance of the inevitability of what might be called 'mainstream globalisation' in terms of neoliberal processes. In Ireland this is evident in the absence of real public debate about the expansion of the market and the rollback of the State through public–private partnerships (PPPs), for example. Dominant discourses of convergence fail to adequately take account of diversity, inequality or of different interests in different contexts. Contesting globalisation therefore requires acknowledgement of both the convergence and divergence tendencies of globalisation (Jones, 2001) and critical engagement with connections and diversity.

In the Irish context, contesting globalisation involves highlighting the challenges related to how neoliberalism has been embraced and mythologised, and the associated contradictory and unequal effects of State policies and practices on different people in Ireland. Issues related to privatisation, employment and migration, for example, highlight just some of the equality challenges associated with market liberalisation in the context of globalisation in Ireland. The unequal effects of globalisation processes suggest that how globalisation is understood or addressed at youth and community level can depend very much on individual and group experiences. For some and in some ways, globalisation represents opportunities, possibilities and freedoms, but for others experiences are of isolation, poverty and uncertainty. This suggests the need for further analysis of inequalities in the Irish context with reference to people's different experiences and how they intersect, for example, in relation to the multiple social divisions that Baker *et al.* (2004) describe. As these divisions highlight power relations at all levels, critical engagements with globalisation and equality are, of necessity, political.

A significant feature of recent debates related to globalisation in the Irish context is that analyses of the effects of globalisation are imbricated with analyses of the sustained economic boom of the 1990s, otherwise known as the Celtic Tiger, and with recent discussions of 'post-Celtic Tiger Ireland' and of 'threats' to the Irish economy and employment. Contemporary Ireland has often been understood in terms of the 'roars' or 'squeals' of the Celtic Tiger, for example, in terms of its relative strength and those it serves. Allen (2000: 2) argues that, in the context of the Celtic Tiger, myths surrounding globalisation have been used to give free rein to market forces in Ireland, where 'the population are repeatedly urged to be grateful for the half a million new jobs that have been created.' Critical of the convergence assumptions of what he calls 'the idealised picture of capitalism as neoliberal economists might like it to appear' (Allen, 2000: 186), he argues that 'the myth of globalism provides a powerful alibi for those who want to discourage resistance and militancy.' Thus, he is critical of the discursive effects of globalisation as a 'taken for granted' series of myths that serve to reinforce the power of capitalism and to disenfranchise trade unions and workers. This raises new challenges in the light of the downturn in the global economy in recent years and its subsequent effects on employment and public spending in Ireland.

In their exploration of social exclusion in Ireland, Jacobson and Kirby (2006: 33) argue that Ireland has become increasingly globalised in recent years and that, in the light of the Celtic Tiger, there was 'a shift in governance towards subordinating social policy to an extremely free-market economic policy, with the result that the latter always took precedence over the former. In other words, the State handed power over to the market' (2006: 33–34). They outline the implications of this in relation to a shift from a 'welfare State' to a 'competition State', which prioritises global competitiveness, resulting in poverty for some and growing inequality in Ireland. There are many issues of concern with regard to neoliberal globalisation and its convergent and divergent tendencies in an Irish context. A central issue is that of equality. Allen (2000) explicitly argues for an analysis of globalisation that interrogates class divisions. He is critical of the unequal effects of the market economy in Ireland and of the role that the State has played through tax concessions to the rich and the destruction of public services. Baker *et al.* (2004) prefer to discuss inequalities in terms of multiple patterns of social division, for example, related to class, gender, ethnicity, disability and sexual orientation, which, among other effects, 'have legitimated discrimination, leading to inequalities of working and learning, of resources and of power' (Baker *et al.*, 2004: 10). Though it would be impossible to discuss all the implications of globalisation in depth here, inequalities in relation to the market economy are associated with issues such as the privatisation of public services, with a shift from a 'welfare State' to a 'workfare State' (Murphy, 2006), and with migration and diversity. These have significant implications in terms of how globalisation relates to people's 'everyday/everynight' lives (Smith, 1999) and offer important challenges for how youth and community work are structured and practised.

Kirby (2006: 197) addresses the 'major challenge to make social inclusion a reality'. Though he explains the parameters of what social inclusion might involve, including what he calls a 'project of active citizenship' (2006: 192), it is important to remember that the concept of 'inclusion' is not one that can easily address the complexities of the unequal and contradictory effects of globalisation in the Irish context. He argues for the need for social inclusion based on a politics of equality and democracy, but observes a gap between the rhetoric of public policy and its economic commitment to inclusion. '[C]ommunity development activists find themselves caught up in a paradox, in which their commitment to tackling social exclusion is co-opted by the State for its own strategic purposes' (Kirby, 2006: 192; see also Chapters 5 and 6). In this context, depending on how it is conceptualised, 'inclusion' can be about being included in the very processes that lead to social exclusion in the first place. Furthermore, it can set up simplistic categories of groups to be 'included', which do not address the complexities of the power relations at work. Meade and O'Donovan (2002: 3) argue that poles of inequality and domination, including 'employee–employer', 'male–female', 'included–excluded', are being redrawn as new 'axes of identity, along which social consensus can be brokered and agreed in State-mediated partnerships'. Furthermore, when applied to the complexities of debates on culture, 'inclusion' can suggest a form of homogenised integration that denies diversity and tries to 'iron out' difference, both within and between social groups.

This presents a challenge for youth and community work to engage critically with structures and processes of inequality in relation to the global and Irish context. This involves a critical engagement with 'inclusions' and 'exclusions', homogeneity and diversity, that takes account of the multiple and contradictory effects of neoliberal globalisation on different young people or different people in a community, for example. Thus, engaging with globalisation is not a matter of accepting the inevitabilities of the 'myths of globalisation', as Allen (2000: 2) has pointed out. Nor is it about engaging with 'the global' as an external 'other', which bears little relation to personal and collective experiences of power and inequality at the local level.

Politics, the State and Civil Society

Some Debates on Politics, the State and Civil Society

Debates on globalisation and politics often focus on State capacity and globalising forces and institutions (Bahnisch, 2002). Key concerns relate to the erosion of State power in the context of the power of 'transnational institutions' and neoliberalism. In this context, questions relate to whether or not the State has any power in the face of institutions such as the European Union or the World Trade Organisation. For many, it is not simply a case of states crumbling in the face of 'external' forces, as states can play an important role in the construction and mediation of globalisation processes and institutions, as outlined by Jacobson and Kirby (2006) in relation to the Irish case. Other debates relating to the political focus on the impact of globalisation on the public sphere. Schirato and Webb (2003: 185) discuss the 'alienation' and 'occupation' of the public sphere of civil society and democracy by 'the interests of globalisation, the market and America/the West'. For others, more hopefully, there are 'new democratic spaces' (Cornwall and Schattan Coelho, 2007: 1) in relation to civil society, new social movements and the media – for example, Indymedia – which offer possibilities for democratisation and the articulation of alternatives. It would be useful here to question the kinds of democracy or citizenship that different approaches to youth and community work represent in Ireland. What kinds of relationship with the State are constructed and possible? How are the fields of youth and community work addressing the challenges presented by mainstream and alternative forms of democratic media, for example?

Debates about the State and the public sphere intersect with considerations about local–global dynamics and understandings of agency. With reference to the latter, the term 'glocalisation' is often used to refer to the interaction between the local and the global, for example, through hybrid or 'glocalised' cultures, 'which incorporate some global scripts into local habits, while rejecting others' (Risse, 2007: 135). In Britain, for example, there has been some debate about what the popularity of chicken tikka masala represents, especially since Robin Cook announced in 2001 that it is 'a perfect illustration of the way Britain absorbs and adapts external influences' (*Guardian*, 2001). The term 'glocalisation' helps to address the criticism that the concept of globalisation tends to mask the complexities of power relations in specific contexts, where local realities are assumed to be externally determined with little acknowledgment of how the local and global intersect. This has important implications for understandings of agency at youth and community level in Ireland and in trying to identify how power works in different spaces, institutions, processes and discourses. Bahnisch (2002: 4) is critical of globalisation theory with its 'absence of social agency and conceptual determinism and reductivism'. If all the power is identified as located at the level of the global, for example, it underestimates agency and power relations at local and State levels, etc. Thus, debates on politics and globalisation suggest the need for an understanding of globalisation that takes account of local–national–global intersections. Furthermore, they highlight structure–agency dynamics, and open the possibility for considerations of globalisation and State–civil society relations.

Contesting Politics, the State and Civil Society – Challenges for Youth and Community Work in Ireland

In analysing globalisation in the Irish context, Jacobson and Kirby (2006) do not give primacy to an externalised understanding of globalisation as an unstoppable force. Instead they review global–local intersections in the light of State policies, priorities and strategies. These, they suggest, are summed up in the shift from State to market, and 'deep integration of the Irish economy into the process of globalisation' (Jacobson and Kirby, 2006: 36). This presents an important challenge for theorisations of contemporary Ireland, asking us to move beyond local–State analysis to recognise local–national–global intersections; for example, not separating analyses of the market economy in Ireland from analyses of global power relations.

Other important debates concern understandings of the 'transnational', the public sphere, civil society and participation. While the 'transnational' construction of globalisation is useful in describing 'transnational' practices and institutions, such as the World Trade Organisation and the United Nations (see Sklair, 1991), in this sense the term 'globalisation' can mask the significance of the role of the State. As outlined in discussions on the Irish context (Jacobson and Kirby, 2006), the State, viewed as an arena and not a discrete bureaucratic institution, still occupies an important position in the negotiation of a variety of interests at local and regional levels. Despite this, State power and positioning is not uniform, nor can it be taken for granted. Such issues highlight the need 'to stress the complexity of the relationship between the local and the global' (Jones, 2001: 7), and to recognise that not all nation-states have equal influence over the processes and institutions of globalisation.

A related important challenge, in the Irish context, concerns the politics of community and youth work. Though addressed elsewhere in this volume in greater detail, a critical analysis of power relations and positions gives an insight into how community and youth work is serving to reinforce or challenge the practices, institutions, structures, discourses and inequalities associated with globalisation in Ireland. How does youth and community work have to be positioned, in relation to the State and other actors, in order to take account of the complexities of globalisation? What does that positioning mean in terms of political or advocacy strategies, for example? Kirby argues, with reference to the Irish context, that 'one can identify a disciplinary strategy on the part of the State towards those sectors of civil society that are adopting a more oppositional stance' (2006: 195; see also Chapter 6).

Such an analysis suggests the need to explore the tensions (Dillon and Madden, 2004) or constraints on youth and community work in relation to its funding, regulation and resources, and to identify strategies for how these can be addressed. Rigorous reflection on the relationships between different civil society actors, and between civil society actors and the State in Ireland – particularly in the light of cuts in State funding to many civil society actors in recent years – presents a major challenge for the youth and community sectors in terms of interrogating any role they might play as critical voices in civil society in Ireland in the context of globalisation.

Alternatives

Some Debates on Alternatives

As discussed above, contesting globalisation suggests the need for alternative responses to globalisation at a number of levels. This involves critical engagement with convergences and diversity, inequalities and various interests, exploring the role of the State and 'local actors', and critical engagement with and articulation of alternative globalisations. Globalisation cannot be taken for granted, nor should we conflate everything into globalisation. At the same time, it is important to address the interrelated political, economic and socio-cultural dimensions of global–local interconnectivities at different levels – local, national, regional and global. Given the complexities of globalisation, any analysis of how to deal with the challenges that it presents is, of necessity, complex. Bahnisch (2002: 7) suggests that responses to globalisation have to move beyond 'a closed dichotomy of globalisation and its other, anti-globalisation'. In this case, reflecting on arguments related to 'alternative forms of globalisation' and 'alternatives to globalisation' from a variety of theoretical perspectives can help to open up considerations of the kinds of strategies and spaces for change that are required. Of particular relevance here is understanding what is involved in constructing a politics of transformation. This has implications for different kinds of youth and community work and their approaches to collective action in the light of State–civil society relations. It also involves critical education, which incorporates an analysis of local–global interactions.

Debates on alternatives are notoriously difficult as they immediately suggest the question: 'alternatives to what?' In the Irish case, they are often alternatives to the inequalities associated with market liberalisation and to the democratic deficits associated with State–civil society relationships. Allen (2000: 193) suggests an analysis of globalisation in the Irish context as one that interrogates class divisions and identifies revolutionary class struggles as a source of possibility in relation to transformation of existing systems: '[W]hat is required is a political movement that starts from the struggles of today, but links them to a strategy for overall change' (2000: 193). As outlined earlier, Kirby (2006: 195–196) discusses alternatives in relation to a 'project of active citizenship' which 'is about building movements with strong local bases but which can impact on national politics' (and which takes account of the 'shift in power points' away from the most vulnerable towards 'an entrenched globally connected elite' (Kirby, 2006: 192)). For him, this involves examining the impacts of changing global economic and political power on 'local lives and communities' (2006: 186).

The above analysts reflect on discourses of 'radical' or 'critical' alternatives that relate to 'struggles', 'change' and 'activism'. They represent alternatives as political, as addressing power relations and institutions, and advocate the necessity for the creation of a movement or movements for change. What kind of implications do such critical analyses hold for the construction of youth and community work as 'movements for change'? Powell and Geoghegan (2004: 272) argue that 'the goal of community development is to "democratise democracy" in a genuinely socially inclusive form.' However they recognise that, while this is a 'task of Herculean proportions' in an Irish society that is dominated by market considerations, 'there is ample evidence of citizens willing to try' (2004: 272). What is involved in constructing alternatives based on a politics of transformation? What does this mean for the kinds of collective action and education processes that youth and community work are engaged in? In the next section, some examples of alternative responses to globalisation in an Irish context will be explored.

Some Examples of Alternative Responses to Globalisation in an Irish Context

In this section, I introduce some examples of alternative responses to globalisation and present some of the challenges of globalisation in Ireland, as identified by three people working in development education in the youth and community sectors.[ii]

Globalisation and the National Youth Council of Ireland (NYCI)

The National Youth Council of Ireland (NYCI) has been involved in organising One World Week since 1989. Though initially through a specific project entitled Development Education for Youth, One World Week now represents part of an overall programme and strategy for development education within NYCI. Hundreds of young people, youth leaders, workers and organisations engage in a myriad of activities related to themes identified annually for One World Week, for example, 'young people and stress'; 'global health and justice'; and 'making a difference'. According to NYCI, the aim of its development education strategy is to mainstream development education into the core programmes of youth organisations through, for example, training, capacity building, the development of relevant materials, support and networking. Recent initiatives of its development education programme have been to form links and exchanges between community workers in Zambia and in Ireland, to develop a strategy for the youth sector to promote access to youth work to people from minority ethnic groups in Ireland, and to develop a development education strategy for the professional development of youth workers.

Johnny Sheehan points out that, from a practical point of view, NYCI has not framed development education specifically as a globalisation issue. He highlights that the purpose of development education is to contribute in some way to the development of people in the Global South ('Global South' or 'South' refer to the countries of Africa, Asia and Latin America) as well as 'people we work with'. He says that 'transformation is critical to why we do development education. You're ultimately trying to transform society, want Ireland to be a place where people act, themselves in an individual way, within youth and society, and influence the Government to act in a way which promotes respect for other people, fairness and so on.'

In terms of the implications of globalisation for development education in youth work, Sheehan points out that 'it is easier to talk about other parts of the world as people are less narrowly focused on their own society and are more aware of the world around them.' For him, 'migration has positive implications, but also poses difficulties, in terms of the communication of ideas and experiences from others and challenging the negative stereotypes about migrants in Ireland.'

He explains that globalisation presents particular challenges in relation to models of action. He argues that 'one of the impacts of globalisation in Ireland is that Irish society is wealthier, but within that there is a bigger gap between the rich and the poor. A lot of young people perceive themselves to be better off financially.' This presents a challenge to youth work when considering responses to global inequalities, in that 'when people become wealthier, the charity model of development that we've been moving away from is being replaced again by a charity model.' He cites the example of an increase in responses to 'What can we do?' type questions being answered as 'fundraising' or 'becoming a volunteer overseas and building houses for them'. This presents a challenge to youth work, Sheehan suggests, to engage with wealth and poverty in critical or justice terms.

Sheehan also presents specific challenges in relation to 'values education and to the role of youth workers'. He argues that the role of development education is not to impose values or to make assumptions about globalisation, but to question where power lies and what can be done about it.

Globalisation and Banúlacht

In the introduction to *Looking at the Economy through Women's Eyes: A Facilitator's Guide to Economic Literacy*, Maeve Taylor writes:

> Banúlacht is a feminist development education organisation that works with locally based women's organisations in Ireland. Banúlacht's particular focus is linking local and global issues in solidarity with Southern women's organisations. These issues include gender and trade, gender budgeting, gender mainstreaming and women's human rights. In challenging global processes which engender power relationships, Banúlacht's work is based on a commitment to new kinds of global relationships informed by solidarity. Our economic literacy work is one aspect of this commitment. (Taylor, 2004: 3)

In an interview, she explains that, as part of its overall development education strategy, Banúlacht organises economic literacy courses for women community activists. The framework for this work is women's human rights and power, but she suggests that economic literacy presents an opportunity for an economic approach and a human rights approach to illuminate each other. Issues addressed in these courses include: gender, care and the economy; economic growth: a measure of well-being?; globalisation and trade; and challenging neoliberalism: a human rights approach.

In terms of the implications of globalisation for community work, Taylor explains that Banúlacht has identified challenges and particular problems for women in relation to political, economic and socio-cultural dimensions of globalisation. She argues that, while the political dimension of globalisation manifests itself in the increasingly determining power of many decisions made at global level, political discourse in Ireland, including that of the community sector, tends toward an outmoded politics which focuses almost exclusively on the national level. Among other effects and challenges, Taylor argues that this 'undermines participation at a local level especially among the marginalised', it 'obscures the global context of power-brokering and decision-making', and it 'perpetuates and reinforces gender inequalities at local, national, regional and global levels'. With reference to the economy, she suggests that 'globalisation driven by neoliberalism, although creating opportunities for some women, has also exacerbated the problems of poor women.' In this regard, a key challenge that Banúlacht identifies is the 'limited recognition in Ireland of the global economic context and its impact on women's experiences at the local, national and international level'. In relation to socio-cultural issues, Taylor points out Banúlacht's position:

> in the context of globalisation, specific forms of gender inequalities, and their complex intersection with other forms of discrimination such as racism, sexism and classism, become reworked against a wider cultural background of increasing Eurocentrism and cultural hegemony ... this creates socio-cultural problems for women, not only at the level of lived experiences, but also in terms of creating intercultural connections between women based on equality and solidarity.

In the light of its analysis of globalisation, Taylor explains that Banúlacht has devised a development education strategy over the past few years, the overarching framework of which

> ... has been to avail of the institutional spaces created by the United Nations human rights instruments, in particular, the Beijing Platform for Action and CEDAW, as global tools for transforming decision-making processes at all political levels. In the context of Beijing+5, Banúlacht's focus was on the need for a National Plan for the Implementation of a Platform for Action which would encompass a global agenda. The development of partnerships with and between women's organisations in Ireland and in the South has been central to that work.

Globalisation and Lourdes Youth and Community Services (LYCS)

Lourdes Youth and Community Services (LYCS) is an integrated community development project based in Dublin's north inner city.

> [The] LYCS adult education programme is committed to individual and community development through education and collective action. The programme seeks to facilitate participants to identify their educational and social needs, to access resources to meet those needs and to effectively challenge any structures and systems which may inhibit their development. (Lourdes Youth and Community Services, 2006: 8)

LYCS's adult education programme is underpinned by a development education perspective on the grounds that it 'enables learners to begin to develop a broader perspective on the root causes of the issues they confront in their everyday lives and to learn from the experiences of other communities across the world. It can also foster a sense of shared experiences and solidarity and an appreciation of diversity' (Lourdes Youth and Community Services, 2006: 8). 'In practice this often means that individuals feel less isolated both as individuals and as members of a community, and more able to take action' (Lourdes Youth and Community Services, 2006: 10). Such an approach has been used, for example, in a joint programme with Cáirde,[iii] Women as Leaders in Equality, in which women from the 'established community' and women from 'new communities' undertook programmes in community and global development. Furthermore, LYCS is currently running a Further Education and Training Awards Council (FETAC) (level 5) course in development for participants and workers in community development.

In relation to the issue of globalisation, Helena McNeill points out that, for LYCS, key issues are those of growing inequality and migration. With regard to the changing nature of communities, she identifies 'community breakdown' or 'atomisation' as central challenges: 'Though some consciously might not put that in the context of debates about globalisation, I would argue that globalisation is exacerbating those problems.' She highlights that 'the pressures of globalisation are also opportunities' and gives the example of migration. She argues that migration 'is not necessarily a problem, but when it is framed as a problem, it can increase the potential for exploitation and for conflict. Migration is also potentially an opportunity for Ireland to look outwards more and to understand the world better and to bring the richness of cultures together.' In this regard, she argues that it is the purpose of community work to work with communities. As communities are changing, there are new and more complex challenges. She highlights one of the challenges for community work as 'finding ways to include a more diverse community', for example, through outreach and identifying communities within communities. This involves addressing different 'isolations' and 'exploitation' within communities, and presents challenges to community organisations that 'want to be a point of connection'. She explains that this requires new and increased resources on the basis of the specific needs identified.

In terms of the relationship between community work and the State, she argues that 'the relationship with the State is always problematic because some of what you do is an implicit or explicit criticism of them.' Critical of the depoliticisation of community work, for example, in relation to 'citizenship' and 'volunteering', she argues that 'community work is struggling to challenge the status quo. It is being pushed into a service delivery role. Many services are provided at community level for good reasons, as community organisations do a good job ... but they do it on the cheap ... they are taking up the slack for the State.' She links the service delivery role of community work to neoliberalism, which is about 'small government' and 'privatisation by the back door'.

In the next section, I will draw together some conclusions from this work and from discourses of alternatives more broadly in order to suggest some of the challenges for youth and community work from contestations of alternatives.

Contesting Alternatives – Challenges for Youth and Community Work in Ireland

A key debate with regard to the construction of alternatives is the normative framework upon which such alternatives are based, for example, the statement 'another world is possible' on its own does not describe that world. The normative content of alternatives has often been filled with concepts such as 'empowerment', 'participation' and 'inclusion'. Such concepts have all been criticised on the basis of their rhetorical value but limited effect, or on their reformist rather than transformist content (Hilhorst, 2003; Hickey and Mohan, 2004; Chapter 3). Though these concepts are commonly associated with discourses of transformation in relation to youth and community work, in terms of processes, strategies and the creation of alternatives, critiques of such concepts suggest that the construction of alternatives is not about the articulation of easy prescriptions. This is evident in each of the cases (NYCI, Banúlacht and LYCS) introduced above, where interviewees explained the complexities and challenges involved in addressing globalisation, and regarded globalisation as presenting pressures and opportunities, difficulties and potential.

Despite the challenge of 'Herculean' proportions involved (Powell and Geoghegan, 2004), consideration of alternatives in the light of globalisation suggests the need for a politics of transformation that takes account of globalised inequalities and local–national–global intersections. Such a politics of transformation impacts upon how normative concepts of transformation are constructed, for example, shifting from notions of 'local development' to 'local-national-global developments'. This presents particular challenges for youth and community work in Ireland in its approaches to participation, volunteering and social change. Drawing on Kirby's (2006) construction of active citizenship, discussed earlier in this chapter, it is clear that citizenship is not just about involvement or volunteering, but about making an 'impact' on national policies. Hickey and Mohan (2004: 5) remind us that 'politics matters' and they argue that 'understanding the ways in which participation relates to existing power structures and political systems provides the basis for moving towards a more transformatory approach.' Who would need to be involved and how would participation need to be structured in such a transformatory approach to youth and community work? This presents some challenges to 'mainstream' community work in its construction of citizenship and in how it addresses inequalities associated with neoliberal globalisation in Ireland today. McNeill and Sheehan are both critical of a reductionist volunteerism approach to citizenship, arguing instead, in the case of Sheehan, for a model of action based on justice.

Of itself, an approach to citizenship based on 'making an impact on national policies' or engaging critically in society and politics can come from a very conservative position, which does not address inequalities or local–national–global intersections. Kirby (2006) argues for citizenship based on 'strong local movements' that take account of 'power shifts' and which challenge the elites of the global market economy. Do youth and community organisations represent such movements? Suggesting that citizenship needs to be based on an 'integrated' understanding of 'the local impacts of national and even global processes and power shifts' (2006: 186–187), Kirby's analysis also presents important challenges to youth and community work to 'move beyond the local'.

What would be the impact on youth and community work if its concerns were addressed to local–national–global intersections, as identified in this chapter? Arguably, it would suggest a radical politicisation of youth and community work, which would challenge inequality and critically engage with participation processes and diversity. It would mean an interrogation of or repositioning of relationships with the State in the context of current neoliberal economic policies such as public–private partnerships (PPPs).[iv] According to McNeill, relationships with the State present particular challenges in this regard, especially when community work is 'being pushed down a service delivery role'. It would involve linking the local to the global in a variety of critical ways, especially in the framing and analysis of issues affecting Ireland today (Kirby, 2006). This integration of the local, national and global is suggested by the kinds of approaches advocated by NYCI, Banúlacht and LYCS (above), through their focus on development, globalisation, transformation and/or human rights. At a practical level, it is evident in their education and training programmes, in partnerships and exchanges with youth workers and communities in 'the Global South' (rather than charity work), and in identifying issues that link communities in Ireland with communities in other contexts.

From a feminist point of view, Rai (2002: 118) argues that 'in order to address the issue not simply of recognition of gender inequality but also of redistribution of resources to overcome this inequality, women's activism has to invoke the politics of structural change – in terms both of patriarchy and of socio-economic structures of power.' In doing so, she argues that this politics is even more challenging in the context of globalisation as it raises dilemmas of 'difference, of elitism, of negotiations, engagements and oppositions to State structures' (2002: 119–120). Such dilemmas and difficulties also apply in relation to the youth and community sectors in Ireland, and Rai's point (2002) highlights the complexities involved in the creation of alternatives, especially in relation to State–civil society relationships and strategies of social change.

In addition to challenges about how 'citizenship' and 'participation' are constructed, considerations of critical education and collective action in the light of globalisation also present some challenges for youth and community work. Maeve Taylor of Banúlacht suggests that 'there is a tendency in community development to over-emphasise the power of locally-based collective action and to ignore the State and transnational actors.' Projects and programmes at a community level can ignore the State and global dimensions or can overlook power inequalities at the 'local' or community levels. Similarly, youth and community work often focuses on the personal to the detriment of the political. Madden and Moane (2006) are critical of the discursive practices involved in framing and regulating personal development, while Ryan (2001: 3) explores how personal development can become a starting point for 'radical adult education' and 'the production of politicised human subjects, capable of successfully resisting oppressive structures and knowledges'. This presents a challenge to youth and community work to engage in different forms of critical education. Johnny Sheehan of NYCI sees development education as about transformation for those participating in it and for society as a whole, and Maeve Taylor argues that critical education should be 'about collective action processes that can bring about change rather than collective action for its own sake'.

In terms of collective action, new social movements are often constructed as offering transformative potential in relation to globalisation and neoliberalism. Indeed, many youth and community organisations would consider themselves to be part of a global movement, for example, a youth movement, human rights movement or feminist movement. Parfitt (2002) cautions against assuming that all new social movements are 'progressive' or 'authentic', and argues that we need to develop criteria for judging them. Considerations such as Parfitt's (2002) reinforce the importance of interrogating collective action and notions of solidarity and development. Global solidarity, associated with new social movements, is often associated with phrases such as 'think global, act local' or 'act locally, while thinking globally'. In order to take account of the complexities of global–national–local intersections identified here, it is perhaps more useful to conceptualise solidarity in terms of 'thinking and acting globally, nationally and locally'. This involves exploring the complex power relations associated with globalisation at all levels and, in particular, challenging the inequalities at the heart of neoliberal globalisation. For youth and community work, the challenges are immense. How can 'inclusion' and 'exclusion' be addressed in processes of collective action whether in processes of critical education or advocacy? How are dialogue and decision-making processes constructed and facilitated in State–civil society partnerships? There are no easy answers. Perhaps a good starting point is to explore the possibilities of alternative forms of politics and education which are based on a contestation of the discursive and material effects of globalisation at local, national and global levels.

Conclusion

Everything about globalisation is complex – how it is understood and its effects on all of us. The complexity of understandings, positions and debates that I have introduced in this chapter presents difficulties for a simple analysis of the questions and challenges posed to youth and community work from globalisation. Despite this, it is important to try to understand and to critically challenge the material and discursive effects of globalisation, and particularly of neoliberalism.

In this chapter, I have argued that inequalities and democratic deficits associated with neoliberal globalisation call for a politics of transformation that moves beyond a dichotomous analysis of global-local relationships and processes. As outlined above, it is not simply a matter of constructing idealised and simple prescriptions for youth and community work. On the other hand, this politics of transformation does call for radical alternatives that address inequalities and power imbalances in State-civil society relationships, and which acknowledge local-national-global intersections. Introducing three examples of 'alternatives' in the Irish context, I have discussed some forms of critical education, collective action and solidarity, which may provide the basis for how youth and community work can respond to the challenges of globalisation.

Notes

i Thanks to Siobhán Madden for her helpful comments on an earlier draft of this chapter, and to Helena MacNeill, Johnny Sheehan and Maeve Taylor for their valuable interview contributions.

ii In preparation for this chapter, I interviewed three people from organisations that I am familiar with in order to try to illuminate some of the challenges related to globalisation for youth and community work in Ireland. I chose three organisations (one from the youth sector – NYCI – interviewee: Johnny Sheehan; one feminist organisation – Banúlacht – interviewee: Maeve Taylor; and one community-based organisation – LYCS – interviewee: Helena McNeill) that are involved in 'development education'. This choice of examples does not represent the range of 'alternatives', nor does it suggest that these are the best examples available. This chapter does not set out to critically evaluate this work, but I introduce it here to illustrate some of the complexities involved in addressing the challenges of globalisation. It is important to state that I was a member of the executive committee of Banúlacht for five years and that I have acted as a co-contributor to its analysis on globalisation. In this section, I use quotations without references to illustrate where I am quoting from the views of the interviewees, as expressed in the interviews, and quotations with references where the material comes from documentary sources.

iii Cáirde is an NGO working to 'tackle health inequalities among ethnic minority communities' in Ireland (see Cairde website: http://www.cairde.ie).

iv See Indymedia Ireland for a discussion of the debacle about PPPs in St Michael's estate, Dublin (http://www.indymedia.ie).

References

Aapola, S., Gonick, M. and Harris, A. (2005), *Young Femininity: Girlhood, Power and Social Change,* Basingstoke: Palgrave Macmillan.

Adshead, M. and McInerney, C. (2006), 'Mind the Gap – An Examination of Policy Rhetoric and Performance in Irish Governance Efforts to Combat Social Exclusion', paper presented to the Governments and Communities in Partnership: From Theory to Practice Conference, University of Melbourne, 25–27 September.

Ahern, B. (2005), speech by the Taoiseach Bertie Ahern TD at The Wheel's Conference on the Future of the Community and Voluntary Sector in Croke Park Conference Centre, Thursday, 14 April, 2005.

Alexander, J. (ed.) (1998), *Real Civil Societies – Dilemmas of Institutionalisation,* London: Sage.

Alinsky, S. (1971/1989), *Rules for Radicals,* New York: Vintage Books.

Allen, K. (2000), *The Celtic Tiger: The Myth of Social Partnership in Ireland,* Manchester: Manchester University Press.

Allman, P. (1987), 'Paulo Freire's Education Approach: A Struggle for Meaning', in G. Allen, J. Bastiani, I. Martin and K. Richards (eds.), *Community Education: An Agenda for Educational Reform,* Milton Keyes: Open University Press, 214–237.

Apple, M. (1982), *Education and Power,* London: Routledge and Kegan Paul.

Aries, P. (1962), *Centuries of Childhood,* London: Jonathan Cape.

Arnett, J.J. (2007), *Adolescence and Emerging Adulthood: A Cultural Approach* (3rd edn), New Jersey: Pearson/Prentice Hall.

Baccaro, L. (2002), *Civil Society Meets the State: A Model of Associational Democracy,* Geneva: International Institute for Labour Studies.

Bacharach, P. and Baratz, M.S. (1962), 'Two Faces of Power', *The American Political Science Review,* 56(4), 947–952.

Back, L. (1997), *New Ethnicities and Urban Youth Culture,* London: UCL Press.

Bahnisch, M. (2002), 'Against "Globalisation" as a Useful Social Scientific Concept', paper presented to the Social Change in the Twenty-First Century Conference, Centre for Social Change Research, Queensland University of Technology, 22 November 2002.

Baker, J., Lynch, K., Cantillon, S. and Walsh, J. (2004), *Equality: From Theory to Action,* Basingstoke: Palgrave Macmillan.

Banks, S. (1999), *Ethical Issues in Youth Work,* London and New York: Routledge.

Banks, S. (2004), *Ethics, Accountability and the Social Professions,* Hampshire: Palgrave Macmillan.

Banks, S. and Jeffs, T. (1999), 'Youth Workers as Controllers' in S. Banks (ed.), *Ethical Issues in Youth Work*, London and New York: Routledge, 93–109.

Barber, B.R. (1984), *Strong Democracy: Participatory Politics for a New Age*, Berkeley: University of California Press.

Barclay, J.M.G. (2007), 'There is Neither Old nor Young? Early Christianity and Ancient Ideologies of Age', *New Testament Studies*, 53(2), 225–231.

Barlow, J. and Rober, M. (1996), 'Steering not Rowing: the Coordination and Control in the Management of Public Services in Britain and Germany', *International Journal of Public Sector Management*, 9(5/6), 73–89.

Barrington-Leach, L., Conoy, M., Hubert, A. and Lerais, F. (2007), *Investing in Youth: An Empowerment Strategy*, Brussels: BEPA.

Batsleer, J. (1996), 'It's Alright for You to Talk: Lesbian Identification in Feminist Theory and Youth Work Practice', *Youth and Policy*, 52, 12–21.

Bauman, Z. (2000), *Liquid Modernity*, Cambridge: Polity.

Bauman, Z. (2007), *Consuming Life*, Cambridge: Polity.

Beck, U. (1992), *Risk Society*, London: Sage.

Beck, U. and Beck-Gernsheim. E. (2002), *Individualisation: Institutionalised Individualism and its Social and Political Consequences*, London: Sage.

Bell, C. and Newby, H. (1976), 'Communion, Communalism, Class and Community Action: the Sources of New Urban Politics' in D. Herbert and R. Johnston (eds.), *Social Areas in Cities, Volume 2*, London: Wiley, 189–207.

Bell, D. (1976), *The Cultural Contradictions of Capitalism*, New York: Basic Books.

Bell, D. (1990), *Acts of Union: Youth Culture and Sectarianism in Northern Ireland*, Basingstoke: Macmillan.

Bellah, R., Madsen, R., Sullivan, W., Swidler, A. and Tipton, S. (1985), *Habits of the Heart: Individualism and Commitment in American Life*, Berkeley: University of California Press.

Benhabib, S. (1996), 'Towards a Deliberative Model of Democratic Legitimacy' in S. Benhabib (ed.), *Democracy and Difference: Contesting the Boundaries of the Political*, New Jersey: Princeton University Press, 67–94.

Berger, P. and Berger, B. (1976), *Sociology: A Biographical Approach*, Harmondsworth: Penguin.

Berger, P. and Luckmann, T. (1967), *The Social Construction of Reality: A Treatise in the Sociology of Knowledge*, Harmondsworth: Penguin.

Berghman, J. (1995), 'Social Exclusion in Europe: Policy Context and Analytical Framework' in G. Room (ed.), *Beyond the Threshold: The Measurement and Analysis of Social Exclusion*, Bristol: The Policy Press, 10–28.

Bernstein, R.J. (1983), *Beyond Objectivism and Relativism: Science, Hermeneutics and Praxis,* Oxford: Blackwell.

Bezanson, K. (2004), 'Rethinking Development: The Challenge for International Development Organisations', *IDS Bulletin,* 35(3), 127–134.

Birch, A. (1997), *Developmental Psychology: From Infancy to Adulthood,* Basingstoke: Palgrave.

Blair, H. (2000), 'Participation and Accountability at the Periphery: Democratic Local Governance in Six Countries', *World Development,* 28(1), 21–39.

Blatterer, H. (2007), 'Contemporary Adulthood: Reconceptualising and Uncontested Category', *Current Sociology,* 55(6), 771–792.

Blau, J.R. (2001), 'Bringing in Codependence' in J.R. Blau (ed.), *The Blackwell Companion to Sociology,* Oxford: Blackwell, 58–70.

Bohman, J. (1998), 'The Coming of Age of Deliberative Democracy', *The Journal of Political Philosophy,* 6(4), 400–425.

Bourdieu, P. (1984), *Distinction: A Social Critique of the Judgement of Taste,* London: Routledge and Kegan Paul.

Bourne, L.E. and Ekstrand, B.R. (1979), *Psychology: Its Principles and Meanings,* New York: Holt, Rinehart and Winston.

Bowden, M. (2006), 'Youth Governance and the City: Towards a Critical Urban Sociology of Youth Crime and Disorder Prevention', *Youth Studies Ireland,* 1(1), 19–39.

Bowie, V. (2002), *Youth Work in Educational Settings,* New South Wales, Australia: University of Western Sydney.

Bowles, S. and Gintis, H. (1976), *Schooling in Capitalist America: Educational Reform and the Contradictions of Economic Life,* London: Routledge and Kegan Paul.

Boyle, R. and Butler, M. (2003), *Autonomy v. Accountability – Managing Government Funding of Voluntary and Community Organisations,* Dublin: IPA.

Bradford, S. (2005), 'Modernising Youth Work: From the Universal to the Particular and Back Again' in R. Harrison and C. Wise (eds.), *Working with Young People,* London: The Open University Press and Sage, 57–69.

Breen, P.J. (2003), 'Ireland's Youth Policy for the New Millennium', *Forum 21: The European Journal on Youth Policy* ,1, 14–21, available at: <http://www.coe.int/t/dg4/youth/Source/Resources/Forum21/Issue_No1/N1_ireland_en.pdf>, accessed August 2007.

Broderick, S. (2002), 'Community Development in Ireland – A Policy Review', *Community Development Journal,* 37(1), 101–10.

Bronfenbrenner, U. (1979), *The Ecology of Human Development,* Cambridge, MA: Harvard University Press.

Brookfield, S.D. (1987), *Developing Critical Thinkers: Challenging Adults to Explore Alternative Ways of Thinking and Acting,* Milton Keyes: Open University Press.

Browning G., Halcli, A. and Webster, F. (2000), *Understanding Contemporary Society: Theories of the Present*, London: Sage.

Budapest Declaration (2004), *Building European Civil Society through Community Development,* Fife: International Association for Community Development.

Butters, F. and Newell, F. (1978), *The Realities of Training,* Leicester: National Youth Bureau.

Bynner, J. (2005), 'Rethinking the Youth Phase of the Life-Course: the Case for Emerging Adulthood', *Journal of Youth Studies*, 8(4), 367–84.

Callinicos, A. (2007*a*), 'Globalization, Imperialism and the Capitalist World System' in D. Held and A. McGrew (eds.), *Globalization Theory: Approaches and Controversies,* Cambridge: Polity, 62–78.

Callinicos, A. (2007*b*), *Social Theory*, Cambridge: Polity.

Cameron, C. (2007), 'Whose Problem? Disability Narratives and Available Identities', *Community Development Journal*, 42(4), 501–511.

Campbell, S. (2007), *Foróige Annual Review 2006–2007,* Dublin: Foróige.

Carr, W. and Kemmis, S. (1986), *Becoming Critical: Education Knowledge, and Action Research,* Lewes: Falmer.

Castells, M. (1997), *The Power of Identity*, Oxford: Blackwell.

Cleary, J. (2007), *Outrageous Fortune: Capital and Culture in Modern Ireland,* Dublin: Field Day Publications.

Cleaver, F. (2001), 'Institutions, Agency and the Limitations of Participatory Approaches to Development' in B. Cooke and U. Kothari (eds.), *Participation: The New Tyranny?* London: Zed Books, 36–55.

Cleaver, F. (2004), 'The Social Embeddedness of Agency and Decision-making' in S. Hickey and G. Mohan (eds.), *Participation: From Tyranny to Transformation?* London: Zed Books, 271–277.

Coakley, A. (2004), 'Poverty and Insecurity' in B. Fanning, P. Kennedy, G. Kiely and S. Quin (eds.), *Theorising Irish Social Policy,* Dublin: University College Dublin Press, 112–127.

Cochrane, A. and Pain, K. (2000), 'A Globalizing Society?' in D. Held (ed.), *A Globalizing World? Culture, Economics, Politics,* London: Routledge, 5–46.

Cohen, J. (1996), 'Procedure and Substance in Deliberative Democracy' in S. Benhabib (ed.), *Democracy and Difference: Contesting the Boundaries of the Political,* New Jersey: Princeton University Press, 95–119.

Cohen, J. and Arato, A. (1994), *Civil Society and Political Theory,* Cambridge, MA: MIT Press.

Cohen, J. and Fung, A. (2004), 'Radical Democracy', *Swiss Political Science Review,* 10(4), 23–34.

Cohen, J. and Rogers, J. (1997), *Can Egalitarianism Survive Internationalization?* Working Paper 97/2, Economic Globalisation and National Democracy Lecture Series, available at: <http://www.mpi-fg-koeln.mpg.de/pu/workpap/wp97-2/wp97-2.html>, accessed March 2009.

Cohen, R. and Kennedy, P. (2000), *Global Sociology*, New York: Palgrave.

Cohen, S. (2002), *Folk Devils and Moral Panics* (3rd edn), London: Routledge.

Coleman, J. and Hendry, L. (1999), *The Nature of Adolescence* (3rd edn), London and New York: Routledge.

Combat Poverty Agency (2007), *Submission to the Minister of State and the Department of Community, Rural and Gaeltacht Affairs on Community Development and Disadvantage and on the Community Development Programme 2007–2013*, Dublin: Combat Poverty Agency.

Comhairle na nÓg Implementation Group (2007), *Report from the Comhairle na nÓg Implementation Group to the Minister for Children, Brian Lenihan*, Dublin: Office of the Minister for Children.

Commins, P. (1985), 'Rural Community Development: Approaches and Issues', *Social Studies* , 8(3/4), 165–178.

Community Platform (2006), 'Social Partnership Tests', January, Galway: Community Workers Co-operative, available at: <http://www.eapn.ie/pdfs/188_Platformdocument0106.pdf>, accessed May 2009.

Community Platform (2008), *Strategic Plan 2009–2011*, Galway: CWC.

Community Workers Co-operative (2001*a*), *Strengthening Our Voice: A Guide for Community Sector Participation in Local Decision Making*, Galway: CWC.

Community Workers Co-operative (2001*b*), *Partnership, Participation and Power*, Galway: CWC.

Community Workers Co-operative (2006*a*), 'CWC Social Partnership Update', 27 February, available at: <http://www.cwc.ie>, accessed February 2009.

Community Workers Co-operative (2006*b*), 'CWC Social Partnership Update', 15 February, available at: <http://www.cwc.ie>, accessed February 2009.

Community Workers Co-operative (2007), *Draft Standards for Quality Community Work – A Statement of Values and Principles*, available at: <http://www.cwc.ie>, accessed February 2009.

Community Workers Co-operative (Undated), 'Areas of Work – CWC Social Partnership', available at: <http://www.cwc.ie>, accessed February 2009.

Connolly, B. (2007), 'Beyond the Third Way: New Challenges for Critical Adult Education and Community Education' in B. Connolly, T. Fleming, D. McCormack and A. Ryan (eds.), *Radical Learning for Liberation 2*, Maynooth: National University of Ireland Maynooth, 109–129.

Connolly, E. (2007), *The Institutionalisation of Anti-Poverty and Social Exclusion Policy in Irish Social Partnership*, Dublin: Dublin City University/ Combat Poverty Agency.

Connolly, L. (2002), *The Irish Women's Movement: From Revolution to Devolution*, Basingstoke: Macmillan.

Connolly, L. (2006), 'The Consequences and Outcomes of Second-Wave Feminism in Ireland' in L. Connolly and N. Hourigan (eds.), *Social Movements and Ireland*, Manchester: Manchester University Press, 58–85.

Conroy, P. (1999), 'From the Fifties to the Nineties: Social Policy comes out of the Shadows' in G. Kiely, A. O'Donnell, P. Kennedy and S. Quin (eds.), *Irish Social Policy in Context*, Dublin: University College Dublin Press, 33–50.

Consultative Group on the Development of Youth Work (1993), *Report of the Consultative Group on the Development of Youth Work*, Dublin: The Stationery Office.

Cooke, B. and Kothari, U. (2001), *Participation: The New Tyranny?* London: Zed Books.

Coombs, P.H. and Abmed, M. (1973), *New Pathways to Learning*, New York: UNICEF.

CORI Justice (2007), *Socio-Economic Review 2007 – Addressing Inequality: Policies to Ensure Economic Development, Social Equity and Sustainability*, Dublin: CORI Justice.

Corney, T. (2004), 'Values versus Competencies: Implications for the Future of Professional Youth Work Education', *Journal of Youth Studies*, 7(4), 513–527.

Corney, T. (2006), 'Youth Work in Schools: Should Youth Workers also be Teachers?' *Youth Studies Australia*, 25(3), 17–25.

Cornwall, A. (2002), *Making Spaces, Changing Places: Situating Participation in Development*, Working Paper 170, Sussex: Institute of Development Studies.

Cornwall, A. (2004), 'Introduction – New Democratic Spaces: The Politics and Dynamics of Institutionalised Participation', *Institute of Development Studies Bulletin*, 35(2), 1–10.

Cornwall, A. and Schattan Coelho, V. (eds.) (2007), *Spaces for Change? The Politics of Citizen Participation in New Democratic Arenas*, London: Zed Books.

Council of Europe (1999), *Council Resolution on Youth Participation* (OJ C 42 17/2/99), available at: <http://europa.eu/scadplus/leg/en/cha/c11604.htm>, accessed August 2007.

Cowen, B. (2009), speech by the Taoiseach Brian Cowen TD to the ICTU Biennial Conference, Tralee, Friday, 10 July, 2009.

Cox, L. (2006), 'News from Nowhere: the Movement of Movements in Ireland' in L. Connolly and N. Hourigan (eds.), *Social Movements and Ireland*, Manchester: Manchester University Press, 210–229.

Craig, G. (1998), 'Community Development in a Global Context', *Community Development Journal*, 33(1), 2–17.

Crook, R.C. and Sverrisson, A.S. (2001), *Decentralisation and Poverty Alleviation in Developing Countries: A Comparative Analysis or, Is West Bengal Unique?* Sussex: Institute of Development Studies.

Crossley, N. (2005), *Key Concepts in Critical Social Theory*, London: Sage.

Crotty, R. (1986), *Ireland in Crisis: A Study in Capitalist Colonial Undevelopment*, Dover, NH: Brandon.

Crowther, J. Martin, I. and Shaw, M. (2000), 'Turning the Discourse' in J. Thompson (ed.) *Stretching the Academy: The politics and Practice of Widening Participation in Higher Education*, Leicester: NICE, 171–185.

Cunningham, M. (2008), *Clár na nÓg Newsletter*, June 2008, available at: <http://www.nyci.ie/what_s_new/clar_na_nog_the_youth_sector_newsletter>, accessed September 2008.

Curley, H. (2005), 'We're Educators, Not Providers of Cannon-Fodder for Multi-Nationals', *Village – Ireland's Current Affairs Weekly*, 2 September.

Curtin, C. and Varley, T. (1995), 'Community Action and the State' in P. Clancy, S. Drudy, K. Lynch and L. O'Dowd (eds.), *Irish Society: Sociological Perspectives*, Dublin: Institute of Public Administration, 379–409.

Dáil Éireann (2000), 'Youth Work Bill, 2000: Second Stage', 23 November, available at: <http://historical-debates.oireachtas.ie/D/0526/D.0526.200011230008.html>, accessed August 2007.

Daly, M.E. (1999), 'The State in Independent Ireland' in R. English and C. Townshend (eds.), *The State: Historical and Political Dimensions* , London: Routledge, 66–94.

Daly, S. (2008), 'Mapping Civil Society in the Republic of Ireland', *Community Development Journal*, 43(2), 157–176.

Davies, B. and Gibson, A. (1967), *The Social Education of the Adolescent*, London: University of London Press.

Davies, B. (1977), 'Phenomenological Sociology and Education: Radical Return or Magic Moment' in D. Gleeson (ed.) *Identity and Structure*, Driffield: Nafferton, 198–203.

Davis, N.Z. (1975), *Society and Culture in Early Modern France: Eight Essays*, California: Stanford University Press.

De Bréadún, D. (2008), 'State Plans Merger of Five Bodies Instead of Just Three', *Irish Times*, 20 August.

Department of Community, Rural and Gaeltacht Affairs (2003), *Local and Community Development Programmes*, February, Dublin: DoCRGA.

Department of Community, Rural and Gaeltacht Affairs (2005), *Many Communities – A Common Focus*, Dublin: DoCRAG.

Department of Community, Rural and Gaeltacht Affairs (2008), *Community Development Programme*, available at: <http://www.pobail.ie/en/

Community LocalDevelopmentProgrammes/CommunityDevelopmentProgramme>, accessed 9 July 2008.

Department of Education (1977), *A Policy for Youth and Sport* (The Bruton Report), Dublin: The Stationery Office.

Department of Education (1980), *Development of Youth Work Services in Ireland, Report of the Committee appointed by the Minister of State at the Department of Education* (The O'Sullivan Report), Dublin: The Stationery Office.

Department of Education (1984), *The National Youth Policy Committee Final Report* (The Costello Report), Dublin: The Stationery Office.

Department of Education (1985), *In Partnership with Youth: The National Youth Policy*, Dublin: The Stationery Office.

Department of Education (1992), *Education for a Changing World: Green Paper on Education*, Dublin: The Stationery Office.

Department of Education (1995), *Charting our Education Future: White Paper on Education*, Dublin: The Stationery Office.

Department for Education and Employment (2001), *Transforming Youth Work. Developing Youth Work for Young People*, London: Department for Education and Employment/Connexions.

Department of Education and Science (2001), *Report of the Action Group on Access to Third Level Education*, Dublin: The Stationery Office.

Department of Education and Science (2003*a*), *National Youth Work Development Plan 2003–2007*, Dublin: The Stationery Office.

Department of Education and Science (2003*b*), *Supporting Equity in Higher Education*, Dublin: The Stationery Office.

Department of Education and Science (2004), *Introduction to the Youth Affairs Section*, Dublin, available at: <http://www.education.ie/servlet/blobservlet/intro_youth_affairs.doc?language = EN>, accessed August 2007.

Department of the Environment, Heritage and Local Government (1996), *Better Local Government: A Programme for Change*, Dublin: The Stationery Office.

Department of the Environment, Heritage and Local Government (2008), *Stronger Local Democracy – Options for Change: A Green Paper on Local Government Reform*, Dublin: The Stationery Office.

Department of Labour (1984), *National Youth Policy Committee Final Report* (The Costello Report), Dublin: The Stationery Office.

Department of Social, Community and Family Affairs (2000*a*), *White Paper on a Framework for Supporting Voluntary Activity and for Developing the Relationship between the State and the Community and Voluntary Sector*, Dublin: The Stationery Office.

Department of Social, Community and Family Affairs (2000*b*), *The National Community Development Programme,* Dublin: The Stationery Office.

Department of Social, Community and Family Affairs (2003), *National Action Plan Against Poverty and Social Exclusion, 2003–2005,* Dublin: Office for Social Inclusion, Department of Social and Family Affairs.

Department of Social Welfare and Combat Poverty Agency (1995), *Working Together Against Poverty: An Information Pack on the Community Development Programme,* Dublin: The Stationery Office.

Department of the Taoiseach (1987), *Programme for National Recovery,* Dublin: The Stationery Office.

Department of the Taoiseach (1991), *Programme for Economic and Social Progress,* Dublin: The Stationery Office.

Department of the Taoiseach (1994), *Programme for Competitiveness and Work,* Dublin: The Stationery Office.

Department of the Taoiseach (1996*a*), *Partnership 2000,* Dublin: The Stationery Office.

Department of the Taoiseach (1996*b*), *Delivering Better Government: A Programme of Change for the Irish Civil Service,* Dublin: The Stationery Office.

Department of the Taoiseach (2003), *Sustaining Progress: Social Partnership Agreement 2003–2005,* Dublin: The Stationery Office.

Department of the Taoiseach (2006), *Towards 2016: Ten-Year Framework Social Partnership Agreement 2006–2015,* Dublin: The Stationery Office.

Devlin, M. (1989), *Official Youth Work Discourse: Aims, Orientations and Ideology in Irish Youth Work Policy,* unpublished M.Soc.Sc thesis, University College Dublin.

Devlin, M. (2003), 'A Bit of the "Other": Media Representations of Young People's Sexuality', *Irish Journal of Sociology,* 12(2), 86–106.

Devlin, M. (2005), '"Teenage Traumas": The Discursive Construction of Young People as a Problem in an Irish Radio Documentary', *Young: Nordic Journal of Youth Research,* 13(2), 167–84.

Devlin, M. (2006*a*), *Inequality and the Stereotyping of Young People,* Dublin: The Equality Authority.

Devlin, M. (2006*b*), 'Editorial', *Youth Studies Ireland,* 1(1), 2–3.

Devlin, M. (2006*c*), *Inequality and the Stereotyping of Young People,* Dublin: Equality Authority.

Dillon, E. and Madden, S. (2004), 'Positioning between Tensions and Connections: A Critical Exploration of Banúlacht's Work in Contesting Globalisation through Linking Local and Global Issues', paper presented at Women's Education Research and Resource Centre

Conference, Feminism Contesting Globalisation, University College Dublin, April, 2004.

Dominelli, L. (2006), *Women and Community Action*, Bristol: Policy Press.

Doorley, J. (2003), 'The National Youth Work Development Plan – A Critique', *Irish Youth Work Scene*, 40, 3–5.

Dryzek, J.S. (1990), *Discursive Democracy: Politics, Policy and Political Science*, Cambridge: Cambridge University Press.

Dryzek, J.S. (1996), 'Political Inclusion and the Dynamics of Democratization', *American Political Science Review*, 90(3), 475–487.

Dryzek, J.S. (2000), *Deliberative Democracy and Beyond: Liberals, Critics, Contestations*, Oxford: Oxford University Press.

Duggan, C. (1999), 'Locally Based Interventions to Combat Poverty and Exclusion: How Effective Can They Be?' *Administration*, 47(2), 56–77.

Duncombe, S. (2007), *Dream: Re-imagining Progressive Politics in an Age of Fantasy*, New York: New Press.

Durkheim, E. (1893/1984), *The Division of Labour in Society*, London: Macmillan. Durkheim, E. (1912/1968), *The Elementary Forms of the Religious Life*, London: George Allen and Unwin.

Durkheim, E. (1956), *Education and Sociology*, New York: The Free Press.

Eagleton, T. (2008), 'Comrades and Colons', *Antipode*, 40(3), 351–356.

Eisenstadt, S.N. (1956), *From Generation to Generation: Youth Groups and the Social Structure*, Glencoe: Free Press.

Eisenstadt, S.N. (1963), 'Archetypal Patterns of Youth', in E. Erikson (ed.), *Youth: Change and Challenge*, New York: Basic Books.

Eivers, E., Shiel, G. and Shortt, F. (2005), *Literacy in Disadvantaged Primary Schools: Problems and Solutions*, Dublin: Educational Research Centre.

Equality Authority, 'About Us: The Role and Functions of the Equality Authority', available at: <http://www.equality.ie/index.asp?locID = 3&docID = -1>, accessed May 2009.

Erikson, E.H. (1963), *Childhood and Society* (2nd edn), New York: Norton.

Escobar, A. (1992), 'Planning' in W. Sachs (ed.), *The Development Dictionary*, London: Zed Books, 132–145.

Escobar, A. (1995), *Encountering Development*, New Jersey: Princeton University Press.

Esping-Andersen, G. (2002), *Why We Need a New Welfare State*, Oxford: Oxford University Press.

Esteva, G. (1992), 'Development' in W. Sachs (ed.), *The Development Dictionary*, London: Zed, 6–25.

Etzioni, A. (1995), *The Spirit of Community*, London: Fontana.

Etzioni, A. (1997), *The New Golden Rule*, London: Profile.

Eurobarometer (2007), *Young Europeans: A Survey Among Young People Aged between 15 and 30 in the European Union*, Brussels: European Commission.

European Commission (2001), *A New Impetus for European Youth*, White Paper, Brussels: European Commission.

European Commission (2005), *European Pact for Youth*, Brussels: European Commission.

European Commission (2006), *Analysis of National Reports Submitted by Member States Concerning Participation by and Information for Young People*, Communication (2006) 417, Brussels: European Commission.

European Social Fund Programme Evaluation Unit (1999), *Evaluation Report on the ESF and the Local Urban and Rural Development Operational Programme*, Dublin: ESF Evaluation Unit.

Fagan, G.H. (1995), *Culture, Politics, and Irish School Dropouts: Constructing Political Identities*, Westport, CT: Bergin and Garvey.

Fanning, B. (1999), 'The Mixed Economy of Welfare' in G. Kiely, A. O'Donnell, P. Kennedy and S. Quin (eds.), *Irish Social Policy in Context* , Dublin: UCD Press, 51–70.

Ferriter, D. (2005), *The Transformation of Ireland 1900–2000*, London: Profile Books.

Finlayson, A. and Martin, J. (2006), 'Poststructuralism' in C. Hay, M. Lister and D. Marsh (eds.), *The State: Theories and Issues*, Basingstoke: Palgrave Macmillan, 155–171.

FitzGerald, G. (2007), 'Flaws Emerge in Social Partnership Model', *Irish Times*, 14 July.

Fitzsimons, A. (2007), 'What Does Michel Foucault Have to Say About Youth Work?' *Youth and Policy*, 95, 83–95.

Forde, C. (1996), 'History of Community Work' in P. Burgess (ed.), *Community Work Reader*, Cork: Centre for Adult and Continuing Education, 3–13.

Forde, C. (2005), 'Participatory Democracy or Pseudo-Participation? Local Government Reform in Ireland', *Local Government Studies*, 31(2), 137–148.

Forde, C. (2006), *Invited Spaces for Participation: A Critical Analysis of Local Social Partnership in Ireland*, unpublished Ph.D. thesis, University College Cork.

Forde, W. (2003), *Joan's People: Limerick Youth Service 1973–2003*, Limerick: Kara Publications.

Foucault, M. (1979), 'On Governmentality', *Ideology and Consciousness*, 6, 5–22.

Foucault, M. (1991), 'Governmentality' in G. Burchell, C. Gordon and P. Miller (eds.), *The Foucault Effect: Studies in Governmentality*, London: Harvester Wheatsheaf, 87–104.

Foucault, M. (1994), *Power: Essential Works of Foucault 1954–84*, Harmondsworth: Penguin.

Fraser, N. (1990), 'Rethinking the Public Sphere: A Contribution to the Critique of Actually Existing Democracy', *Social Text*, 25/26, 56–80.

Fraser, N. (1992), 'Rethinking the Public Sphere: A Contribution to the Critique of Actually Existing Democracy' in C. Calhoun (ed.), *Habermas and the Public Sphere*, Cambridge, MA: MIT, 109–142.

Fraser, N. (1997), *Justice Interruptus*, New York: Routledge.

Fraser, N. (2000), 'Rethinking Recognition', *New Left Review*, 3(May/June), 107–120.

Fraser, N. (2003), 'Social Justice in the Age of Identity Politics: Redistribution, Recognition, and Participation' in N. Fraser and A. Honneth (eds.), *Redistribution or Recognition?* London: Verso, 7–109.

Freeman, J. (c.1972), 'The Tyranny of Structurelessness', available at: <http://www.jofreeman.com>, accessed November 2008.

Freire, P. (1971), *Pedagogy of the Oppressed*, New York: Scabury Press.

Freire, P. (1972*a*), *Pedagogy of the Oppressed*, Harmondsworth: Penguin.

Freire, P. (1972*b*), *Cultural Action for Freedom*, Harmondsworth: Penguin.

Freire, P. (1973), *Education for Critical Consciousness*, New York: Continuum.

Freire, P. (1974), *Education: the Practice of Freedom*, London: Writers and Readers Publishing Co-operative.

Fremeaux, I. (2005), 'New Labour's Appropriation of the Concept of Community: A Critique', *Community Development Journal*, 40(3), 265–274.

French, S. and Swain, J. (1997), 'Young Disabled People', in J. Roche and S. Tucker (eds.), *Youth in Societ*, London: Sage/Open University, 199–206.

Frith, S. (1984), *The Sociology of Youth*, Ormskirk: Causeway Press.

Frost, L. (2003), 'Doing Bodies Differently? Gender, Youth, Appearance and Damage', *Journal of Youth Studies*, 6(1), 53–70.

Fung, A. and Wright, O.W. (2001), 'Deepening Democracy: Innovations in Empowered Participatory Governance', *Politics and Society*, 29(1), 5–41.

Furedi, F. (undated), 'Consuming Democracy: Activism, Elitism and Political Apathy', available at: <http://www.geser.net/furedi.html>, May 2009.

Gaetz, S. (1993), 'Who Comes First? Teenage Girls, Youth Culture and the Provision of Youth Services in Cork' in C. Curtin, H. Donnan and T.M. Wilson (eds.), *Irish Urban Cultures*, Belfast: Institute of Irish Studies, Queens University Belfast, 143–160.

Gaetz, S. (1997), *Looking Out for the Lads: Community Action and the Provision of Youth Services in an Urban Irish Parish*, Newfoundland: Institute of Social and Economic Research.

Galland, O. (1995), 'What Is Youth?' in A. Cavalli and O. Galland (eds.), *Youth in Europe*, London: Pinter, 1–6.

Gallie, W.B. (1968), *Philosophy and the Historical Understanding*, New York: Shocken.

Galvin, A.E. (1994), *Contrasting Models of Youth Work, A Conceptual and Empirical Analysis of the Work Practices Implemented by Youth Groups in the North Clondalkin Area of West Dublin*, Master of Education thesis, University College Dublin.

Galvin, A.E. (1995), *Contrasting Models of Youth Work*, Dublin: Catholic Youth Council.

Gamson, W.A. (1995), 'Constructing Social Protest' in H. Johnston and B. Klandermans (eds.), *Social Movements and Culture*, London: UCL Press, 85–106.

Garvin, T. (2005), *Preventing the Future: Why Was Ireland so Poor for so Long?* Dublin: Gill & Macmillan.

Gaventa, J. (1980), *Power and Powerlessness: Quiescence and Rebellion in an Appalachian Valley*, Clarendon: Oxford.

Gaventa, J. (2004), 'Towards Participatory Governance: Assessing the Transformative Possibilities' in S. Hickey and G. Mohan (eds.), *Participation: From Tyranny to Transformation?* London: Zed Books, 25–41.

Giddens, A. (1990), *The Consequences of Modernity*, Cambridge: Polity.

Giddens, A. (1995), *Politics, Sociology and Social Theory*, Cambridge: Polity.

Giddens, A. (1998), *The Third Way*, Cambridge: Polity.

Gilligan, C. (1982), *In a Different Voice: Psychological Theory and Women's Development*, Cambridge, MA: Harvard University Press.

Gillis, J.R. (1974), *Youth and History: Tradition and Change in European Age Relations 1770–present*, New York/London: Academic Press.

Giroux, H. (2000), 'Counter-Public Spheres and the Role of Educators as Public Intellectuals: Paolo Freire's Cultural Politics' in M. Hill and W. Montag (eds.), *Masses, Classes and the Public Sphere*, London: Verso, 202–225.

Gore, G. (1993), *The Struggle for Pedagogies: Critical and Feminist Discourses as Regimes of Truth*, New York: Routledge.

Gouldner, A.W. (1980), *The Two Marxisms*, New York: Seabury Press.

Gramsci, A. (1971), *Selections from the Prison Notebooks*, trans. and ed. Q. Hoare and G. Nowell Smith, London: Lawrence and Wishart.

Granovetter, M. (1995), *Getting a Job: A Study of Contacts and Careers* (2nd edn), London: University of Chicago Press.

Green, M. (1999), 'The Youth Worker as Converter' in S. Banks (ed.), *Ethical Issues in Youth Work*, London and New York: Routledge, 110–124.

Griffin, C. (1997), 'Representations of the Young', in J. Roche and S. Tucker (eds.), *Youth in Society*, London: Sage/Open University, 17–25.

Guardian (2001), 'Robin Cook's Chicken Tikka Masala Speech', 19 April.

Habermas, J. (1984), *The Theory of Communicative Action Volume 1: Reason and the Rationalisation of Society*, London: Heinemann.

Habermas, J. (1989), *The Theory of Communicative Action, Volume 2 – Lifeworld and System: The Critique of Functionalist Reason*, Cambridge: Polity Press.

Habermas, J. (1992), 'Further Reflections on the Public Sphere' in C. Calhoun (ed.), *Habermas and the Public Sphere*, Cambridge, MA: MIT Press, 421–461.

Hall, S. and Jefferson, T. (eds.) (1975), *Resistance Through Rituals: Youth Subcultures in Postwar Britain*, London: Hutchinson.

Hall, S., Jefferson, T. and Clarke, T. (1976), 'Youth: A Stage of Life?' *Youth in Society* , 17, 17–18.

Hall, T., Williamson, H. and Coffey, A. (2000), 'Young People, Citizenship and the Third Way: A Role for the Youth Service', *Journal of Youth Studies*, 3(4), 461–476.

Hannan, D. and Ó Riain, S. (1993), *Pathways to Adulthood in Ireland*, Dublin: Economic and Social Research Institute.

Harcourt, W. (2003), 'The Impact of Transnational Discourses on Local Community Organizing', *Development*, 46(1), 74–79.

Hardiman, N. (1998), 'Inequality and the Representation of Interests' in W. Crotty and D.E. Schmidt (eds.), *Ireland and the Politics of Change*, New York: Longman, 122–143.

Hardiman, N. (2006), 'Politics and Social Partnership: Flexible Network Governance', *The Economic and Social Review*, 37(3), 343–374.

Harland, K. and Morgan, T. (2006), 'Youth Work in Northern Ireland: An Exploration of Emerging Themes and Challenges', *Youth Studies Ireland*, 1(1), 4–18.

Harper, L. (2007), *Final Evaluation of Children and Young People's Forum 2005–2006*, Dublin: National Children's Office.

Harrison, R.J. (1980), *Pluralism and Corporatism: the Political Evolution of Modern Democracies*, London: George Allen and Unwin.

Harvey, B. (1994), *Combating Exclusion: Lessons from the Third EU Anti-Poverty Programme in Ireland 1989–1994*, Dublin: Combat Poverty Agency, DTEDG, FORUM, Paul Partnership.

Harvey, B. (2002), *The Role of the Community Sector in Local Social Partnership: A Study of the Community Sector's Capacity to Participate in Local Social Partnership Structures*, Dublin: Area Development Management.

Harvey, B. (2004), *Implementing the White Paper: Supporting Voluntary Activity*, Report for the CV 12 Group.

Harvey, B. (2008), *Community Sector Funding*, report commissioned by a consortium of anti-poverty networks.

Hayes, N. (2002), *Children's Rights – Whose Right: A Review of Child Policy Development in Ireland,* Dublin: Policy Institute.

Haynes, F. (1988), *The Ethical School,* London: Routledge.

Healy, K. and Meagher, G. (2004), 'The Reprofessionalisation of Social Work: Collaborative Approaches for Achieving Professional Recognition', *British Journal of Social Work,* 34(2), 243–260.

Hendrick, H. (1990), *Images of Youth: Age, Class and the Male Youth Problem 1880–1920,* Oxford: Clarendon Press.

Henriksson, B. (1983), *Not For Sale: Young People in Society,* Oxford: Pergamon.

Hickey, S. and Mohan, G. (2004), 'Towards Participation as Transformation: Critical Themes and Challenges', in S. Hickey and G. Mohan (eds.), *Participation: From Tyranny to Transformation?* London: Zed, 3–24.

Hickey S. and Mohan, G. (2005), 'Relocating Participation within a Radical Politics of Development', *Development and Change,* 36(2), 237–262.

Higgins, Michael D. (2006), 'Citizen, not Consumer, Should Be King', *Irish Times,* 22 April.

Hilhorst, D. (2003), *The Real World of NGOs: Discourses, Diversity and Development,* London: Zed.

Hill, M. (2005), *The Public Policy Process,* Harlow: Longman.

Hirst, P. (2000), 'Democracy and Governance' in J. Pierre (ed.), *Debating Governance – Authority, Steering and Democracy,* Oxford: Oxford University Press, 13–35.

Hodgson, L. (2004), 'Manufactured Civil Society: Counting the Cost', *Critical Social Policy* , 24(2), 139–164.

Hughes, I., Clancy, P., Harris, C. and Beetham, D. (2007), *Power to the People: Assessing Democracy in Ireland,* Dublin: TASC.

Hugman, R. (1991), *Power in Caring Professions,* Basingstoke: Macmillan.

Hugman, R. (2005), *New Approaches in Ethics for the Caring Professions,* Hampshire: Palgrave Macmillan.

Hunt, S. (2005), *The Life Course: A Sociological Introduction,* Basingstoke: Palgrave Macmillan.

Hurley, L. (1990), *Youth Participation: The Context of Irish Youth Work,* unpublished M.A. Thesis, University College Cork.

Hurley, L. (1992*a*), *The Historical Development of Irish Youth Work: Youth Work Research Series No.1,* Dublin: Irish Youth Work Centre.

Hurley, L. (1992*b*), *Irish Youth Work Policy: Unresolved Issues,* Dublin: Irish Youth Work Centre.

Hurley, L. (1999), 'Mapping the Youth Work Sector', *Irish Youth Work Scene,* 26, 5–7.

Hurley, L. (2003), *Policy Context of Youth Work, ADM Discussion Paper 2,* Dublin: ADM.

Hurley, L. and Treacy, D. (1993), *Models of Youth Work: A Sociological Framework*, Dublin: Irish Youth Work Press.

Husein, F. (1997), 'Issues as a Focus for Work with Young People' in I. Ledgerwood and N. Kendra (eds.), *The Challenge of the Future: Towards the New Millennium for the Youth Service*, Dorset: Russell House Publishing, 63–72.

Ife, J. (2002), *Community Development*, Frenchs Forest: Longman.

Illich, I. (1977), 'Disabling Professions' in I. Illich, J. McKnight, I. Zola, J. Caplan and H. Shaiken (eds.), *Disabling Professions*, London: Marion Boyars, 11–39.

Indymedia.ie (2008), 'Housing Protest 2', 1 July, available at: http://www. indymedia.ie/article/88189, accessed November 2008.

Irish Examiner (2008), 'Poverty Agency Demands Plans for Future', 28 July.

Irish Times (2006*a*), 'Taoiseach Calls on Citizens to Do More for Society', 10 April.

Irish Times (2006*b*), 'Partnership Deal to Be Wrapped Up this Week', 12 June.

Irish Times (2008*a*), 'Culling of the Combat Poverty Agency Would be a Wicked Ploy', 9 July.

Irish Times (2008*b*), 'Combat Poverty Agency Can Play a Vital Role but It Must Remain Independent', 22 September.

Irish Youth Justice Service (2008), *National Youth Justice Strategy 2008–2010*, Dublin: The Stationery Office.

Istituto de Ricera (2001), *Study on the State of Young People and Youth Policy in Europe*, Milan: IARD, available at: <http://europa.eu.int/comm/dgs/education/youth>, accessed July 2007.

Jacobson, D. and Kirby, P. (2006), 'Globalisation and Ireland' in D. Jacobson, P. Kirby and D. Ó'Broin (eds.), *Taming the Tiger: Social Exclusion in a Globalised Ireland*, Dublin: TASC at New Island, 23–44.

Jeffs, T. and Banks, S. (1999), 'Youth Workers as Controllers' in S. Banks (ed.), *Ethical Issues in Youth Work*, London: Routledge, 93–110.

Jeffs, T. and Smith, M. (eds) (1987), *Youth Work*, Baskingstoke: Macmillan.

Jeffs, T. and Smith, M. (1988), 'Youth Work, Welfare and the State' in T. Jeffs and M. Smith (eds.), *Welfare and Youth Work Practice*, London: Macmillan, 14–41.

Jeffs, T. and Smith, M. (1990), *Young People, Inequality and Youth Work*, Hampshire and New York: Palgrave.

Jeffs, T. and Smith, M. (1994), 'Young People, Youth Work and the New Authoritarianism', *Youth and Policy*, 46, 17–32.

Jeffs, T. and Smith, M. (1996), *Informal Education: Conversation, Democracy and Learning*, Derby: Educational Now Publishing Co-operative.

Jeffs, T. and Smith, M. (1998/99), 'The Problem of Youth for Youth Work', *Youth and Policy*, 62, 45–66.

Jeffs, T. and Smith, M. (2002), 'Individualisation and Youth Work', *Youth and Policy*, 76, 39–65.

Jenkins, R. (1983), *Lads, Citizens and Ordinary Kids: Working Class Youth Lifestyles in Belfast*, London: Routledge and Kegan Paul.

Jenkinson, H. (1996), 'History of Youth Work' in P. Burgess (ed.), *Youth and Community Work Course Reader*, Cork: UCC, 35–43.

Jenkinson, H. (2000), 'Youth Work in Ireland: The Struggle for Identity', *Irish Journal of Applied Social Studies*, 2(2), 106–124.

Joint Committee on Education and Science (2003), National Youth Work Advisory Committee Presentation, 11 March 2003, available at: <http://www.irlgov.ie/committees-29/c-education/20030311-J/Page1.htm#1>, accessed August 2007.

Jones, E. and Gaventa, J. (2002), *Concepts of Citizenship: A Review, Institute of Development Studies Development Bibliography 19*, Brighton: Institute of Development Studies.

Jones, M. (2001), 'The Contradictions of Globalisation', *Journal of Australian Political Economy*, 48(1), 5–22.

Kampmann, B. (1996), 'Anti-Racist Youth Work Approaches in Germany' in A. Aluffi-Pentini and W. Lorenz (eds.), *Anti-Racist Work With Young People*, Dorset: Russell House Publishing, 120–133.

Kane, L. (2006), 'The World Bank, Community Development and Education for Social Justice', *Community Development Journal*, 10.1093/cdj/bsl043.

Keane, J. (1988), *Civil Society and the State*, London: Verso.

Keane, J. (1998), *Civil Society: Old Images, New Visions*, Cambridge: Polity Press.

Kearney, D. (2006*a*), 'Youth Work Assessor and Garda Vetting Finally in Place', *Irish Youth Work Scene*, 49, 2.

Kearney, D. (2006*b*), 'Is it time for a Professional Association for Youth Workers?' *Irish Youth Work Scene* , 50, 2.

Kearney, D. (2007*a*), 'Editorial', *Irish Youth Work Scene*, 54, 2.

Kearney, D. (2007*b*), 'Do We Know What Youth Work Is Anymore?' *Irish Youth Work Scene*, 51, 2.

Kearney, D. (2007*c*), 'Editorial', *Irish Youth Work Scene*, 52, 2.

Kelleghan, T., Weir, S., O hUallacháin, S. and Morgan, M. (1995), *Educational Disadvantage in Ireland*, Dublin: Department of Education, Combat Poverty Agency and the Educational Research Centre.

Kenny, E. (2005), *Volume 607, Leaders Questions*, Dáil Éireann, 27 September 2005.

Kenny, S. (2002), 'Tensions and Dilemmas in Community Development: New Discourses, New Trojans', *Community Development Journal*, 37(4), 284–299.

Keogh, D. (2005), *Twentieth Century Ireland*, Dublin: Gill & Macmillan.

Kiely, E. and Kennedy, P. (2005), 'Youth Policy' in S. Quin, P. Kennedy, A. Matthews and G. Kiely (eds.), *Contemporary Irish Social Policy* (2nd edn), Dublin: University College Dublin Press, 186–205.

Kilkelly, U. (2007), *Obstacles to the Realisation of Children's Rights in Ireland*, Report Commissioned by the Ombudsman for Children, Dublin: Office of the Ombudsman for Children.

Kirby, P. (2002), *The Celtic Tiger in Distress: Growth with Inequality in Ireland*, Basingstoke: Palgrave.

Kirby, P. (2006), 'Bringing Social Inclusion to Centre Stage: Towards a Project of Active Citizenship' in D. Jacobson, P. Kirby and D. Ó Broin (eds.), *Taming the Tiger: Social Exclusion in a Globalised Ireland*, Dublin: TASC, 180–199.

Koehn, D. (1994), *The Ground of Professional Ethics*, London: Routledge.

Kohlberg, L. (1963), 'The Development of Children's Orientations towards a Moral Order', *Vita Humana*, 6, 11–33.

Kolb, D. and Fry, R. (1975), 'Towards an Applied Theory of Experiential Learning' in C.L. Cooper (ed.), *Theories of Group Processes*, London: John Wiley and Sons, 33–58.

Kumar, K. (1993), 'Civil Society: An Inquiry into the Usefulness of an Historical Term', *British Journal of Sociology*, 44(3), 375–395.

Lally, C. and Healy, A. (2007), 'Pavee's Roma Role Questioned', *Irish Times*, 27 July.

Lalor, K. and Baird, K. (2006), *Our Views, Anybody Listening?* Dublin: Centre for Social and Educational Research.

Lalor, K., de Róiste, Á and Devlin, M. (2007), *Young People in Contemporary Ireland*, Dublin: Gill & Macmillan.

Langford, S. (1999), 'The Impact of the European Union on Irish Social Policy Development in Relation to Social Exclusion' in G. Kiely, A. O'Donnell, P. Kennedy and S. Quin (eds.), *Irish Social Policy in Context*, Dublin: University College Dublin Press, 90–113.

Langman, L. (1992), 'Neon Cages: Shopping for Subjectivity', in R. Shields (ed.), *Lifestyle Shopping: the Subject of Consumption*, London: Routledge, 40–82.

Law, A. and Mooney, G. (2006), 'We've never Had It so Good: The "Problem" of the Working Class in Devolved Scotland', *Critical Social Policy*, 26(3), 523–542.

Ledwith, M. (2005), *Community Development*, Bristol: Policy Press.

Lee, A. (2006), *Community Development: Current Issues and Challenges*, Dublin: Combat Poverty Agency.

Leighton, J.P. (1972), *The Principles and Practices of Youth and Community Work*, London: Chester House Publications.

Lentin, R. and McVeigh, R. (2006), *After Optimism: Ireland Racism and Globalisation*, Dublin: Metro Éireann.

Leonard, P. (1995), 'Postmodernism, Socialism and Social Welfare', *Journal of Progressive Human Services*, 6(2), 3–19.

Levitas, R. (2004), 'Lets Hear it for Humpty: Social Exclusion, the Third Way and Cultural Capital', *Cultural Trends*, 13(50), 41–56.

Lewin, K. (1952), *Field Theory in Social Science: Selected Theoretical Papers*, London: Tavistock.

Low, N. and Gleeson, B. (1998), *Justice, Nature and Society – An Exploration of Political Ecology*, London: Routledge.

Lukes, S. (1974), *Power: A Radical View*, Basingstoke: Macmillan Education.

Lukes, S. (2005), *Power: A Radical View*, Basingstoke: Palgrave Macmillan.

Lourdes Youth and Community Services (2006), *Connecting Communities*, Dublin: LYCS.

Lynch, K. (1999), *Equality in Education*, Dublin: Gill & Macmillan.

Lynch, K. (2006), 'Neo-liberalism and Marketisation: The Implications for Higher Education', *European Educational Research Journal*, 5(1), 1–17.

McAliskey, B. (2007), 'The Role of the Community and Voluntary Sector in Building Peace and Democracy' in Community Workers Co-operative (ed.), *Building Peace and Democracy in Ireland North and South: The Role of the Community and Voluntary Sector*, Galway: Community Workers Co-operative, 27–30.

McCready, S. (2006), 'Review of the Youth Work Liaison Forums' Strategy for the Delivery of Youth Work in Northern Ireland (2005–2008)', *Youth Studies Ireland*, 1(1), 99–101.

Macdonald, K.M. (1995), *The Sociology of the Professions*, Sage: London.

McGonagle, D. (2007), 'A New Deal: Art, Museums and Communities – Re-imagining Relations', *Community Development Journal*, 42(4), 425–434.

McIlveen, R. and Gross, R. (1997), *Developmental Psychology*, London: Hodder and Stoughton.

McInerney, C. (2006), *Evaluating the Tralee RAPID Programme*, Tralee: Kerry County Council.

Macpherson, C.B. (1977), *The Life and Times of Liberal Democracy*, Oxford: Oxford University Press.

McRobbie, A. (2000), *Feminism and Youth Culture* (2nd edn), London: Routledge.

Madden, S. and Moane, G. (2006), 'Critical Psychologies in Ireland: Transforming Contexts and Political Possibilities', *Annual Review of Critical Psychology*, 5, 1–24.

Magnuson, D. (2005), 'Response to "Captured by Capital"', *Child and Youth Care Forum*, 34(2), 163–166.

Mahon, E. (1995), 'From Democracy to Femocracy: the Women's Movement in the Republic of Ireland' in P. Clancy, K. Lynch, S. Drudy and L. O'Dowd (eds.), *Irish Society: Sociological Perspectives*, Dublin: Institute of Public Administration, 675–708.

Manley, J.F. (1983), 'Pluralism I and Pluralism II', *American Political Science Review*, 77(2), 368–383.

Mannheim, K. (1927), 'The Problem of Generations', in K. Mannheim (ed.) *Essays on the Sociology of Knowledge*, London: Routledge and Kegan Paul, 276–320.

Mansbridge, J. (1996), 'Using Power / Fighting Power: The Polity' in Benhabib, S. (ed.) *Democracy and Difference: Contesting the Boundaries of the Political*, New Jersey: Princeton University Press, 46–66.

Marcia, J.E. (1980), 'Identity in Adolescence' in J. Adelson (ed.), *Handbook of Adolescent Psychology*, New York: Wiley.

Marsden, T. (2003), *The Condition of Rural Sustainability*, Assen: Royal Van Gorcum.

Marx, K. (trans. 1973), *Surveys from Exile*, trans. and ed. David Fernbach, Harmondsworth: Penguin.

Mayo, M. (1975), 'Community Development: A Radical Alternative?' in R. Bailey and M. Brake (eds.), *Radical Social Work*, London: Edward Arnold Publishers, 129–143.

Mead, G.H. (1934), *Mind, Self and Society from the Standpoint of Social Behaviourism*, Chicago: University of Chicago Press.

Meade, R. (2005), 'We Hate It here, Please Let Us Stay! Irish Social Partnership and the Community/Voluntary Sector's Conflicted Experiences of Recognition', *Critical Social Policy*, 25(3), 349–373.

Meade, R. (2008), 'Mayday, Mayday! Newspaper Framing Anti-globalisers! A Critical Analysis of the *Irish Independent*'s Anticipatory Coverage of the "Day of the Welcomes" Demonstrations', *Journalism*, 9(4), 330–352.

Meade, R. and O'Donovan, O. (2002), 'Editorial Introduction: Corporatism and the ongoing Debate about the Relationship between the State and Community Development', *Community Development Journal*, 37(1), 1–9.

Melucci, A. (1992), 'Youth Silence and Voice: Selfhood and Commitment in the Everyday Experience of Adolescents' in J. Fornäs and G. Bolin (eds.), *Moves in Modernity*, Stockholm: Almqvist and Wiksell International, 51–71.

Merton, B. (2004), An *Evaluation of the Impact of Youth Work in England, Research Report 606*, De Monfort: De Monfort University.

Merton, B. and Wylie, T. (2002), *Towards a Contemporary Curriculum for Youth Work*, Leicester: National Youth Agency.

Mestrum, F. (2004), 'The World Social Forum: A Democratic Alternative' in F. Polet and CETRI (eds.), *Globalizing Resistance*, London: Pluto Press, 188–205.

Midgley, J. (1986), 'Community Participation: History, Concepts and Controversies', in J. Midgley (ed.), *Community Participation, Social Development and the State*, London: Methuen, 13–44.

Milburn, K. (1996), *Peer Education: Young People and Sexual Health: A Critical Review*, Health Education Bureau for Scotland, Working Paper No.2, Edinburgh: HEBS.

Miles, S. (2000), *Youth Lifestyles in a Changing World*, Buckingham: Open University Press.

Misztal, B.A. (2001), 'Civil Society: A Signifier of Plurality and Sense of Wholeness', in J.R. Blau (ed.), *The Blackwell Companion to Sociology*, Oxford: Blackwell, 73–85.

Mizen, P. (1999), 'Ethics in an Age of Austerity' in S. Banks (ed.), *Ethical Issues in Youth Work*, London and New York: Routledge, 21–36.

Monro, S. (2006), 'Growing Up Transgender: Stories of an Excluded Population' in C. Leccardi and E. Ruspini (eds.) *A New Youth? Young People, Generations and Family Life*, Aldershot: Ashgate, 298–320.

Morgan, M., Hickey, B. and Kellaghan, T. (1997), *International Adult Literacy Survey: Results from Ireland*, Dublin: The Stationery Office.

Motherway, B. (2006), *The Role of Community Development in Tackling Poverty in Ireland*, Dublin: Combat Poverty Agency.

Mouffe, C. (1999), 'Deliberative Democracy or Agonistic Pluralism', *Social Research*, 66(3), 745–758.

Mouffe, C. (2000), *The Democratic Paradox*, London: Verso.

Mowbray, M. (2005), 'Better Together – Restoring the American Community', *Community Development Journal* , 39(4), 458–465.

Murphy, M. (2002), 'Social Partnership – Is it "the only Game in Town"?' *Community Development Journal*, 37(1), 80–90.

Murphy, M. (2006), 'The Emerging Irish Workfare State and its Implications for Local Development' in D. Jacobson, P. Kirby and D. Ó Broin (eds.), *Taming the Tiger: Social Exclusion in a Globalised Ireland*, Dublin: TASC at New Island, 85–112.

Murphy, T. (2005), *Review of Comhairle na nÓg and Dáil na nÓg*, report submitted to the National Children's Office, Dublin: NCO.

Musgrove, F. (1964), *Youth and the Social Order*, London: Routledge and Kegan Paul.

Narayan, D., Chambers, R., Shah, M.K. and Petesch, P. (2000), *Voices of the Poor: Crying Out for Change*, New York: Oxford University Press for the World Bank.

National Children's Office (2004), *Ready, Steady Play: A National Play Policy*, Dublin: The Stationery Office.

National Development Plan/Community Support Framework (1999), *Community Support Framework, 2000–2006*, Dublin: Government of Ireland.

National Development Plan/Community Support Framework (2007), *Transforming Ireland – A Better Quality of Life for All, National Development Plan 2007–2013*, Dublin: Government of Ireland.

National Economic and Social Council (2005), *The Developmental Welfare State*, Dublin: NESC.

National Economic and Social Forum (1997), *A Framework for Partnership – Enriching Strategic Consensus through Participation*, Forum Report No. 16, Dublin: NESF.

National Economic and Social Forum (2003), *The Policy Implications of Social Capital*, Forum Report No. 28, Dublin: NESF.

National Traveller Accommodation Consultative Committee (2004), *Review of the Operation of the Housing (Traveller Accommodation) Act, 1988*, Dublin: Department of the Environment, Heritage and Local Government.

National Youth Council of Ireland (1973), *The Development of Youth Services*, Dublin: NYCI.

National Youth Council of Ireland (1978), *A Policy on Youth Work Services*, Dublin: NYCI.

National Youth Council of Ireland (1994), *Towards the Development of a Comprehensive Youth Service* (the Youth Policy of the National Youth Council of Ireland), Dublin: NYCI.

National Youth Council of Ireland (2002), *Identifying Priorities and Pursuing Goals: Submission to the Work Plan of the European Youth Forum*, Dublin: NYCI.

National Youth Council of Ireland (2003*a*), *Presentation to the Joint Committee on Education and Science*, available at: <http://www. housesoftheoireachtas.ie/viewdoc.asp?DocID = 299>, accessed May 2009.

National Youth Council of Ireland (2003*b*), 'Budget could Signal Beginning of the End of the Youth Sector in Ireland warns NYCI President', *NYCI Press Release Archive*, available at: <http://www.youth.ie/what_s_new/nyci_press_releases>, accessed August 2007.

National Youth Council of Ireland (2004), 'Youth Council Angry and Disappointed with Education Estimates and Calls on Minister to Redress Balance before Budget Day', NYCI Press Release Archive, available at: <http://www.youth.ie/what_s_new/nyci_press_releases>, accessed August 2007.

National Youth Council of Ireland (2005*a*), 'Disappointing Budget for the Youth Sector', NYCI Press Release Archive, available at:

<http://www.youth.ie/what_s_new/nyci_press_releases>, accessed August 2007.

National Youth Council of Ireland (2005*b*), *Budget 2006: Youth Forgotten – Post Budget Analysis*, available at: <http://www.youth.ie/resources/pre_and_post_budget_submissions>, accessed August 2007.

National Youth Council of Ireland (2006*a*), *Annual Report 2006*, Dublin: NYCI.

National Youth Council of Ireland (2006*b*), 'National Youth Council of Ireland Welcomes Appointment of Youth Work Assessor', NYCI Press Release Archive, available at: <http://www.youth.ie/what_s_new/nyci_press_releases>, accessed August 2007.

National Youth Council of Ireland (2006*c*), 'Youth on the Agenda in Social Partnership', NYCI Press Release Archive, available at: <http://www.youth.ie/what_s_new/nyci_press_releases>, accessed August 2007.

National Youth Council of Ireland (2006*d*), 'Youth Groups Vote in Favour of Social Partnership', NYCI Press Release Archive, available at: <http://www.youth.ie/what_s_new/nyci_press_releases>, accessed August 2007.

National Youth Council of Ireland (2008), *What Is Youth Work?* available at: <http://www.youth.ie/youth_work>, accessed May 2008.

National Youth Policy Committee (1984), *Final Report* (The Costello Report), Dublin: The Stationery Office.

Navarro, V. (2002), 'A Critique of Social Capital', *International Journal of Health Services*, 32(3), 423–432.

Newby, H., Bell, C., Rose D. and Saunders, P. (1978), *Property, Paternalism and Power*, London: Hutchinson.

O'Carroll, J.P. (2002), 'Culture Lag and Democratic Deficit in Ireland: Or, "Dat's outside de terms of d'agreement"', *Community Development Journal*, 37(1), 10–19.

Ó Cinnéide, S. and Walsh, J. (1990), 'Multiplication and Divisions: Trends in Community Development in Ireland since the 1960s', *Community Development Journal*, 25(4), 326–336.

Ó Cinnéide, S. (1998), 'Democracy and the Constitution', *Administration*, 46(4), 41–58.

O'Connell, P.J., Clancy, D. and McCoy, S. (2006), *Who Went to College in 2004? A National Survey of New Entrants to Higher Education*, Dublin: Higher Education Authority.

O'Dalaigh, D. (2005), 'Tara', *Chimera*, 20, 142–146.

O'Donnell, R. and O'Reardon, C. (2000), 'Social Partnership and Ireland's Economic Transformation' in G. Fajertag and P. Pochet (eds.), *Social*

Pacts in Europe – New Dynamics, Brussels: European Trade Union Institute, 79–95.

O'Donnell, R. and Thomas, D. (1998), 'Partnership and Policy Making' in S. Healy and B. Reynolds (eds.), *Social Policy in Ireland: Principles, Practice, Problems,* Dublin: Oak Tree Press, 117–146.

O'Donovan, O. (2000), 'Re-theorizing the Interactive State: Reflections on a Popular Participatory Initiative in Ireland', *Administration,* 35(3), 224–232.

O'Ferrall, F. (1983), 'Irish Youth Work, Challenges and Issues', *Social Studies* 7(2): 99–109.

Office of the Minister for Children (2008), *Garda Youth Diversion Project Guidelines* , available at: <http://www.justice.ie>, accessed May 2009.

Ó hAodain, M. and Forde, C. (2007), 'Challenges in the Education and Training of Youth and Community Workers: Experiences from the Republic of Ireland', *Youth and Policy,* 97 and 98, 29–45.

O'Hara, P. (2002), 'Social Partnership and Regional Development' in B. Reynolds and S. Healy (eds.), *Choosing a Fairer Future: An Agenda for Social Partnership after the Celtic Tiger,* Dublin: Conference of Religious of Ireland, 113–137.

Oldfield, C. (2001), '"The Worst Girl has at least 5% Good in Her": The Work of the Girl Guides and the YMCA with "Difficult" Girls during the Inter-War Period' in G. Gilchrist, T. Jeffs and J. Spence (eds.), *Essays in the History of Community and Youth Work,* Leicester: National Youth Agency, 133–148.

Ó Riain, S. and O'Connell, P.J. (2000), 'The Role of the State in Growth and Welfare' in B. Nolan, P. J. O'Connell and C.T. Whelan (eds.), *Bust to Boom? The Irish Experience of Growth and Inequality,* Dublin: Institute of Public Administration, 310–339.

Ortega y Gasset, J. (1923), 'The Concept of the Generation', in *The Modern Theme,* New York: Norton.

O' Sullivan, D. (2005), *Cultural Politics and Irish Education since the 1950s: Policy Paradigms and Power,* Dublin: Institute of Public Administration.

Pakulski, J. and Waters, M. (1996), *The Death of Class,* London: Sage.

Papadopoulos, Y. (2003), 'Cooperative Forms of Governance: Problems of Democratic Accountability in Complex Environments', *European Journal of Political Research,* 42(4), 473–502.

Parfitt, T. (2002), *The End of Development: Modernity, Post-Modernity and Development,* London: Pluto.

Parkin, S. and McKeganey, N. (2000), 'The Rise and Rise of Peer Education Approaches', *Drugs: Education, Prevention and Policy,* 7(3), 293–310.

Parsons, T. (1951), *The Social System,* Glencoe, Ill.: Free Press.

Parsons, T. (1972), 'Age and Sex in the Social Structure of the United States', in P.K. Manning and M. Truzzi (eds.), *Youth and Sociology*, New Jersey: Prentice Hall.

Pateman, C. (1970), *Participation and Democratic Theory*, Cambridge: Cambridge University Press.

Peace, A. (2001), *A World of Fine Difference – The Social Architecture of a Modern Irish Village*, Dublin: UCD Press.

Peillon, M. (1995), 'Interest Groups and the State' in P. Clancy, S. Drudy, K. Lynch and L. O'Dowd, (eds.), *Irish Society: Sociological Perspectives*, Dublin: IPA, 358– 379.

Pena, D.G. (2003), 'Identity, Place and Communities of Resistance' in J.Agyeman, R. Evans, R.D. Bullard (eds.), *Just Sustainabilities: Development in an Unequal World*, London: Earthscan, 146–67.

Peters, M. (1996), *Poststructuralism, Politics and Education*, Connecticut: Bergin and Garvey.

Peters, M. (1998), *Naming the Multiple: Poststructuralism and Education*, Connecticut: Bergin and Garvey.

Phillips, A. (2004), 'Democracy, Recognition and Power' in F. Engelstad and O. Osterud (eds.), *Power and Democracy, Critical Interventions*, Aldershot: Ashgate, 57–78.

Piaget, J. (1926), *The Language and Thought of the Child*, London: Kegan Paul.

Piven, F.F. and Cloward, R.A. (2002), 'Eras of Protest, Compact and Exit' in S. Aronowitz and P. Bratsis (eds.), *Paradigm Lost – State Theory Reconsidered*, Minneapolis: University of Minnesota Press, 143–169.

Ploeg, J.D. van der, Renting, H., Brunori, G., Knickel, K., Mannion, J., Marsden, T., de Roest, K., Sevilla-Guzmán, E. and Ventura, F. (2000), 'Rural Development: From Practices and Policies towards Theory', *Sociologia Ruralis*, 40(4), 391–408.

Pobal (2007), *Inclusion through Local Development Newsletter* (Summer), Dublin: Pobal.

Polanyi, M. (1966), *The Tacit Dimension*, New York: Doubleday.

Popple, K. (1995), *Analysing Community Work*, Buckingham: Open University Press.

Popple, K. (2005), 'Community Development in the 21st Century: A Case of Conditional Development', *British Journal of Social Work*, 36(2), 333–340.

Porter, S. (1998), *Social Theory and Nursing Practice*, London: Macmillan.

Powell, F. and Geoghegan, M. (2004), *The Politics of Community Development*, Dublin: A & A Farmar.

Putnam, R.D. (2000), *Bowling Alone: The Collapse and Revival of American Community*, New York: Simon and Schuster.

Putnam, R.D., Feldstein, L.M. and Cohen, D. (2003), *Better Together*, New York: Simon and Schuster.

Radio Telefís Éireann (2008), 'Crackdown on Jobless Benefit Claims', available at: <http://www.rte.ie/news/2008/0721/welfare.html>, 21 July 2008, accessed July 2008.

Rai, S. (2002), *Gender and the Political Economy of Development: From Nationalism to Globalization*, Cambridge: Polity.

Rapley, J. (2004), *Globalization and Inequality: Neoliberalism's Downward Spiral*, London: Lynne Rienner.

Reed Jr., A. (2000), *Class Notes*, New York: The New Press.

Regan, S. (2005), 'CWC Roundtable Highlights Gap in our Democracy', *News and Views*, 15, 1.

Richardson, J. (1997), 'The Path to Adulthood and the Failure of Youth Work' in I. Ledgerwood and N. Kendra, (eds.), *The Challenge of the Future: Towards the New Millennium for the Youth Service*, Dorset, England: Russell House Publishing, 89–122.

Risse, T. (2007), 'Social Constructivism Meets Globalization' in D. Held and A. McGrew (eds.), *Globalization Theory: Approaches and Controversies*, Cambridge: Polity, 126–147.

Rist, S., Chidambaranatham, M., Escobar, C., Wiesmann, U. and Zimmermann, A. (2006), 'Moving from Sustainable Management to Sustainable Governance Processes: the Role of Social Learning Processes in Rural India, Bolivia and Mali', *Journal of Rural Studies*, 22(1): 1–15.

Rixon, A. (2007), 'Practitioners' in M. Robb (ed.), *Youth in Context: Frameworks, Settings and Encounters*, London: Sage, 15–52.

Robinson, L. (1997), 'Black Adolescent Identity and the Inadequacies of Western Psychology', in J. Roche and S. Tucker (eds.), *Youth in Society*, London: Sage/Open University, 151–57.

Ronayne, T. (1992), *Participation in Youth Service Provision*, Dublin: Work Research Centre.

Rosseter, B. (1987), 'Youth Workers as Educators' in T. Jeffs and M. Smith (eds.), *Youth Work*, London: Macmillan, 52–65.

Rossport 5 (2006), *Our Story*, Wicklow: Small World Media.

Ryan, A.B. (2001), *Feminist Ways of Knowing: Towards Theorising the Person for Radical Education*, Leicester: NIACE.

Sandwell's Young People's Service (undated), *Planning for Learning: Sandwell's Youth Work Curriculum*, Sandwell Metropolitan Borough Council, available at: <http://www.laws.sandwell.gov.uk>, accessed May 2009.

Savoie, D.J. (1995), 'What Is Wrong with the New Public Management', *Canadian Public Administration*, 38(1), 112–121.

Schirato, T. and Webb, J. (2003), *Understanding Globalization*, London: Sage.

Scott, J. (1995), *Sociological Theory – Contemporary Debates*, Aldershot, UK: Edward Elgar.

Sen, A. (1987), *On Ethics and Economics*, Oxford: Blackwell.

Sercombe, H. (2007), 'Embedded Youth Work: Ethical Questions for Youth Work Professionals', *Youth Studies Australia*, 26(2), 11–19.

Shapiro, I. (2004), 'Power and Democracy' in F. Engelstad and O. Osterud (eds.), *Power and Democracy: Critical Interventions*, Aldershot: Ashgate, 11–32.

Share, P., Tovey, H. and Corcoran, M.P. (2007), *A Sociology of Ireland* (3rd edn), Dublin: Gill & Macmillan.

Shaw, M. (2003*a*), '"Community" Community Work and the State' in R. Gilchrist, T. Jeffs and J. Spence (eds.), *Architects of Change, Studies in the History of Youth and Community Work*, Leicester: National Youth Agency, 215–331.

Shaw, M. (2003*b*), 'Gilding the Ghetto' and 'In and Against the State', *Community Development Journal*, 38(4), 361–366.

Shaw, M. (2005*a*), 'Outcome-Based Funding for Community Groups: Professional Contradictions and Challenges', Seminar of Scottish Community Development Alliance, 3 June 2005, Glasgow, available at: <http://www.communitydevelopmentalliancescotland.org>, accessed May 2009.

Shaw, M. (2005*b*), Introductory Presentation to Community Development Exchange Annual Conference, 23–25 September.

Shaw, M. (2006), 'Community Development – Everywhere and Nowhere? Rediscovering the Purpose and Practice of Community Development', transcript from seminar organised by CDX and Scottish Community Development Network, <http://www.scdn.org.uk/id52.html>, accessed April 2009.

Shaw, M. (2008), 'Community Development and the Politics of Community', *Community Development Journal* , 43(1), 24–36.

Simmel, G. (1997), 'The Metropolis and Mental Life', in D. Frisby and M. Featherstone (eds.), *Simmel on Culture*, London: Sage, 174–186.

Sklair, L. (1991), *Sociology of the Global System*, London: Harvester.

Skott-Myhre, H.A. (2005), 'Captured by Capital: Youth Work and the Loss of Revolutionary Potential', *Child and Youth Care Forum*, 34(2), 141–157.

Small Firms Association (2008), 'SFA calls for Decrease in Minimum Wage', 15 July 2008, available at: <http://www.sfa.ie/>, accessed March 2009.

Smith, D.E. (1999), *Writing the Social: Critique, Theory and Investigations*, Toronto: University of Toronto Press.

Smith, G. (2005), *Power Beyond the Ballot: 57 Democratic Innovations from Around the World*, London: The Power Inquiry.

Smith, M.K. (1980), *Creators Not Consumers: Rediscovering Social Education*, Leicester: NAYC Publications.

Smith, M.K. (1988), *Developing Youth Work*, Milton Keynes: Open University Press.

Smith, M.K. (1994), *Local Education, Community, Conversation, Praxis*, Buckingham: Open University Press.

Smith, M.K. (2002), 'Transforming Youth Work – Resourcing Excellent Youth Services: A Critique', the Informal Education Homepage, available at: <http://www.infed.org/youthwork/transforming.htm>, accessed July 2007.

Smith, M.K. (2003*a*), 'From Youth Work to Youth Development: The New Government Framework for English Youth Services', *Youth and Policy*, 79, 46–58.

Smith, M.K. (2003*b*), 'From Youth Work to Youth Development: The New Government Framework for English Youth Services', the Informal Education Homepage, available at: <http://www.infed.org/archives/jeffs_and_smith/smith_youth_work_to_youth_development.htm>, accessed June 2009.

Smith, M.K. (2007), Keynote Speech at Directions in Youth Work in Ireland Policy and Practice Seminar, 3 April, University College Cork.

Smoke, P. (2003), 'Decentralisation in Africa: Goals, Dimension, Myths and Challenges', *Public Administration and Development*, 27, 7–16.

Smyth, S.S. and Kulynych, J. (2002), 'It May Be Social but Why Is it Capital?' *Politics and Society*, 30(1), 149–186.

Sorensen, E. (1997), 'Democracy and Empowerment', *Public Administration*, 75, 553–567.

Spence, J. (1996), 'Feminism in Work with Girls and Women', *Youth and Policy*, 52: 38–53.

Spence, J. (2001), 'Edwardian Boys and Labour in the East End of Sunderland: Welfare and Work' in G. Gilchrist, T. Jeffs and J. Spence (eds.), *Essays in the History of Community and Youth Work*, Leicester: National Youth Agency, 75–94.

Spence, J. (2004), 'Targeting, Accountability and Youth Work Practice', *Practice*, 16(4), 261–272.

Spence, J. (2007), 'What Do Youth Workers Do? Communicating Youth Work' *Youth Studies Ireland*, Autumn/Winter, 2(2), 3–18.

Spence, J. and Devanney, C. (with Noonan, K.) (2007), *Youth Work: Voices of Practice*, Leicester: National Youth Agency.

Spence, J. and Jeffs, T. (2007/2008), 'Farewell to All That? The Uncertain Future of Youth and Community Work Education', *Youth and Policy*, 97/98, 135–166.

Stacey, K. (2001), 'Achieving Praxis in Youth Partnership Accountability', *Journal of Youth Studies*, 4(2), 209 -231.

Stoecker, R. (2003), 'Understanding the Development-Organizing Dialectic', *Journal of Urban Affairs*, 25(4), 493–512.

Storper, M. (2005), 'Society, Community and Economic Development', in S. de Paula and G.A. Dymski (eds.), *Reimagining Growth – Towards a Renewal of Development Theory*, London: Zed Books, 198–229.

Storper, M. and Scott, A.J. (eds.) (1992), *Pathways to Industrialisation and Regional Development*, London: Routledge.

Strasser, H. and Randall, S. (1981), *An Introduction to Theories of Social Change*, London and Boston: Routledge and Kegan Paul.

Sweeney, J. and Dunne, J. (2003), *Youth in a Changing Ireland*, Dublin: Foróige.

Taskforce on Active Citizenship (2006), *Taskforce on Active Citizenship: Public Consultation Document*, available at: <http://www.activecitizen.ie/index.asp?docID = 61>, accessed May 2009.

Taylor, M. (2004), *Looking at the Economy through Women's Eyes: A Facilitator's Guide for Economic Literacy*, Dublin: Banúlacht.

Taylor, P. and Mayo, M. (2008), 'Editorial', *Community Development Journal*, 43 (3), 263–268.

Taylor, T. (1987), 'Youth Workers as Character Builders: Constructing a Socialist Alternative' in T. Jeffs and M. Smith (eds.), *Youth Work*, London: Macmillan, 133–156.

Tett, L. (2000), 'Working in Partnership', *Youth and Policy*, 68, 58–71.

Tett, L. (2006), *Community Education, Lifelong Learning and Social Inclusion*, Edinburgh: Dunedin Academic Press.

Tocqueville, A. de (1856), *The Old Regime and the French Revolution*, New York: Anchor Books.

Todaro, M.P. and Smith, S.C. (2006), *Economic Development* (9th edn), Harlow: Pearson Education.

Tönnies, F. (1957), *Community and Society*, trans. C.P.Loomis, East Lansing: Michigan State University Press.

Tovey, H. (1993), 'Environmentalism in Ireland – Two Versions of Development and Modernity', *International Sociology*, 8(4), 413–30.

Tovey, H. and Share, P. (2003), *A Sociology of Ireland* (2nd edn), Dublin: Gill & Macmillan.

Treacy, D. (1989), *Youth Work: An Investigation of Purpose and Practice*, unpublished MA thesis, Department of Adult and Community Education, National University of Ireland Maynooth.

Treacy, D. (1994), *A Review of Youth Work Practice in Community-Based Projects*, Dublin: The Stationery Office.

Twelvetrees, A. (1991), *Community Work*, Basingstoke: Macmillan.

United Nations Capital Development Fund (UNCDF) (2003), *Local Government Option Study – Draft Report*, East Timor: (unpublished).

Usher, R. and Edwards, R. (1994), *Postmodernism and Education*, London: Routledge.

Varley, T. and Curtin, C. (2002), 'Communitarian Populism and the Politics of Rearguard Resistance in Rural Ireland', *Community Development Journal*, 37(1), 20–32.

Wallace, C. (1987), *For Richer, For Poorer: Growing Up In and Out of Work*, London: Tavistock.

Wallace, C. and Kovatcheva, S. (1998), *Youth in Society: The Construction and Deconstruction of Youth in East and West Europe*, London: Macmillan.

Walsh, K. (2005), *Social Inclusion Units in Local Authorities: Going Forward – the Lessons Learned*, Dublin: Combat Poverty Agency.

Walther, A., Stauber, B., Pohl, A. and Seifert, H. (2004), *Yo-Yo- National Report Transitions to Work: Youth Policies and 'Participation' in Germany*, Dresden, Germany: University of Technology.

Walther, A., Moerch, H., Bechmann, G. and Jensen, T. (2002), *Youth Transitions, Youth Policy and Participation: A Comparison in Ten European Regions*, Tubingen: IRIS.

Wates, N. (2000), *The Community Planning Handbook*, London: Earthscan.

Weber, M. (1947), *The Theory of Social and Economic Organisation*, trans. A. Henderson and T. Parsons, Glencoe: Free Press.

Weiler, K. (1991), 'Freire and a Feminist Pedagogy of Difference', *Harvard Educational Review*, 61(4), 449–474.

Whelan, M. (1989), 'Training and Professionalisation in Community Work' in CPA and CWC (eds.), *Community Work in Ireland: Trends in the 80's, Options for the 90's*, Dublin, CPA, 145–161.

Williams, R. (1983), *Keywords*, London: Fontana.

Williamson, H. (2005), 'Challenging Practice: A Personal View on "Youth Work" in Times of Changed Expectations' in R. Harrison and C. Wise (eds.), *Working With Young People*, London: Sage and Open University Press, 70–84.

Willis, K. (2005), *Theories and Practices of Development*, London: Routledge.

Willis, P. (1977), *Learning to Labour*, Westmead: Saxon House.

World Social Forum (2002), *World Social Forum Charter of Principles*, available at: <http://www.forumsocialmundial.org.br/main.php?id_menu = 4andcd_language = 2>, accessed March 2009.

Wyn, K. and White, R. (1997), *Rethinking Youth*, London: Sage.

Young, I.M. (2000), *Inclusion and Democracy*, Oxford: Oxford University Press.

Young, K. (1999*a*), *The Art of Youth Work,* Dorset, England: Russell House Publishing.

Young, K. (1999*b*), 'The Youth Worker as Guide, Philosopher and Friend: The Realities of Participation and Empowerment' in Banks, S. (ed.), *Ethical Issues in Youth Work,* London and New York: Routledge, 77–92.

Index